THE LIFE AND TIMES OF
MAJOR JOHN MASON OF CONNECTICUT

THE MAJOR JOHN MASON STATUE AT MYSTIC, CONNECTICUT

THE LIFE AND TIMES OF
MAJOR JOHN MASON
OF CONNECTICUT: 1600-1672

By LOUIS B. MASON

Illustrated

G. P. PUTNAM'S SONS

NEW YORK :: LONDON

1935

To
My Dear Wife
IDA

PREFACE

*"Every loyal American ought to know the prin-
ciples and motives which led to the founding of
this Republic.   These cannot be understood without an acquaintance with the men and women who
first came to New England."* [1]

IT was with that idea in mind that this book was written. The life of the New England colonies' first great
military leader, with accounts of the laws, religions, superstitions and supreme difficulties of the period in which he
lived, will give a picture, it is hoped, at least in part, of
the early history of the colonies.

The indomitable courage with which the settlers met
and overcame the seemingly insurmountable obstacles that
beset them at every turn, proved the stern integrity with
which they were endowed. Their bigotry and intolerance
can be forgiven when we realize the manner in which they
had been persecuted in their homeland and the religious
fervor of the times, when each sect regarded its beliefs as
the only road to salvation. Also the haven they sought
and founded in the new world for themselves, was an
abode of peace until those of different religious views
forced themselves and their doctrines on the Puritans, and
this aroused a spirit of persecution in the settlers.

A sad part in the history of our country which began

[1] From A. E. Dunning's Introduction to the American edition of John
Brown's "The Pilgrim Fathers of New England and their Successors."

with the first settlements, is the treatment of the Indians by the whites, and which is still an unsettled problem. Unfortunately we have no written record by the Indians of that period to help form an unbiased opinion.

In regard to the Pequot war, there was no alternative for the colonists; omitting the question as to their rights to the possession of the land, it was a fight to save the lives of themselves and their families.

To return to the principal character of this history, there is no better description and index to the man than the one given by Miss Caulkins in her "History of Norwich," and from which it is a pleasure to quote.

"With the residence of Captain Mason at Windsor, all the stirring scenes of the Pequot war are connected. This was the great event of the early history of Connecticut, and the overshadowing exploit of Mason's life. He was instrumental in originating the expedition, formed the plan, followed out its details, fought its battles, clinched, as it were, with iron screws, its results, and wrote its history. . . . From this period he became renowned as an Indian fighter, and stood forth a buckler of defence to the exposed colonies, but a trembling and a terror to the wild people of the wilderness. . . . Mason is one of the prominent figures in our early history. He shines forth as a valiant soldier and a wise counselor. He was prudent, and yet enterprising; fertile in resources, prompt and heroic in field of action. The natural ardor of his mind, fostered by early military adventures, and continually called into exercise by great emergencies, made him a fearless leader in war. Sturdy in frame, and hardy in constitution; regardless of danger, fatigue, or exposure;

he was invaluable as a pioneer in difficult enterprises, and a founder of new plantations. He was also a religious man and a patriot; of virtuous habits, and moderate ambition. Though he sustained many high and honorable offices in the infant colony, he was best known by the simple title of *Captain*. . . . Yet viewing the character of Mason at this distance of time, we become aware of some rigid and imperious features. Though faithful to his convictions of duty, he was stern and unrelenting in the execution of justice, and as a magistrate and commander, dictatorial and self-reliant."

LIST OF ILLUSTRATIONS

THE LIFE AND TIMES OF
MAJOR JOHN MASON OF CONNECTICUT

CHAPTER I

I

"I NEVER had thought that this should have come to the Press, until of late: If I had, I should have endeavoured to have put a little more Varnish upon it, . . . I shall only draw the Curtain and open my little Casement, that so others of larger Hearts and Abilities may let in a Bigger Light; that so at least some small Glimmering may be left to Posterity what Difficulties and Obstructions their Forefathers met with in their first settling these desert Parts of America. . . . For how can History find Credit, if in the Beginning you do not deliver Plainly and clearly from whence and how you do come to the Relation which you presently intend to make Actions?" Thus wrote John Mason in the introduction to his "History of the Pequot War."

Following this principle it is well to "deliver plainly and clearly" the setting of the scene at the time when he was born and the years in which he passed his youth in the old world before he took an active part in making history in the new world.

The year 1600 found Europe in a more peaceful condition than had existed for some time previous, and which was only to last for a short interval. England, still under the rule of the virgin queen, was prosperous and happy. Elizabeth's scepter was a rod of iron, and while mentally as alert as ever, she was failing physically. She kept herself erect, as she did until the last, but she realized her condition, and the mirrors, which she had the courage to have replaced, told her that she was not the dazzling epitome of "Spring and Beauty" that her courtiers endeavored to make her believe, hoping by this flattery to further their advancement. England's troubles in Ireland still continued after four centuries due to the cruelties which she had inflicted, and the religious fanaticism on both sides. These were some of the major worries of the queen, and they were added to by the seeming disloyal conduct of her favorite Essex. Probably, however, her chief concern was her knowledge that her advancing age was bringing her nearer to the horror which had haunted her for years. She had signed the death warrant countless times during her reign, but as the time approached for her to meet the grim conqueror, she quailed.

Yet withal, England was merry at this time. Shakespeare was writing and producing his plays; trade was good; the queen granted a charter to the East India Company; St. Helena was acquired, which two hundred years later was to serve as the prison of England's greatest enemy. And even at this period the law makers were frivolous enough to pass an act called the "Anti-effeminancy Law," which prohibited men from riding in coaches, and the times rolled merrily on.

Up in Scotland James was eagerly waiting for the news of the death of the woman who had signed his mother's death warrant. It is difficult to conceive that this awkward, ungainly, vacillating, but kind-hearted man, could have been the son of the handsome and graceful Mary

Stuart, and the debonair Lord Darnley. Nearly three years would elapse before Elizabeth's demise, but in the meanwhile James was busy anticipating the event, and had his agents at all of the principal courts in Europe interceding for his recognition as the legitimate heir to the throne of England.

While James was engaged in "watchful waiting," what was the political state of France?

The popular Henry of Navarre, the founder of the House of Bourbon, was the fourth of his name to reign over the French. Some seven years before the beginning of the seventeenth century he had renounced his religion, and had become a Catholic, and two years previous to this period, he had issued the Edict of Nantes, but in spite of that, the religious conflicts continued. However the beginning of the century promised well for the happiness of the gay Henry. The peace proclaimed with Spain in 1599, and the annulment of his marriage with Marguerite de Valois, famous for her intrigues, as well as her writings, was concluded in December of 1599. This left him free to send his ambassadors to Florence on the 9th of January following, to negotiate for his marriage to Marie de' Medici, daughter of Francis, the late Grand Duke of Tuscany. The marriage took place by proxy, and what a surprise for the king some time later, when he entered the bridal chamber fresh from his trip to Marseilles, still clad in his armour and boots! To see for the first time, instead of the beauty whose portrait had been shown him eight years previous and which had captivated him with its charm, a tall, fat woman, no longer in her first youth with "staring eyes" and a "forbidding air." No wonder that

Henrietta, Marquise de Verneuil, one of Henry's mistresses, exclaimed when she saw her, "So this is the fat bankeress from Florence!"

At this time Sweden was ruled by the catholic king Sigismund Third of Poland, who had recently made peace with Russia, and Michael "The Brave" of Russia had freed his country from the Turks. The Low Countries were fighting for their freedom from Spain. But in the midst of all the religious intolerance and conflicts which were growing more and more severe, the great artists were painting world-famous pictures. In Florence Ferdinand reigned in peace, and was adding to his collection of art that still keeps Florence the Mecca of the art world. Clement VIII occupied the papal throne, and Philip III of Spain who drove out the Moors, was continuing the wreck that his father had begun.

What was the condition in America at that period? The permanent settlements made on the Northern Hemisphere were in southern California, and Florida. An attempt was made by Sir Walter Raleigh in July, 1585, to establish a colony at Roanoke, North Carolina. The settlement was in charge of a kinsman of Raleigh's, named Sir Richard Grenville. It was there that Virginia Dare was the first English child born on the North American continent now in the confines of the United States. What the fate was of the settlers was never known, but the place was found abandoned by later expeditions. Thirteen years later, the Marquis de la Roche tried to plant a colony on the Isle of Sable in Canada. Numerous navigators had made exploring expeditions along the eastern coast, but no attempts at a real settlement were made previous to the first part of the seventeenth century.

During the year 1600 several people were born who exerted great influence over the destinies of the early colonists. First of all was Charles the First, who saw the light of day in Scotland, and who as king, gave and revoked charters; Roger Williams who came into the world a year previous and who was the first to preach and practice tolerance among the fanatics of New England; John Mason, whose courage and initiative advanced the growth of the colonies, and gave peace and freedom from Indian warfare to the plantations for many years.

II

About a hundred miles northeast of London in the County of Norfolk, England, lying romantically between the river Wensum, is old Norwich, with its ancient castle and Gothic cathedral dating back long centuries before the Reformation. From this city came some of the early settlers of the New World, and among them, perhaps, was John Mason. It is only supposition that Norwich was his native town, based on the fact that he was the promoter, and leader of the town of the same name in Connecticut. Much time and money have been spent endeavoring to learn the place of his birth, and the names of his parents, but without success. It is known, however, from the data that have been gleaned, that he was of the gentry class, otherwise he could not have held a commission in the British army. His people were probably Puritans, since he evinced such strong tendencies for that faith at an early age, while the composition of his letters, and government

documents preserved in the Connecticut and Massachusetts archives, prove him to have been a man of education
and refinement.

The age in which his youth and early manhood were
spent, was one of religious complexes and general wars,
founded, in most cases, by a fanaticism hardly paralleled
in history. Eighty years had passed since Martin Luther
had proclaimed—"Here stand I; I can none other; God
help me. Amen." At the beginning of the seventeenth
century all the western world was absorbed in religious
questions. Both the aristocracy and the common people
gave little thought to any other subject. One writer of
the times states, "Sunday after Sunday, day after day, the
crowds that gathered round the Bible in the nave of St.
Paul's, or the family group that hung on its words in the
devotional exercises at home, were leavened with a new
literature." There had been many wars caused by religious conflicts, and all Europe was embroiled in 1618
when the Thirty Years' War broke out.

Heretics, the name applied to the converts of all religions save the one to which one belonged, were burnt
at the stake in practically all European countries, including England. A Catholic League was formed in Germany
to fight the Protestants, and a Protestant League was
established to fight the Catholics. In Bohemia, which was
one of the first countries in which the Protestant faith
gained fast recognition was finally won over to catholicism,
and in 1624 the Jesuits, protected by the military, "ransacked private houses, and boasted of having burned over
sixty thousand volumes, all published previous to 1414."
Jews were expelled from London at an early date.

Unprincipled politicians were as much in evidence or even more so than in our time. They practiced their knavery, pulled the wires, flattered and deceived those in authority as they do now. Titles were sold, as well as offices. King James, like the other reigning monarchs, had spent large sums on his favorites, and the treasury had to be replenished. Scotland was unusually critical of James, and one preacher is said to have called out in his sermon, that "all kings' children were the devil's children," and even went so far as to call the queen an atheist. While in England, James in a speech in Parliament pleaded for tolerance, stating that "nothing can be more hateful than the uncharitableness of the Puritans, who condemned alike to eternal torments even the most inoffensive partisans of Popery," and "that the blood of the martyrs was the seed of the church." Later, proving the inconsistency of human nature, he had a law passed which required the members of both houses of Parliament to partake of the Sacrament.

Lazy, indolent, pleasure-loving James, who indulged in all sports, especially hunting, was gracious enough to allow his subjects the same privileges, permitting sports on Sunday after divine services, and a little later a book was published advocating this idea. This act, as can well be imagined, was especially irritating to the Nonconformists, and Puritans, and aroused a greater hatred of the king and the prescribed church.

Parliament, and also the people at large in the meanwhile were growing in their desire for freedom, which was to burst out into a mighty conflagration in the following reign. The gunpowder plot in 1605 probably did, for a time, awaken James to the dangers of his position, but it was soon forgotten, and he continued to lavish wealth and titles on his favorites.

In spite of wars and rumors of wars, in spite of the religious conflicts and persecutions, the arts flourished. Shakespeare, Chapman, Beaumont and Fletcher were writing and producing plays. Rubens, Van Dyck and other artists were painting portraits and other works of art—masterpieces that were to grow in beauty and value in the passing of the centuries. Colleges and hospitals were founded, as well as Botanical Gardens, and even a submarine was invented in 1620 by a Dutchman named Drebbel. It was not until one hundred and fifty-five years later that David Bushnell, a Yale student, invented the first one in America. The trades were making rapid advancement. Broadcloth, tapestries, silks and other fabrics were being manufactured. The principal streets in London were being paved. Printing presses were kept busy producing books, newspapers, and even a journal was established in the English metropolis devoted only to foreign news. William Harvey had discovered the circulation of the blood. King James' version of the Bible was printed, and "God Save the King" was first sung to music.

James' reign was much influenced by the opening of the possibilities in the New World, and the emigration of the Pilgrim Fathers first to Leyden, Holland, and later to Plymouth, New England. The execution of Sir Walter Raleigh caused the indignation of all classes, for it was thought to have been instigated by the Spanish government. The feeling against Raleigh that had been so pronounced when he was committed to the Tower had been greatly modified during the thirteen years of his confinement, especially so, after he had written his "History of the World." It was with sympathy for him and perhaps an eagerness for gold that the populace greeted King James' final permission for him to sail with his twelve armed ships to Guiana for the fabulous gold mine which was found to exist only in Raleigh's fertile imagination. The result was the destruction of the Spanish town of St. Thomas on the Orinoco River, and in Raleigh's imprisonment and final execution. Thus perished one of the most romantic figures in the history of that time.

An event that complicated international affairs was the blow to the Huguenots at the fall of La Rochelle in France in 1628.

Another of the greatest mistakes made in the two reigns both from a political and religious standpoint, was creating Laud, bishop, and depending upon his counsels regarding the Puritans. This latter act was to bear bitter fruit for all parties.

Frederic, Count of Palatine, had married Elizabeth, the only surviving daughter of James, who had joined the Protestant forces. Later his father-in-law raised an army and sent it to his aid, and again, in 1624. The following year another army of several thousand men was sent to the Low Countries to join the English contingent under General Sir Francis Vere. In his battalions, as well as in those sent later by Charles I, then in command of Sir Horace Vere, brother of Sir Francis, were several men who were later to distinguish themselves in the military forces of New England: Captain Patrick, Captain Underhill, Captain Miles Standish, Captain Lion Gardiner, and Captain John Mason. Nearly all were young men at that period, and their experiences in the military forces in the Low Countries were to serve them so well in their adopted one later.

In the same year that King James died, in 1625, Frederick Henry succeeded his brother as Prince of Orange who continued his country's fight for freedom from the Spanish yoke, and Charles I became King of England.

Charles' marriage with Henrietta Marie, daughter of Henry IV of France, proved a happier one than is generally credited to, or falls to the lot of royal marriages. The queen was a Catholic, and this was a strain on the principles of the Puritans who every day were becoming stronger in Parliament. Charles also made the fatal mistake that his father had made before him, in following the counsels of the Duke of Buckingham and Bishop Laud. The first was a knave, the latter a bigot and cruel fanatic. Buckingham had been raised from obscurity on account of his handsome person, by King James, to a leading position in the aristocracy and government. His evil temper and abnormal vanity made him a danger to the nation in which he played a leading rôle. He was abhorred by Parliament, as well as by the people, and this sentiment was aggravated by the king's continually showering him with titles and wealth. The unfortunate results of the visit Buckingham and Charles, then Prince of Wales, paid to Philip IV of Spain, when Charles was betrothed to the Infanta, was one of the principal causes of war between the two countries. Charles had at once been welcomed and loved by royalty and the Spanish people, but for Buckingham, with his arrogance and insulting ways, they had only contempt. The English favorite resented this attitude, and it was due to his machinations that the Spanish match was broken. This may have pleased the English people, since the Infanta was a Catholic, but it grieved and embarrassed King James, as the two million dowry was not easy to give up. Also Buckingham's vanity was wounded by being repulsed by the Queen of France, at his absurd advances, which determined him to persuade Charles to declare war on France. This all happened when not only the King was bankrupt, but the country as well. Parliament refused to advance the expenses incurred, and the forced loans exacted from the people, raised the first distant rumbles of the approaching revolution.

Research has not revealed the date of the enlistment of John Mason in the English army, nor the year in which he first went to Holland. We only know that in 1630 he was in the forces under Sir Horace Vere, and at that time Thomas Fairfax, who was later to fill the distinguished office of commander of the Parliamentary army during the civil war, joined the army in the Low Countries in time for them both to be in the battle of Bois-le-Duc, in April of that year. "The Maid Brabant," as Bois-le-Duc was called, owing to her never having been taken, was the most important military station in the Brabant. Sieur de Grubbendonck [1] was governor of the town, Anthony Schets was in command of the fortress, and Count

1 Antoine, the Lord de Grubbendonck, is referred to by Mason in his "History of the Pequot War." He held Bois-le-Duc in three sieges and also at the attack of Levain.

Note: Sir Ferdinando Gorges, who later was to be such a thorn in the side of the Puritans in New England, fought side by side with Lord Vere in this battle.

Henry de Berghe was in the field with a large force. The Dutch were under the command of Prince Ferdinand and Lord Vere led the English, which were said to number over thirty thousand men.

"The place was gallantly defended" was stated in a letter written at Bois-le-Duc under date of May 12, 1630, by Thomas Fairfax, to his grandfather. He described the place "as one of great strength, with marshy ground on one side," and mentions that "the enemy kept up a sharp fire when the siege commenced, which had slackened." Bois-le-Duc surrendered in July, and shortly after, Thomas Fairfax followed the wishes of his grandfather, and left the camp to "travel in France, where he remained for about eighteen months, learning the language and other accomplishments."

Fairfax's stay in the Low Countries was of short duration, but long enough for him to win the heart of Anne de Vere and the approval of her father. They were married a few years later in England.

It was during this period that Fairfax and Mason became comrades. This friendship was based not only upon a mutual liking, but also on the high opinion Fairfax had formed of Mason's military talents. Later, when Lord Fairfax was the commander of the Parliamentary forces, he urged Mason to return to England to accept a commission of high rank in that army.

III

Many changes had occurred in North America since the beginning of the century. Several voyages of discovery

had been made along the coast of Maine, Cape Cod and
Buzzards Bay. Samuel Champlain had sailed up the St.
Lawrence as early as 1603, and later discovered the lake
named in his honor. George Weymouth, together with
John Knight, had attempted an expedition to the Arctic
Circle. A colony had been founded in Nova Scotia, but
the only settlements in the country now included in the
United States were a few by the Spanish in Florida, southern California, Santa Fé in 1605, and the first one in
New England at St. Croix, Maine, in 1603, which was
abandoned the following year. Weymouth returned from
his cruise along the southern coast that year bringing
reports that resulted in a charter being granted for the
settlement of Virginia. The colony was established the
following summer, and was named Jamestown in honor
of the King. In the same year an attempt was made to
found a colony on the coast of Maine, but the severe
climate and general disappointment so discouraged the
colonists, who numbered over a hundred, that they soon
returned to England.

The year 1607 was a propitious one in the history of
America. Henry Hudson made his second voyage and
discovered the Hudson River. This year records the first
literature of the New World, the first book written on
America which led others to venture to this great land
of mystery, for the exaggerated and curious accounts were
spread over England, and induced many to try their for-
tunes in America. John Mason had passed his seventh
birthday, old enough to begin to be thrilled by the stories
of Indians and bears that he heard on every side. He

was much too young, however, to dream then that he would one day play such an important part in that land which had just been opened.

The first book written in America of which there is any record is by Captain John Smith, entitled "A True Relation of Virginia" which gives a graphic account of the country and its inhabitants, as well as the experiences, trials, quarrels, and attacks of the Indians. The title page reads as follows—

"A True Relation of such occurrences and accidents of note as hath happened in Virginia since the first planting of the colony, which is now resident in the South part therof, till the last return from thence. Written by Captain Smith, Colonel of the said colony, to a worshipful friend of his in London, England. Printed for John Tappe, and are to be sold at the Grey-hound in St. Paul's church-yard, by W. W. 1608." [1]

Captain Smith was most prolific in the histories of his adventures, and the complete works gave the author the modest title of "President of Virginia and Admiral of New England." He gives an interesting account of Pocahontas; how she saved his life, and also the lives of the other colonists by notifying them that her father planned to massacre the settlers. He also tells of her romance and marriage to John Rolfe and of her triumphs in England where she was recognized as a royal princess, and where her portrait was painted by the famous artist Sully. This depicts her as a handsome young woman, while another is the likeness of a more mature woman. The European costume is an incongruous setting for her Indian features.

[1] A first edition of this work sold in New York City in 1934 for $800.

This portrait is labeled—"The Portrait of Rebecca, daughter of the Great Emperor of Powhatan . . . and wife of John Rolfe." [1]

Another book on Virginia appeared about the same time, written by George Percy, brother of the Earl of Northumberland, entitled—"Discovery of the Plantations of the Southern Colony in Virginia by the English." It gives an account of the settlement from the time he left England to the autumn of that year. He describes the beauties of the country, and then adds this pathetic account, so different from the glowing descriptions given by some of the other writers. "Our men were destroyed with cruel diseases, as swellings, flixes, burning fevers, and by wars; and some departed suddenly. But for the most part they died of mere famine. There were never Englishmen left in a foreign country in such misery as we were, in this new discovered Virginia. We watched every three nights lying on the bare ground, what weather soever came; warded all the next day which brought our men to be most feeble wretches. Our food was but a small can of barley sod in water to five men a day; our drink cold water taken out of the river, which was at flood very salt, at a low tide full of slime and filth, which was the destruction of many of our men. Thus we lived for the space of five months in this miserable distress, not having five able men to man our bulwarks upon any occasion. If it had not pleased God to put a terror in the savages' hearts, we had all perished by those wild and cruel pagans, being in that weak estate as we were; our men night and

---

1 Pocahontas left a son who came to Virginia to live. It is interesting to note that three hundred years later a descendant of hers should become the First Lady of the Land, as mistress of the White House.

day groaning in every corner of the fort most pitiful to hear. If there were any conscience in men, it would make their hearts to bleed to hear the pitiful murmurings and outcries of our sick men, without relief every night and day for the space of six weeks; some departing out of the world, many times three or four in a night, in the morning their bodies trailed out of their cabins like dogs to be buried."

These small volumes were followed in 1610 by William Strachey's book: "A True Reportory of the Wreck and redemption of Sir Thomas Gates, Kt., upon and from the islands of Bermuda: his coming to Virginia, and the estate of that colony then and after, and under the government of the Lord LeWare." This work gives an interesting account of the shipwreck on the Bermuda Island, how they built new boats salvaged from the wrecks and finally, months later, arrived at Jamestown, long after they had thought to have been lost. The description given in this history is supposed by many to have been the inspiration of Shakespeare's "Tempest."

It must have been encouraging to the friends remaining at home to read the Rev. William Whitacker's "Good News from Virginia," published in 1613. This work is remarkable in that it expresses sympathy for the Indians, albeit, more for their souls than for the treatment by the whites. He writes—"let the miserable condition of these naked slaves of the devil move you to compassion toward them. They acknowledge that there is a great God, but know him not. . . . They live naked in body, as if the shame of their sin deserved no covering. . . . They esteem it a virtue to lie, deceive and steal, as their master teacheth them. . . . If this be their life, what think you shall become of them after death, but to be partakers with the devil and his angels in hell for ever more."

The secretary of Governor Sir George Yeardley, one George Pory, wrote some very interesting accounts of the early days in the Virginia colony. He lived there from 1619 to 1622, and being of a very gay nature and a lover of adventure, his descriptions, one can imagine, were greatly exaggerated though amusing, and perhaps were written, as some suppose, while under the influence of liberal potations. In describing his interview with Namenacus the chief of the Pawtuxent tribe of Indians, to whom he had given a Bible with explanations, the chief remarked "that he was like Adam in one thing, for he never had but one wife at once."

During the early period wives were much needed in the Virginia settlement, and numbers of women were sent over at different times to be chosen, but generally bought by prospective husbands, who often paid as much as 150 pounds of tobacco for a helpmate. There were as many as sixty women sent over at one time.

Changes were rapidly taking place also in other harbors of the eastern coast of the Atlantic. Colonizing of Canada had begun at an early date, and at different times had been discouraged by the armed expeditions sent out by the English against the French settlements. Especially devastating was the force sent out in three ships under command of Argall, who was accompanied by a Jesuit named Biard. They burned St. Sauveur, St. Croix and at Port Royal, not satisfied with destroying the buildings during the absence of the inhabitants, they cruelly robbed them of all their household goods and even food, and this at the beginning of winter.

In the meanwhile the English had founded a colony at New Foundland, with Captain John Mason as governor (as far as known he was not related to Major Mason). The proclamation in 1630 established peace for the time between France and England. Gorges and Popham sent out an expedition to Maine in 1607, but as said before, one winter was sufficient to discourage them, and they soon returned to England. Not discouraged, Gorges fitted out another boat to trade furs and fish with the Indians, and is said to have kept men in his employ in the Kennebec section for the next several years. That explains how some of the Indians living there, and a few taken captive to England, learned the English language.

It is generally taken for granted, save by the students of history, that the aborigines of the country were free from all diseases and epidemics before the arrival of the whites, but history has proved this to be an erroneous idea. One of the worst epidemics, of what nature is unknown, swept over and destroyed entire tribes of Indians in New England in 1614 to 1616. The Europeans, as well as the tribes of Pequots and Narragansetts, escaped. Six years later an early settler when passing over the land once occupied by these Indians which were believed to have numbered several thousand, said that "they died in heaps . . . and the bones and skulls upon several places of their inhabitants made such a spectacle after my coming into those parts, that, as I travailed in that Forest nere the Massachusetts, it seemed to mee a new found Golgotha." This was described many years later by the intolerant Mather in his "Magnalia," as "the woods were almost cleared of those pernicious creatures to make room for a better growth."

It is known that two French trading vessels visited Cape Cod at an early date, which had been discovered and named by Bartholomew Gosnold in 1602. One of the ships was wrecked and all the crew murdered by the natives, save two. One of these joined the Indian tribe, married a squaw, leaving issue. The other boat anchored in the Boston bay. It was visited by the Indians who came in their canoes, ostensibly to trade, stealthily covering and concealing their weapons. On gaining the deck of the vessel, they murdered the crew—a feat they told with much boasting and joy to the settlers who came later.

Captain Smith was accompanied on his voyage to New England, by a companion ship, manned by Thomas Hunt. After the departure of Smith, Hunt remained behind to load a cargo of dried fish. When about to sail, he persuaded some twenty Indians, by promises of presents, to go on board, and among the number was one named Squanto, who later was to be of great value in aiding the planters. The Indians were no sooner on the vessel, when the sails were unfurled, the anchor hoisted, and the ship sailed away with the Indian captives, called by Hunt, "silly savages," to be sold as slaves in Spain. Fortunately for the prisoners, the priests at Malaje saw in the Indians an opportunity to make converts to the Faith, and due to their interest, Squanto and one other were rescued from slavery; the others, as far as known, did not escape that fate. This incident was the beginning of the Indian hostilities, and was one of others, which eventually led to the Pequot war.

Colonies were being founded both north and south along the coast. The Dutch, save an occasional ship sent over for the fur trade, did not make any attempt to settle in New Amsterdam until seventeen years after Hudson had discovered the river that bears his name. Even then they sailed by the island that was to be the site of the largest city in America, to Albany, which they named "Orange." They erected Fort Auraina there, and at once began to branch out in every direction. They did not establish a colony on the island of Manhattan until 1626, when Peter Minuit, a director in the Dutch East India Company, purchased the island for goods worth 60 guilders, equivalent to $25. In 1643, when a French priest visited the plantation, he noted but little growth of the colony.

In the meantime the Dutch were trading in the adjoining country to Albany, and it is said that they discovered the Connecticut River as early as 1614, which they named the "Fresh River." Later, when the English forced their way into that region, disputes arose between the two colonies which led to trouble during many years, as to which had the right to the land. The Dutch based their claims by the right of discovery and purchase from the Indians. It is worth noting in passing, that the Indians living on the disputed land were glad of the white settlement, as they believed they would be protected from the domination of their Pequot enemies, who had treated them with great cruelty.

The little band of Pilgrims that fled from England in

1607, and settled in Holland, found, after years of struggle, that it was practically impossible for them to gain a
living in a country so foreign to their early training and
language.   After much difficulty, both with the English
government, and eventually with the elements, they set
sail on that memorable voyage in the now famous *Mayflower*. The discomforts and trials that beset them, as well
as all of the early colonists on their passages, can hardly be
realized by us of this generation.   Not only the shortage
of food, but the quality was of a most unappetizing kind.
Storms threatened their small craft, and disputes that came
near to a mutiny arose among the passengers.   It was a
question who should have the authority to rule the land to
which they were then sailing.   Fortunately the Compact
that was drawn up on board the *Mayflower,* "was intended
not only as a basis for the government of the colony in the
absence of the patent," but also, according to Bradford,
" 'as an effect to the discontented and mutinous speeches'
of some of the company."

The courage and perseverance of the colonists was put
to the most extreme tests.   These hardy pioneers possessed an indomitable spirit in braving these unknown
hardships—a spirit of courage which they bequeathed to
their descendants.   Landing in the midst of a wilderness
in a New England winter, beset by all kinds of trials, it is
not surprising that many did not survive the first few
months of the settlement.   It is impossible for us living in
this age of comforts to thoroughly realize the sufferings
which our ancestors endured.   Sick, without the necessary
drugs to heal or alleviate the pain, not sufficient food, nor
of the kind that should be administered to the sick, they

were nursed by the layman whose kindness was his only recommendation to aid, and often the conditions were so nauseating, that only those with unusually strong stomachs could perform the revolting tasks. One can imagine, then, the joy of the planters when the first Indian made his appearance and greeted them in English, with the word "welcome." The man's name was Samoset, who had learned a few words of English from the fishermen who had visited the coast from time to time, but it was the friendship of Squanto, the only surviving Indian of the Pokanokat tribe that proved invaluable to the whites. He had escaped the epidemic which had destroyed his people, that Smith described in 1614 when he visited their land, as a "goodly, strong, well proportioned people," who dwelt in a "paradise of all these parts," so that his capture by Captain Hunt had saved his life, and which had given him the opportunity to learn the language of the settlers. He instructed the colonists in planting corn and in renewing the land by fertilizing it with fish. He also acted as interpreter between the English and the Indians.

Human nature being what it is, it is not strange that the planters had other problems than those of climate and the adverse conditions of adjusting themselves to a wilderness home. The threats of the London Company, their demands for payments for money advanced, their endeavors to force the newcomers to accept the Church of England service, though they had emigrated for the free exercise of their religious beliefs, all combined to harass the colony. Then came the grant in 1622 to Gorges and Mason [1] to

---

[1] This John Mason is not known to have been a relative of Major John Mason.

all the land along the coast of Maine and extending west to an indefinite point, which in reality included most, if not all, of the present New England states. At the same time the Indians were combining forces and planning to massacre all the white intruders. They did not realize that the planters had Captain Miles Standish with whom they would have to contend. He was short in stature, though of a military bearing, but not the romantic person in appearance we are led to believe. He had had a classical education, judging by his library. Standish had joined the Pilgrims, though he was not a member of their sect. It was even thought by some that he was inclined to catholicism. He was a man of great courage and insight, which was well illustrated on several occasions—one of which was when he went in search of corn for the famished planters, to the town known as Sandwich, where danger threatened him and his men and he paced before the fire through the long, winter night, knowing his life as well as the lives of his comrades were in danger. Standish was trying one time, to learn the number of the Indians in that vicinity. His experience when camping with friendly savages was far from pleasant. The food was badly cooked, the sleeping quarters were poor, and what with lice, bedbugs and Indians as sleeping companions, he and his fellow men were glad to make their visit short.

There was much jealousy among the Indians owing to the position that Squanto held with the whites. Corbitant, an Indian chief of a neighboring tribe, hated Squanto, as well as his English friends, and he said that if Squanto were dead "the English had lost their tongue." This jealousy on account of Squanto led to several con-

spiracies to murder him. His enemies tried to persuade
the planters that he was only acting as a spy to eventually
betray the whites into the hands of the unfriendly red
men. These accusations, after a time, aroused the suspicions of the Pilgrims, who were on the point of prosecuting him. Fortunately, perhaps, "he died on a voyage with
some of the whites, and 'proved his loyalty' by giving his
belongings to his English friends in testimony of his affection." He died in November, 1622.

The colonists had at an early date won the friendship
of Massasoit, sachem of the remnant tribe of the Massachusetts Indians. The authorities had received gifts from
him, and the peaceful relations were cemented when
Winslow and Stephen Hopkins went as envoys to his home,
taking presents of clothing. This friendship proved of
great value both to the whites and red men. When Massasoit was threatened by the Narragansetts, the Plymouth
authorities sent counter threats if any injury befell either
Squanto or Massasoit due to their emnity. Massasoit's
warning to the settlers of the massacre which the warlike
Indians planned, saved them from annihilation, a fate
that befell the colonists of Virginia. It is sad to relate that
this great service that saved the lives of the Plymouth
planters was forgotten during King Philip's war, when the
whites sold the infant grandchild of Massasoit, the unfortunate son of Philip, into West Indies slavery. The treaty
between Massasoit and the Plymouth colony was kept for
fifty-four years.

Another trouble that beset the Plymouth colony was
when Weston, an adventurer of bad repute, attempted a
settlement at Wessagusset, with men of the lowest type.

This led to complications which would have terminated in the annihilation of the New England settlers had it not been for the quick action of Standish upon receiving a message from Massasoit of the plot to kill the planters. Weston's band of adventurers had stolen corn from the Indians, took familiarities with their women, and had become so poor that without help from the savages, would have died of starvation.   But in spite of this help to Weston, they had planned to massacre the whites.   Standish realized the seriousness of the situation and took means to overcome it which has led to a blot on his memory.   He invited Peeksnot and Wittowamat, who were leaders in the plot against the English, to meet him in the stockade, where they came in good faith, and unarmed.   They were no sooner in the white man's camp, than they were set upon by Standish and his men and murdered.   This act, cruel as it was, no doubt saved the English from being wiped out, and which Bradford said was "the just judgment of God."

To add to the discomfort of the planters, several of their buildings burnt.   Then John Oldham and John Lyford, the latter, "the sneaking, cowardly minister," were planning to undermine the London Company's faith in the leaders of the Pilgrims.   Bradford's success in intercepting the letters which the traitors were sending to England, resulted in their banishment.   He describes them as "most unsavory salt" and that it was another means of the devil to persecute God's anointed.   They were both banished. Oldham at once, and Lyford a little later, being allowed to remain until the weather was more seasonable to leave with his family.   Oldham, however, reappeared some time

after, when he was "clapt up a while" and then told to
"goe and mend his manners." Morton of Merry-Mount
gives a good description of his exit. "After a solemne invention in this manner; A lane of Muskitiers was made
and hee compelled in scorne to passe along betweene, and
to receive a bob upon the bumme by every musketier."

The letter episode illustrates a practice that was quite
common at that time. There seemed to have been no
compunction in regard to opening other people's mail.
This happened on several occasions, and regardless of the
lack of principle involved, it no doubt saved the colonies
from disastrous consequences.

With all of these misadventures, Winslow who returned
from a visit to England, must have been most welcome, as
he brought news from friends at home, and four head of
cattle, said to be the first to arrive in that colony.

Another great trial to the Pilgrim fathers, one incident
of which, regarded from our present standpoint, is a little
amusing. It was the conduct of Thomas Morton of
Merry-Mount, and his gay companions. It was in 1625
that one Captain Wollston arrived in the colonies accompanied by four or five followers, one of whom was the
famous Thomas Morton, as Bradford said, "and a great
many servants . . . all lavish Fellows." Of Morton, he
wrote that he was "a man of pretie parts." Later Wollston,
with most of his "redemptioners" went to Virginia, where
the latter were sold for slaves for the stated time for
which they had signed. Morton at once took possession
of the settlement, where, according to Bradford, they conducted themselves "as if they had anew revived and celebrated practices of ye madd Baccanalians." There seemed

to be no distinction of race in the Merry-Mount carousals, as the Indian women took part in the May-Pole dances. This was all as bad as could be from the Plymouth moral and religious standpoint, but the promiscuous way in which they were selling fire arms and ammunition to the savages, was much more serious, as it was a menace to the safety of the colonists. In addition, it gave the Merry-Mount men a monopoly of the fur trade, for the Indians would sell anything they possessed for guns and powder. The clothing, hatchets and gewgaws which had hitherto pleased the natives in barter with the Plymouth colony lost their value in comparison to what Morton and his band paid. Consequently the magistrates decided to arrest "mine hoste," as Morton called himself, which they accomplished by a ruse, and to be sure of their prisoner, several guards were set about the camp where he was kept for the night, even one of them sleeping with him, but for all of that he made his escape, only to be recaptured the following day at Mt. Wollston. He was tried and instead of giving him the death penalty, which some of the English, including Standish, desired, he was banished to England. Within two years he was back again at his former home, carrying on his life as formerly. He not only antagonized Plymouth, but which was more serious for him, the new settlement at Salem. With the stern Endicott and the intolerant Dudley, there was little chance of Morton's escaping their vindictiveness, and he was accordingly brought to trial in 1630. A trial, so called, since it was a farce from the beginning. Morton was not allowed to make any defense, and the verdict, which was no doubt decided beforehand, was that he "be set in the bilbowes, and after sent prisoner into England . . . that all his goods shall be seized upon to defray the charge of his transportation, payment for his debts and to give satisfaction to the Indians for a canoe he unjustly took away from them; and that his home, after his goods are taken out, shall be burnt to the ground in the sight of the Indians for their satisfaction." It is said he saw his house in flames as he sailed away.

Morton described all of these experiences in his book "New English Canaan" in which he refers to Endicott as "Captain Littleworth." His version varies from those given by Winthrop and Bradford, and makes very interesting reading. Regardless of the dissolute life that was led by Morton and his men, the accusations brought against him by Endicott were not sufficient for the verdict that was given. It not only showed the intolerance of the Puritans, but also their shortsightedness in sending Morton to the homeland where the New England colonies had so many enemies, for Morton and Sir Christopher Gardiner, the latter another colonial adventurer, were followers of Sir Ferdinando Gorges. They, together with Radcliffe, who had been severely punished on account of his religious beliefs differing from the founders, were all banished to England where they had an opportunity of testifying before the Privy Council of the conditions in New England, and endeavored to assist Gorges and Mason to have the Massachusetts' charter revoked. A committee of twelve Lords was appointed to investigate the matter, but as King Charles decided with the magistrates of New England, the matter, for the time, was dropped. However, two years later, the king reversed his decision and decided to appoint Gorges governor-general of the northern colonies.   When this information reached this side of the Atlantic, it caused the authorities to reinforce the fort and train the militia for any emergency.   Fortunately for the colonists, the troubles in England, and finally the death of Mason and later of Gorges, saved the planters from that misfortune.   Fourteen years later Thomas Morton was again in New England, this time a broken-down old man, and was thoughtless enough to venture into Massachusetts where the ever-watchful Endicott had him seized and immediately tried for having appeared before the Privy Council.   He was imprisoned for a year, tried again, given his freedom, though fined a hundred pounds.   He died two years later in extreme poverty.

One of the strangest occurrences in the early Plymouth settlement was the first recorded duel ever fought there, which happened in 1621, when two servants with sword and dagger engaged in a fierce encounter.   It is told that they were both wounded.   Their punishment was "to be tied for twenty-four hours with their hands and feet together."

John Endicott and his company numbering a hundred planters not including servants, arrived in 1628, and founded Salem, the first settlement in Massachusetts, and the second in New England.   This was the first of the sect known as Puritans to be established in the New World.   This term given by the members of the Church of England to followers of this religion, was first heard of in 1564 and was a term of contempt.   Fuller in his ecclesiastical history says "it was improved to abuse pious people, who endeavored to follow the minister with a pure heart, and

labored for a life pure and holy." To be called a Puritan
at that time, was considered an insult by those not of that
sect. They were also called "The Unspottyd Lambs of
the Lord."

The Massachusetts Bay Colony was established in England in 1629, and Governor Winthrop and his company
sailed in the spring of 1630. He wrote to his wife on
board the *Arabella* from Cowes under date of March 28,
of that year, "I can write the good news, that we are all
in very good health, and having tried our ship's entertainment now more than a week, we find it agree very well
with us. . . . We have only four ships ready, and some
two or three Hollanders go along with us. The rest of
our fleet, (being seven ships) will not be ready this sen-
night. We are all in our eleven ships, about seven hundred persons, passengers, and two hundred and forty cows,
and about sixty horses. And now (my sweet soul) I must
once again take my last farewell of thee in Old England.
It goeth very near my heart to leave thee." They arrived
in Charlestown harbor June 17. He recorded in his diary
under July 2, "My son Henry was drowned at Salem."

From this time the Massachusetts colony grew rapidly
so that new towns were continually being established.
Often as many as fourteen to seventeen ships would arrive
within a year. Many of the passengers died on the long
trips across the Atlantic in their miniature vessels, and it is
almost unbelievable that not one of their boats was lost
previous to the sinking of the *Angel Gabriel* in 1635 off
the coast of Maine.

Increase Mather was one of the immigrants, on board
the shipwrecked vessel. An excerpt from his diary record-

ing this event may be of interest. "Aug. 14. While
anchored on the Ile of Shoaler, when wee had slept sweetly
ye night till break of day. . . . But yet ye Lord had not
done with us, nor yet let us see all his power and goodness
which he would have us take knowledge of, and therefore
on Saturday morn, at break of day, ye Lord sent forth a
most terrible storme of raine, and easterly wind, whereby
wee were in as much danger as I think ever people were.
For we lost in ye morning three great anchors and cables,
one having cost fifty pounds, broken by ye violence of ye
waves, and ye third was cut by ye seamen in extremity
and distress to save ye ship and our lives, and ye Angel
Gabriel," and he ends the account with "The Lord's name
be blessed forever." Hubbard's account reads—"It was on
the terrible 15th of August, 1635 that Parson Avery perished with these words upon his lips—'Lord I cannot challenge a preservation of life, but according to the covenant,
I challenge heaven,' which words, as soon as he had ever
expressed, the next wave gave him a present dismission
into eternal rest." How the parson's words could have
been heard in the torrent of the storm, and memorized, is
quite beyond our understanding, nevertheless, it inspired
Whittier to later write the following poem entitled "The
Swan Song of Parson Avery" 1853 edition.

> "There was wailing in the shallop;
>   Woman's wail and man's despair;
> A crash of breaking timbers on the rocks
>   So sharp and bare;
> And through it all the murmur of
>   Father Avery's prayer.

The ear of God was open to his servant's
  last request.
As the strong wave swept him downward,
  the sweet hymn upward pressed,
And the soul of Father Avery went sinking
  to its rest."

By 1636 the settlers were beginning to push farther back
into the country toward the Connecticut River.   Large
numbers of immigrants were arriving, people of a superior
class, many of them of note, not only in their own country,
but were to add to the prestige of the New World.   Those
of the lower order were mostly servants.   Boston, Dorchester, Watertown and Roxbury were founded, while
Charlestown, owing to the poor water and no sanitary arrangements, was depopulated by an epidemic when several
hundred died under most pathetic conditions.

The passing of time since the establishment of Plymouth, had brought many improvements and comforts,
and even luxuries, in exchange for the furs and dried fish
that were sent to England.   Even literature had made its
advent, though not to be recognized as such until many
years later.   William Bradford's "History of Plymouth,"
one of the most valuable records, which was lost for many
years, now gives us a most intimate account of the Pilgrims' settlement, of the lives of the people and of their
leaders, Bradford, Brewster, Winslow and John Carver.
The generosity of the latter's fortune had made it possible
for the settlement, and his fate was to die within three
months after he landed.   Another work which does for
Massachusetts, what Bradford did for Plymouth, was the

journal kept by Winthrop.   Much of the early history of the northern colonies is based on these two journals.

This brings us to the time when the subject of this history came to America.

CHAPTER II

THE fleet of boats from the mother country to New England grew larger year by year. On one of the vessels, sailing early in 1632, was a young man of fine appearance, over six feet in height, well proportioned, and of a military bearing. This was John Mason, sailing to his new home in America. The tedious voyage of several weeks' duration, in a 400-ton ship, was probably not trying to this man who had roughed it for years in the military operations in the Low Countries. He had become accustomed to privations, and hardships with all the annoyances that are a part of a soldier's life. Free from care, and ready for any emergency for which his early life had trained him, he looked forward to the New World with hope and courage. His commission as a lieutenant in the English army gave him a standing among his fellow passengers, as it was to do among the settlers later. The irregular life of a campaigning soldier in a foreign country was not conducive to matrimony, and he, like most of the men who had served in the army abroad, and were now emigrating to America, was a bachelor.

The laws of the colonists, however, were severe against men remaining single. Bachelors were looked upon with suspicion, and in many settlements they were fined. No one wished to take them into their homes as boarders. Every pressure and inducement was used to do away with "single blessedness," which the planters claimed was not according to the teachings of the Scriptures. A law was passed in the colonies a few years later regarding this subject, forbidding any young man from keeping house by himself without permission of the town, under penalty of twenty shillings a week, and any master of a family entertaining unmarried young men without the permission of the town was subject to the same fine. Consequently it is not surprising that the young lieutenant turned Benedict. Just when this occurred, and where, and with whom, is not recorded, all we know is that it happened some time soon after his arrival.

The settlements of the New England colonies in 1632 were far from being attractive, and it is not difficult to imagine the homesickness and disappointment that must have filled the hearts of the immigrants on their arrival, even though it was a joy to be once more on land. Roger Clap in his "Memoirs" describes his first impressions of the country as a "vacant wilderness." The houses were in most cases mere shacks, thatched with grass. Even the "Meeting House," as it was sacrilegious to call the place of worship a church, was only a rough, square boarded building. The streets of the towns were paths, where swine, cattle and chickens had freedom to wander where they would. In spite of the crudeness of the dwellings, the ships were beginning to bring new finery to tempt the inhabitants. Food was becoming more plentiful, as corn was shipped from Virginia, and in 1631 sold "at ten shillings the bushel," while a year later the price was reduced to four shillings sixpence.

Potatoes were brought to the colony at an early date, some authorities say as early as 1630, and it is possible that

the Pilgrims had them previous to that time. Many did
not consider them fit to eat, since they were not mentioned
in the Bible, and those believing these superstitions, said
that any one who ate them would surely die within seven
years. Evidently the planters soon learned to free themselves from this fear, as Winthrop notes that in 1636 "the
Rebecka came from Bermuda with thirty thousand weight
of potatoes, and a store of oranges, and (limes). Potatoes
were brought there for two shillings and eight pence the
bushel, and sold here for two pence the pound." Beverages seemed plentiful, and "beers and ales were preferred,"
wrote Roger Clap, and it was "not accounted a strange
thing in these days to drink water." "Strong waters" were
forbidden by law, and alcohol in any form was not allowed
to be sold to the "inflamed devilish bloody savages."
Cattle, and horses were being shipped from southern colonies, and also from England, so that scarcity of food from
which the first planters suffered, was past, though this
scarcity occurred in Connecticut following the Pequot
war.

The clergy, from the first, were all-powerful. They
were not supposed to hold any office, though no law could
be passed without their approval, which made them, in
fact, the real dictators of the commonwealth, and they
used their authority in directing, or rather instructing,
the members of their congregations how to vote. The
ballot was first used in America July 20, 1628, to elect
John Wilson pastor. Occasionally the deputies and magistrates did not agree on points of law, and at such times,
the preachers and elders of the church would be called in
to hear the arguments and make decisions. At one of

these disputes, the question arose as to whether the magistrates should give a verdict as the law dictated, or whether it could be modified or varied according to the circumstances. The elders decided after a long speech, that the penalty must vary according to the nature of the crime, and added as an example, "So any sin committed with an high hand, as the gathering of sticks on the Sabbath day may be punished with death, when a lesser punishment may serve for gathering sticks privily and in some need."

The services in the meeting house began at nine in the morning of the "Lord's Day," and lasted until noon. The afternoon session followed immediately after the cold, noon repast. Cold, as nothing could be cooked on the seventh day of the week, which began at sundown on Saturday. The sermons and prayers were often hours in length, during which time the worshipers in winter sat in unheated buildings where the temperature was often so low during the winter months, that the preachers wore cloaks and mittens while they preached. The members of the congregation were likewise protected from the cold, and the men, as well as the women carried muffs. When one realizes that these primitive meeting houses were not as well built as the old-fashioned barns, often having cracks through which the cold, winter winds swept, it is astonishing that so many of the settlers survived and were able to go on with their work. These extremes of temperature did not, however, prevent babes from being baptized. Judge Sewall wrote in his diary as late as "Lord's Day, January 15, 1716. An Extraordinary Cold Storm of Wind and Snow . . . . Bread was frozen at the Lord's Table. . . . Though Twas so Cold, yet John Tucerman was bap-

tized.   At Six o'clock my ink freezes so that I can hardly
write by a fire in my Wife's Chamber." Children were
baptized within a day or two after birth, and as we have
noted, regardless of the weather, where in some instances,
the ice in the baptismal fonts had to be broken before
proceeding with the ceremony.   No wonder that mortality
among the children was appalling.   Sometimes in a family
of eighteen or twenty, only two or three of the children
would survive to reach maturity.

Next in importance to the services on the Lord's day,
were the Thursday lectures which originally began in the
morning and lasted all day, and occasionally into the night.
So much time was given to attendance to the lectures, that
as early as 1633, it was found necessary to change the hour
to one o'clock in the afternoon.   The preachers at once
raised objections to the limited time.   They felt that it was
an intrusion by the magistrates on their rights and privileges.   The matter was not adjusted satisfactorily, and
finally six years later, another law was passed limiting lectures to not over two a week.   In spite of these laws, which
the clergy felt was a restriction on the exercises of the
Lord's work, the ministers were held in great reverence.
A good illustration was shown by the congregation rising
when the parson entered the meeting house and walked to
the pulpit.   He was generally dressed in black, and wore
a German cloak and skull cap.

There was nothing more thrilling these days than the
Sunday sermon, the religious lectures on Thursday after-
noons, and the pleasure of watching transgressors of the
law being punished.   Hunting and even skating were permitted, though swimming was prohibited.   It would be

interesting to know what John Mason thought of these Puritanical restrictions, though he was a member of this sect. He had lived for some years in easy, sport-loving European countries, where all forms of amusements were enjoyed, especially the theater. Regardless of what he thought, he adjusted himself to the new conditions, for all that is known of his public and private life prove that he always advised and practiced moderation, never extremes except where actually necessary.

His ability as a leader was soon recognized, and although he had only been a member of the colony for a few months, yet at the first need for a military leader, they called on him to protect the colonies from the maraudings of a gang of pirates. The increasing wealth of New England, and the richly laden ships entering her ports, soon became known not only among the colonies, but also in Europe. The apparent ease with which these freighted ships could be captured, caused a captain of a vessel in the eastern trade, named Dixy Bull, together with his English crew, to become pirates. He was at first successful in plundering several boats, and also some of the settlers in outlying districts. It was not long before Governor Winthrop learned of these crimes, and he at once brought the matter before the magistrates of the colony who commissioned Lieutenant Mason to start in pursuit of the robbers. The pirates had sent word to the different colonies that they would not injure any of their countrymen, and that if they were attacked, they would sink their boat, rather than be taken. The missives were signed "Fortune le garde," but no name was added.

The Court directed Mason and his men to bring the

marauders to the colony for punishment. The cold of the early winter of 1632 had already set in which made the undertaking all the more hazardous. Mason fitted out a shallop of twenty tons, and sailed in search of the bandits. The vessel was a small boat, and most of his men were inexperienced, with the exception of Captain Gallup. It took both courage and prudence, but with the confidence he possessed, and which he instilled into the members of his crew, he felt confident to rid the colonies of this danger. The expedition of two months' duration was not successful in capturing the pirates, but succeeded in frightening them away, and freed the settlements from that menace. It was learned later that Bull's vessel was attacked from the Virginia shore, that he made his escape, and finally reached London, "where," to quote from Roger Clap, "God destroyed this wicked man."

This commission brought Mason at once prominently before the planters, and the Court book records under date of July 2, 1633, "Order is given to the Treasurer to deliver to Lieutenant Mason £10 for his voyage to the eastward, when he went about the taking of Bull." In November of the same year, "Serjeant Stoughton is chosen Ensign to Captain Mason."

Two years later Massachusetts established a Commission of Military Affairs giving them unlimited power "over life and limb," and Mason was appointed captain of the Militia.

In 1634-5 Mason became a freeman. The requirements to be one were, that the candidate should be "21 years of age, of sober and peaceable conversation, orthodox in fundamentals of religion, and possessed of a ratable estate of twenty pounds." This meant that he was a citizen of good standing, allowed to become a church member, and had the privilege of the franchise. No one not a freeman could become a church member, and no one not a member of the church was allowed to vote. Mason evidently did not avail himself of this privilege at the time, as he did not join the church, at least his name is not among the members of that year.

In order to become a member of the church it was necessary for the applicant to testify before the congregation not only that he felt conviction for his sins, but had to tell his special experience that made him feel that he was redeemed. These strict rules enforced by the Puritans was an ordeal that many feared to undergo especially in public. Consequently not more than one-fifth of the inhabitants were church members. They were therefore debarred from communion and from any participation both in church and community affairs. It not only affected them, but their children as well who were forbidden baptism, which meant in the eyes of the preachers, eternal damnation.

Not being a church member did not relieve the non-members from attending service, or free them from all the rules and expenses of the enrolled flock. Not to attend meeting meant a fine of five shillings. To be absent for a month was punished by being placed in the stocks, whipped or worse. In the first six towns in Connecticut there were ten ministers to look after the spiritual welfare of the inhabitants. That is, about one minister to every fifty families. Trumbull estimated that at that time there were about two hundred and seventy souls in the new settlement, including New Haven. In addition to the ministers in some communities, there were "Seven Pillars," men of high standing in the church, and at the installation of a minister, were the ones appointed to the "laying on of hands."

Caste was always recognized in the colonies. There were three distinct classes: first the clergy, second the gentry, mostly those descended from English families of that class and education and wealth. "They monopolized the chief offices, and were not sentenced by the Court to degrading punishment, such as whipping." The third grade was the commonalty who were accustomed from early environment to recognize the superiority of the upper classes. These distinctions were illustrated in the "seating of the meeting." Next to the pulpit, or immediately in front of it, was the "foreseat," which was the place of honor for the highest magistrate, or most prominent member of the town. The high places next to the foreseat were for the deacons, the next in honor were for the magistrates, then came the gentry, while at the rear sat the servants, slaves and negroes. There was also a place reserved near the pulpit for the preacher's family. This necessarily had to be spacious, as minister's families were generally large. One parson could boast of twenty-six children. Those afflicted with deafness were not kept from hearing the Lord's word as delivered from the pulpit, and had a place in front which was called the "Deaf Pue." The men sat on one side of the room and the women on the other, and no flirtations or signs ever passed between them. It was not for over a century later, when the first meeting house built of brick in Connecticut at Wethersfield, that the congregation had the courage to permit the two sexes to sit together, which, at the time, caused much criticism and condemnation. The mere thought of such an idea in the early days of the settlements would probably have merited punishment.

The religious services were very serious institutions. A word, or even a look that could be construed as criticism of the Lord's word, as interpreted by the preacher, was punishable by hours in the stocks, or even a public whipping, and extreme cases would warrant a sentence of death. A good example is the case of Philip Radcliffe, who was supposed to have been tempted by the "lying spirit of Satan" to blaspheme against "the church of all the holy land," for which he was publicly whipped, had both ears cut off, and banished. Many of the church members thought he deserved the sentence of death.

Morton of Merry-Mount gives a different version of the trouble. He said that "Innocence Fairecloath," as he called Radcliffe, was a member of the Church of England, and had been imposed upon by some of the citizens. Radcliffe allowed them to become greatly in his debt so that when he was ill and needed payment, he received "an epistle full of zealous exhortations to provide for the soul, and not to mind these transitory things that perish with the body, and to bethink himself whether his conscience would be so prompt with to demand so great a sum of Beaver as he has contract for. . . . The perusal of this (paper) was as bad as poison to the creditor, to see his debtor, Master Subtilety (Endicott), a serious professor, as he thought, to deride him in this extremity, that he could not choose, in admiration of the deceit, but cast out these words:—'Are these your members? if they be all like these, I believe the Devil was the scttcr-up of their church.'"

Radcliffe, like Morton, was banished to England, where later they had the opportunity of having their revenge on the treatment they had received from the magistrates of the colonies, by testifying in Gorges' interests before the Privy Council.

Religious fanaticism had reached such a stage that even a gesture or the expression on the face, might be interpreted as sacrilege and be punished. A maidservant for smiling at meeting, was threatened with banishment as a "vagabon," but the sentence was modified, probably owing to the fact that servants were rare and difficult to get, so that she remained in the colony.

To speak ill or criticize the preacher was equally criminal and severe punishments were inflicted. A man named Haddock was whipped on account of saying he got nothing from the minister's sermons. Another planter Maule received the same punishment, as he said the parson preached only lies; while still another man, for saying he "had rather hear a dog bark than to hear the minister preach," felt the strong hand of the law. And Mistress Oliver for "reproaching the elders," had to stand in public with a cleft stick on her tongue.

Lack of attention to the spoken word was also punishable, and to prevent such mishaps, the sleepers of the sterner sex were awakened by a rap on the head by the tithing man in charge. He stood on watch with a long pointer, at one end of which was a ball to hit the men, and at the other end a bunch of fur or a rabbit or fox tail, with which to tickle any member of the women's section who showed such a lack of respect and attention as to fall asleep during a sermon of hours in length.   However, sometimes even the tithing man must have dozed off, as there is the record of one divine, who, in order to overcome the humiliation of seeing his flock sleeping, called out in the middle of his sermon—"Fire—fire—fire!"   And when the suddenly awakened congregation started up and demanded "Where?"   The preacher shouted, "In hell, for sleeping sinners!"   Another ingenious preacher in a later time when acting as a substitute in a neighboring town where he learned some of the members of the church broke the rigid rule by leaving the meeting house before the end of the services, announced that he would preach to the sinners first, who could then leave, and the saints last.   It is said that this subterfuge met with success.

The meetings were no place for the expression of happiness or brotherly love, as such sentiments were suppressed.   The stern and scorching words of the prophets were shouted out in tones to create terror in the hearts of the strongest, as only fear and damnation were preached. No doubt the religious fear that was instilled into our forefathers has taken generations to eradicate.   But men who could conform and live up to such strict laws, proved, at least, that they had the courage and stern character to enable them to triumph over the difficulties they encountered.   A sermon preached some hundred years later by the noted Jonathan Edwards, first president of "Old Nassau," can probably express the religious sentiments of the time, as well as any of those by Revs. Wells, Nathaniel Ward, or other divines of the early days of New England.

"The God that holds you over a pit of hell," shouted Edwards, "much as one holds a spider or some loathsome insect over the fire, abhors you and is dreadfully provoked . . . he looks upon you as worthy of nothing else, but to be cast into the fire. . . . You are ten thousand times more abominable in his eyes than the most hateful, venomous serpent in ours." This was the same minister who was the leader in the great revival that took place in Northampton in 1735, when he said, "the noise among the Dry Bones waxed louder and louder, and Souls did as it were come by Flocks to Jesus Christ." This revival led to the "Great Awakening" that spread over New England four years later.

Infants, whose parents did not have them baptized, were doomed to everlasting torment, or, as one preacher said, that "the soul of a baby was a pestilence in the eyes of God, if it died before baptism, it would go to hell forever."

The noted poem entitled "The Day of Doom," written many years later by Wigglesworth, shook the hearts of the good New Englanders for a century or more. When referring to the misfortune of unbaptized children, it reads—

> *"You sinners are: and such a share*
> *As sinners, may expect;*
> *Such you shall have, for I do save*
> *None but mine own elect.*
> *Yet to compare your sin with their*
> *Who lived a longer time,*
> *I do confess yours is much less,*
> *Though every sin's a crime."*

But the severe sentence was somewhat tempered with mercy, as will be seen by the remainder of the verse.

> *"A crime it is; therefore in bliss*
> *You may not hope to dwell;*
> *But unto you I shall allow;*
> *The easiest room in hell."*

The Puritan laws in some settlements were so strict regarding baptism that a child could not be baptized unless it was a "child of the covenant," that is, a child of a member of the church.

While sermons were preached and mortals were being damned to the torments of the lower regions, there were some among the colonists who were of a more tolerant order, though they dared not, except in a few cases among the bravest, give expression to their belief. Those who did, were persecuted, often to their death.

In a time of such religious intolerance, superstition reigned supreme. All troubles, sickness, and accidental death, were the signs of the Almighty's wrath. A combat between a mouse and a snake in which the mouse was victorious, was explained thus, by the Rev. Wilson. The snake was the devil and the mouse "a contemptible people who God had brought thither to overcome Satan." A man worked one hour after sunset on a Saturday, and the next day the Lord punished him by drowning one of his children. In a collection of books owned by the younger John Winthrop, there was a volume containing the Greek Testament, psalms, and the Common Prayer. The latter part was eaten by mice, the other parts were not touched,

which was proof that the Lord did not approve of the
Book of Common Prayer. Savage, however, amusingly
explained, that "the mice not liking Psalmody, and not
understanding Greek, took the food from another part of
the volume." Johnson in his "Wonder-Working Providence" in describing a winter that was unusually severe
said, "the Lord being pleased to send us a very sharp
winter . . . Here the reader will take notice of the sad
hand of the Lord," and then goes on to say how a maid
and a barber were found frozen to death in separate places
during this winter, and all because they both had offended
the Lord. Then again in 1633 "the Lord was pleased to
send a severe epidemic."

Some idea can be gained of the reverence in which the
preachers were held at that time, by the adjectives used
by Johnson to express his admiration, as—"the grave,
godly, and judicious Hooker, the Reverend and much-
desired Mr. John Cotton, the rhetorical Mr. Stone, the
reverend, and holy of God, Mr. Nathaniel Rogers, the
holy, heavenly, sweet effecting and soul ravishing minister, Mr. Thomas Shepard." The Grave and Reverend
Mr. John Wilson, "the holy Man of God," who wished to
burn all of the Quakers in the world. Rev. John Cotton,
so "much desired," was the broadest and best educated of
the preachers of the first days of the colonies. He, it was,
whose inspiring sermons in England, persuaded Anne
Hutchinson to come to Massachusetts, much to the regret
later of both the colony and Rev. Cotton.

The "ravishing Mr. Shepard" was the minister who
Bishop Laud called in his interview with him, as "a prat-
ing coxcomb" and told him to "never read, marry, bury

or exercise any ministerial function in any part of my diocese," and threatened him if he disobeyed his orders. Another well-known preacher of the time was William Hooke, a relative of Cromwell, and an advocate of peace. His views on that subject were forcibly expressed in a long sermon on the subject, and which in closing, he said— "Every battle of the warrior is with confused noise and garments rolled in blood. Death reigns in the field and is sure to have the day, which side soever falls. . . . A day of battle is a day of harvest for the devil."

Even with all the adoration and reverence in which the preachers were held, their flocks failed to pay them enough on which to live, although salaries were at first underwritten by the government. The Sunday collections often, if not generally, proved disappointing. They often contained bullets, broken pieces of wampum and other worthless articles. Perhaps in most cases, such contributions were given through pride, and the wish to be seen dropping something into the box, in order to cover their poverty. The ministers had not only to preach practically all day on Sunday, but also several times during the week, including Lecture day, all of which gave them but little time to do other work to add to their incomes. To do so they drew up wills and deeds, other clerical work, and often menial work as well, as it is known one preacher added to his income by sweeping out the meeting house for which he received one dollar a year. Many of them had to till the ground in order to get enough to keep body and soul together of their generally large families. Rev. John Cotton said that "ministers and milk were the only cheap things in New England."

An aftermath of this parsimony on the part of the worshipers, was seen at the latter part of the nineteenth century, when the congregations helped to make up the minister's pittance of a salary by "donation parties."

In spite of the religious zeal of the planters, they were occasionally imposed upon by false prophets. "Wolves in sheep's clothing," rogues who announced themselves as ordained ministers, but who were eventually discovered and banished from the colony.

Yet with all of the fanaticism, often carried to the point of cruelty, we find instances where the settlers showed deep affection and kindness. There was John Winthrop, the chosen governor before sailing from England, who wrote his work entitled "A Model Christian Charity," on his voyage to America in 1630. In that he states, "We must entertain each other in brotherly affection. We must delight in each other; make others' conditions our own; rejoice together, mourn together, labor and suffer together." To be sure, he was more lenient than Thomas Dudley, who censured Winthrop for his lack of severity, yet his ideas of "Christian Charity" were certainly not practiced in the several religious trials over which he presided, and passed sentence. Nor did he say a word in defense of the kindly Roger Williams when he was brought to trial. It is difficult to reconcile the rigor with which he conducted his administrations as governor with the man who wrote to his wife in his farewell letter on leaving England, in such tender terms as "my sweet soul."

The Court enacted in 1633 "a provision for all refugees from religious persecution on their arrival, except Jesuits; priests; blasphemy; idolatry; witchcraft; which was made

punishable with death. Immoralities are severely punished; money is not to be loaned on interest; extravagance
in dress is a crime; and the Bible is accepted as the ulti-
mate tribunal when the laws are defective."

Toleration, however, was looked upon as a sin and Rev.
John Norton believed in correcting error that "the holy
tactics of the civil sword should be employed." The lines
found in the pocket of Governor Dudley after his death
emphasize this idea. They read—

> "Let men of God in Courts and Churches watch
> O'er such as do a Toleration hatch,
>   Lest that ill Egg bring forth a Cockatrice,
> To poisen all with heresie and vice."

Yet Cromwell, supposed to be a Puritan of the Puritans,
preached tolerance. In his speech when Parliament was
dissolved in January, 1655, he said, "Those that were
sound in the faith, how proper was it for them to labor
for liberty . . . that men might not be trampled upon
for their consciences! Had not they labored but lately
under the weight of persecution? And was it fit for them
to sit heavy upon others? Is it ingenious to ask liberty
and not give it? What greater hypocrisy than for those
who were oppressed by the bishops to become the greatest
oppressors themselves so soon as their yoke was removed?
I could wish that they who call for liberty now also had
not too much of that Spirit, if the power were in their
hands." On another occasion the Protector said that ministers were "helpers of, not lords over God's people." The
New England preachers did not agree with these ideas.

It is difficult to reconcile these sentiments of Cromwell's with the man who directed the sack of Drogheda where over a thousand Catholics were slain at St. Peter's Church.

The literature of the day was practically all based on religious subjects, or it was woven in all they wrote; diaries, histories, sermons, as fiction was not permitted, and the first American novel was not published until 1789. William Bradford's "History of Plymouth" stands out as the best account of the Pilgrim's settlement. He was a student, and knew the French, Dutch, Latin and Greek languages. He also studied Hebrew in his later years. John Winthrop in his "History of New England" gave odd and historic facts and data as they happened to come to his notice, between the years 1639 and 1649, the year of his death. Among other writers were Winslow who aided Bradford in his work; Francis Higginson's "A True Relation of the Last Voyage to New England"; William Wood's "New England's Prospects," which is unusually well written. At times he breaks into poetry in his descriptions. This was published in London in 1634. Rev. Nathaniel Ward's "The Simple Cobbler of Agawam," was written under the nom-de-plume of Theodore de la Guard in which he diatribes the vanity of women. Thomas Lechford, the only known lawyer in the colony, who, after three years' residence, with only one case in the meanwhile, returned to England, and wrote "Plain Dealing." Roger Williams wrote several books from which extracts will be made in this volume at different times. Quotations from Joselyn and Johnson have been already noted, and numerous volumes of sermons were penned by the preachers. All of these works give valuable information regarding the people and the times and conditions under which they lived. These authors were men of education. Moses Coit Tyler, in his "History of American Literature," when describing the men of education in New England in early colonial days, states—"It is probable that between the years 1630 and 1690 there were in New England as many graduates of Cambridge and Oxford as could be found in any population of similar size in the mother-country. At one time, during the first part of that period, there was in Massachusetts and Connecticut, a Cambridge graduate for every two hundred and fifty inhabitants, besides some of Oxford not a few."

The Massachusetts Bay Colony's charter was revoked in 1634. A governor-general was appointed by the King, who was to rule, and with the possibility of enforcing the established church on the colonists. Gorges, who claimed Massachusetts as part of the territory granted him at an earlier date, was probably one of the factors that had brought about this radical change. He and his party had great influence in London, and were there to enforce their claims. This news was appalling and obnoxious to the settlers, arousing their indignation to the boiling point. The clergy, magistrates and principal citizens took part in the controversy and debated how to act in the emergency. They began at once to prepare for an invasion if it should come to that, the same as their descendants did so successfully in 1776.

Captain Mason was at once appointed head of a commission by the General Court in September, 1634, to inspect the land on the Boston peninsula to see where it would be best to erect a fortification for the protection of

Charlestown, and Dorchester. Also to decide regarding alterations and additions that were required to be made to the fort at Boston. Mason took charge of the work at the Boston fort. It is said that the first fortification was a simple affair, built of clay, which served as a defense against the Indians. Later one was made of pine trees and earth, and still later one built of brick and stone. The work on the fort did not advance fast enough to suit the magistrates, and in September, 1635, nearly a year since the news of the change in government was learned, they gave directions that "Captain Mason is authorized by the Court to press more carts to help towards finishing the fort at Castle Island, for all manner of work that is to be done there." Mason's worth and qualifications were recognized by those in authority in his appointment, first when he was commissioned to search for the pirate Bull, and again in appointing him the engineer and superintendent to select the sites and oversee the constructions of the forts. In March of the same year, and the year following, he was a representative to the General Court at Newtown (now Cambridge). At that session of the Court it was decided that the officers of the militia should be paid from the treasury of the country. Previously they had been maintained by their respective companies. From that time until his death, Mason was active as a magistrate, representative, and commander of the military forces of the colonies in which he resided.

CHAPTER III

THE Connecticut River was said to have been discovered by the Dutch as early as 1614, who named it the "Fresh River," and a little later established a few trading stations in that vicinity. In 1627 they made advances to the Plymouth colony, hoping to join forces with them in developing that part of the country. Their envoy was Captain de Rassieres, who was "welcomed with trumpets and drums" by Bradford and his associates. They assured De Rassieres, that the Pilgrims could never forget the kindness with which they were treated when exiled in Holland. The Dutch envoy invited the English to go to Connecticut to see the advantages which that fertile land had to offer for development. The reports of the Plymouth agents who visited the valley a little later, did not encourage the colony or interest them sufficiently to give the matter much thought at the time, and they made no effort to continue further negotiations with the Dutch. Soon after this some sachems of the Indian tribes who inhabited the land along the Connecticut River, visited the Plymouth settlement, but not receiving a cordial response to their mission, they went to Boston and brought before the governor the advantages of founding a colony on their land, pointing out the great possibilities of the fur trade, and making promises to help the settlers. They had heard that the white men with their guns were invincible, and the Indians hoped that with a white settlement in their midst they would be free from the tyranny of their Pequot enemies. Governor Winthrop mentions this visit of the Indian chiefs under date of April 4, 1631, naming for the first time the word Connecticut. He tells how "Wahquimacut a Sagamore upon River Quonehatacut, with John Sagamore, and Jack Straw with divers of the sannops came to Boston." Jack Straw, who had served Sir Walter Raleigh, spoke English, and acted as interpreter. Winthrop received the sachems kindly even entertaining them at dinner, but made no promises.

Endicott was most enthusiastic regarding Connecticut, and wrote in that vein to Winthrop, describing the great advantages of the fur trade, and the promises the Indians had made, all of which convinced him that possession should be taken of the land at once. The country abounded in many fur-bearing animals proving a source of great wealth to the Dutch. Beavers were especially numerous, and as many as ten thousand skins were sold to the English annually. The Plymouth and Massachusetts colonies often sent cargoes of beaver and otter skins to England valued as high as thousands of pounds, and with the prospects of adding to this amount, it was a great point to be considered.

In 1633, Governor Winslow and Mr. Bradford went to Boston to consult with Winthrop and the magistrates regarding the proposition of establishing a settlement in the Connecticut country, but it was thought too dangerous, owing to the country's swarming with thousands of warlike Indians. The same year a party of four men, John Oldham, Samuel Hall, and two others went to investigate.

They returned much impressed with the fertile land and the possibilities of the fur trade. This was the beginning of the disputes between the English and the Dutch, as to the rightful ownership of the Connecticut valley.

In 1632, the Dutch had bought large acreage around Saybrook from the Indians, and the year following at Hartford, where they erected a fort. Massachusetts claimed the country as part of the patent of the land west of the Narragansetts, which was granted March, 1631-2, by the Earl of Warwick, who was president of the Council of New England to Lord Say and Seal, Brook, and nine others, while the Dutch based their claims to the land on the right of prior discovery, occupation, grants and purchase from the Indians.

The kindness the Pilgrims had received when they sought a haven in Holland, and which Bradford said would always be remembered, was quickly forgotten, in the desire to obtain possession of the Connecticut country. A commander of an English vessel visited New Amsterdam, and showed to Governor Van Twiller the commission which the King of England had granted to the colonists. In Van Twiller's reply that he sent to the magistrates, he gave the reasons for his government's claiming the land, as already stated, and hoped no settlement would be made by the English until those in authority should decide the matter, in order that "as Christians (they) might dwell together in these heathenish parts."

The Plymouth authorities gave no heed to this request, but immediately sent an expedition of seventy men to the disputed territory. The bark was under the command of Lieutenant William Holmes who sailed up the river a mile above the Dutch fort, ignoring the latter's threat of opening fire on them, and which only resulted in talk and protests. The English at once erected a collapsible frame house they had brought with them, as a fort. This was probably the first portable house ever erected in America.

The location of the English station north of the Dutch fort gave them every advantage, and control of the much-desired fur trade. Eventually the Hollanders moved away, though it was a cause of bitter contention for many years, causing much friction and warlike skirmishes between Connecticut and New Amsterdam, and even the murder of several settlers. The Connecticut line at that time extended to the east banks of the Hudson River, including all of Westchester and Long Island. A final settlement was not concluded until 1663.

No sooner had the English taken possession of the Connecticut valley, than they began quarreling among themselves as to which colony the new territory belonged. Plymouth claimed a prior right, and Massachusetts strongly opposed her claims. In the meanwhile some of the planters in the latter colony were discussing the possibility of moving to the much-talked-of valley.

An amusing incident of Indian psychology happened at the time of these disputes. Winslow visited the country in 1634. He sailed to the Narragansett country, but decided to return by land. On visiting the chief Osamekin, whom he had known for some time, the sachem told him that he would act as his guide back to Plymouth. Before doing so, however, he sent one of his warriors to Plymouth to tell them that Winslow had been killed, and to give them all particulars and descriptions of the place where the tragedy had happened.   The shock the planters experienced on receiving this news can easily be imagined, as well as their pleasure when Winslow and Osamekin appeared the following day.   The sachem explained when questioned as to the reason of this action, that his people often did that in order to give more pleasure and a greater welcome on the supposed deceased's return.

A severe smallpox epidemic broke out at the time of the Holmes expedition, which gave the English a stronger hold on the land they had taken, by their assistance to the Indians.   The descriptions giving account of the sufferings of the natives are most pathetic.   Having no facilities of caring for themselves, they were said to have died like rats, though the English were not affected.   Let it be said to their credit that they cared for the sufferers, did what they could to help them.   All of this was done at the risk of contracting the disease.   Several towns cared for the Indian children during the epidemic, and took entire charge of the sick, when they were abandoned by their own people.   Some of the English practically gave all of their time in caring for the stricken and in burying the dead.   It is told that one of the settlers buried thirty Indians in one day.

The most conspicuous Indian who died during this affliction, was John Sagamore, probably the first Indian convert to the Christian faith.   He asked to be brought among the English so that he might live with them when he recovered.   Realizing that he was dying, he gave presents to the governor and other English friends, and died, it is said, "in a persuasion that he should go to the Englishmen's God."

There are many incidents that prove the friendship that existed between the whites and the red men. Winthrop entertained Indians not only under his roof, but at his table. He also noted in his diary, how he had a suit of clothes made for the Indian Chickabot, who wished to be dressed like Englishmen. There are also many records where white settlers were severely punished for committing crimes against the aborigines, or defrauding them in their barter.

The immigrants were descended from families that had lived for generations in the same parish or county, and most of them had seldom ventured any distance from the place of their birth. No sooner, however, were they settled in some plantation in the New World than they began to move to other settlements, or found new ones. It was not unusual for a family within the first few years to have lived in several towns. This continual change of residence, probably arose from a wish to locate in a more desirable place where the soil was more fertile, or on account of the rapid crowding of the original settlements by the new arrivals. The spirit of adventure is not likely to have had any influence on these decisions. Whatever the cause, the result was the founding of many new towns in all parts of New England within a few years.

This unrest, like the bees in an overcrowded hive, affected a large number of the inhabitants of Dorchester. In this instance, there were several legitimate reasons for them to migrate. It was not only owing to the increasing

population of the immediate vicinity, nor the rocky nature
of the soil, though both may have had their effect, but
probably the main incentive, for most of them at least, was
to found a colony with a social system in which the church
and state would be separate, and the civil franchise not
founded on church membership. John Mason, who took
a prominent part in this migration, always advocated religious liberty. The late Thomas Collier when speaking
of the Windsor settlement at the dedication of the Major
John Mason statue said—"The part taken in it by John
Mason discloses the bent of his mind in the direction of
freedom of conscience."

The application to the Court was made during Mason's
first term as a representative. It asked permission for the
petitioners to leave the colony, and found one in the Connecticut valley. The request at first met with great opposition. The Court was not willing to have so many families with their prominent leaders go out of the jurisdiction
of Massachusetts. The Court argued that it might encourage others to do likewise, and also they foresaw that
a separate colony, over which they might lose control,
would lead to complications, as well as competition in the
future. After long and heated discussions, permission was
granted. It is said that the influence of Rev. John Cotton
had much to do with this decision. It is also believed
that the great popularity of Rev. Hooker's sermons, together with his pleasing personality, was the cause of
Cotton's favoring the settlement in Connecticut, as Hooker
was the leader of the band that settled Hartford. With
Hooker in the wilds of that fertile valley, Cotton could
have no fear of being supplanted in the hearts of the

Massachusetts church. At any rate, he was asked to preach on the subject and bring harmony to the settlers. The favorable grant was at once acted upon by a few men of the prospective colony, by going to Connecticut to inspect the country and to decide the best place on which to locate the new town.

The Dorchester company had no sooner begun to make their plans to move and establish the new settlement, than the authorities of Plymouth began at once to protest. They stated that the country in the Connecticut valley belonged to them, that Massachusetts had no right to it. While these arguments were taking place, the Dorchester band went on with its preparations, and in spite of the lateness of the season, set forth on their hazardous journey. They probably thought that those first established on the land could claim it as their own, and moving at once they would keep out the Dutch.

It can hardly be realized by us of this generation what such a migration meant. Ellis said that "Without such men as Mason to nerve the feeble and fainting, and to guide the willing and strong, such an undertaking would have rested in mere conception." Among the prominent men besides Mason who formed the company were John Maverick, Rositer, Ludlow, and Henry Wolcott.

The company set out on foot, winding their way through the forests, over narrow Indian paths, and often, no paths. No roads had been cut. No horses to ride, no bridges over streams, and worst of all, no arranged places to camp at night. The cold which presaged an early winter, was already felt, and footsore, and weary, with lack of provisions, save the little they could carry, made the conditions most trying. Women carried their young children which were fed on the milk from the cows they were driving, and the men were loaded down with their firearms, ammunition and a few needed utensils. Up hill and down dale, too tired to admire the beauties of the gorgeous autumn foliage, they were probably often too exhausted to continue for a while the long, tedious march. Can any one question the courage of a people who, in order to have a new home, could make such a pilgrimage? It took the company fourteen days to make the journey that can now be made by airplane in less than an hour.

The settlement was made on the west bank of the river, but how they crossed has not been recorded. The cattle could not be taken over and after driving them one hundred miles, through forest and marsh, they were forced to leave them on the east bank, where many of them perished during the severe winter that followed.

They called the place Dorchester, after the town that they had left, but later changed it to Windsor, the name it now bears. Roger Ludlow called it the "Lord's Waste." It was also known as "Palisado Green," the name given to the Common which surrounded the fort.

While the site was principally meadow land, trees had to be cut down and used for shelter to be made before the snows of winter came, and the land had to be cleared for the spring planting. Also there was the ever-present fear of an attack by the unfriendly Indians who lurked about the place. It took all their physical strength and will power to cope with such a situation. It can readily be understood what it meant to the company to have such a man as Captain Mason as their leader. His experience in the army taught them how best to protect themselves in case of an Indian attack, and his engineering ability could instruct them how to build their homes. By that time Mason was always referred to as "the Captain," until it seems at times that his surname was almost forgotten.

To add to the settlers' troubles, they had only been at the new settlement a few days before they learned that the shallops on which they had shipped their household goods, had been wrecked, which meant an entire loss. Several of the crew had been drowned, and when the news was brought to the attention of the Rev. John Cotton, he made the consoling reflection regarding the unfortunates lost in the vessel, that "they went to Heaven in a chariot of water, as Elijah long before in a chariot of fire."

In the early part of November, six of the company left the settlement in a vessel to return to Boston. The boat was wrecked, and although the survivors managed to reach shore, they did not find their way to town until ten days later, and then in a state of exhaustion from cold and hunger. By December Windsor had its first taste of winter, which so discouraged thirteen more that they started to return to Boston, and on the way one of the party was drowned in a stream they crossed. No doubt that helped to confirm the "13" superstition. A few days later seventy more decided to leave and went to the mouth of the river for provisions that had been promised to be shipped by water, but there were no signs of the ship. However another vessel was there, a sixty-ton bark which eventually took them back to Dorchester, which they had left but a few weeks before filled with so much hope. They also met with accidents: first their boat was ice bound, then the sand bar would not permit of the boat's passing, and it had to be unloaded in order to get it to the sea, and then reloaded. In the meanwhile a winter storm added to their discomfort and danger.

In speaking of the atrocities of the Indians, it must not be forgotten that there were many kind-hearted ones among them. The first group of settlers would have starved on their way back to Massachusetts had not some friendly Indians furnished them with food. The same good Samaritan acts were performed for the planters, the men, women and children, who had the courage to remain at Windsor, and it was due to the red man's help that they were able to survive. All they had besides the provisions given by the Indians, were "acorns, nuts, malt and grain," and what they were able to procure in the way of game.

Early the following spring the little band at Dorchester began once more to make arrangements to return to the settlement they had abandoned the winter before. Governor Winslow of Plymouth once again tried to stop the colonization of Connecticut. A peaceable arrangement was finally made, and the Dorchester company set forth to the promised land with probably Mason once more as their leader. We have no knowledge that he remained at Windsor during the winter, though it would have been like him to have done so. In the party this time must have been Mason's wife and Rev. Wareham and his family. The one-hundred-mile tramp through the forest was not beset with so many of the hardships of the previous autumn, but the pest of flies and mosquitoes must have been almost as unbearable. The complaints that the Pilgrims had made to Bradford when attacked by the same

pesky insects, had brought forth the severe rebuke that
they "were too delicate and unfit to begin new plantations
and colonies, that cannot endure the biting of a mosquito.
We would wish such to keep at home, till at least they
be mosquito proof."

One among many sights that interested and amused the
planters as they trudged along in their march, were the
flocks of pigeons that were so numerous as to obscure the
light of the sun, and as one historian wrote, "It passed
credit, if but the truth be written."

Everything demanded the attention of the newcomers
on their arrival. They needed houses to live in, the fort
to protect them, and the land to be cleared for planting
to save them from famine the following winter. But few,
perhaps, of the band had ever felled a tree, and the tools
they possessed were inadequate for such work. Only the
greatest courage, perseverance and belief in their doctrines, made it possible for them to overcome all of the
many obstacles that met them at every turn.

The Windsor company, however, allowed nothing to
stop them, and on their arrival they had at once set about
building their homes around which they erected the "Palisado" enclosing the Green with high stakes, with a wide
ditch surrounding it. This enclosure was over three
fourths of a mile in length, comprising sixty rods on the
south, sixty-nine rods west, eighty rods east, and fifty rods
on the north. What a gigantic task!

This achievement of the Connecticut pioneers is regarded as Rockwell said, "one of the most remarkable on
the pages of the early history of this or any other country."
They had left the comparative comfort of their homes in

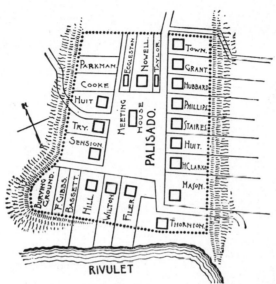

PLAN OF THE PALISADO (ENLARGED BY J. H. HAYDEN).

(By courtesy of the publishers of "The Memorial History of Hartford County.").

REPRINTED FROM PLATE IN "THE MEMORIAL
HISTORY OF HARTFORD COUNTY"

Dorchester against the remonstrances of the Massachusetts as well as that of Plymouth colonies, and they had ventured into the territory claimed by the Dutch and surrounded by the largest and most powerful Indian tribes in New England.

Only one house that was built at the time of the first settlement has survived these three hundred years, and that is the Fyler house, erected in 1640, and seemingly still as staunch as when it was built. Thanks are due to the Windsor Historical Society for preserving the house of one of the founders for posterity. It faces the Palisado as it did when first enclosed in the stockade. It is interesting to know that this protection against Indian attacks was never needed, as the Indians feared Mason's courageous leadership, and Windsor was never attacked. Mason's reputation had been established by previous minor conflicts with them.

One of the first matters that had to be decided after the erection of the fort and the dwellings, and always in the case of a new settlement, was selecting the site for the meeting house. It was generally built on the highest part of the town, often on a hill. It was therefore in sight of the inhabitants as an inspiration, and also a vantage point in case of an Indian attack during the services. John Eliot, the Indian missionary, said, as he climbed the hill to the meeting house at Roxbury, when he was old, and feeble, "this is very like the way to heaven; 'tis uphill. The Lord by his grace fetch us up."

When the question regarding the site of the house of worship was settled, next came the location for the home of the minister, and fifty acres of land were given to him.

The first meeting house in Windsor had a platform built on the roof in 1638, so that "from the Lanthorne to the ridge to walk conveniently to sound a trumpet or a drum to give warning to meeting."

Other settlements were made about the same period besides the one at Windsor. Hooker led his band of followers to Hartford, taking with them one hundred and sixty head of cattle. Pynchon had established a town at Springfield, and Wethersfield was also founded. There have been many disputes among the citizens of the three towns which one was actually settled first. About this time Lieutenant Lion Gardiner went to Saybrook, which had first been claimed by the Dutch, where he admitted in the brief history of his time, "that he was disappointed to find so few men there, and so little work done, and so much to be completed."

In passing it seems a fact worth stating, to the citizens of Connecticut, which was later to have the monopoly of the brass business in the country, that in this year of 1635, the first cannon was cast in brass.

Many things were happening in the New and the Old World. New settlements were being founded along the entire coast of the Atlantic. Strict laws were enacted to hold desirable planters in the colonies, and to make it unpleasant to return to the mother-country. The following is recorded under date of 1631, "that no planter within the limit of this jurisdiction, returning for England, shall carry either money or beaver with him, without leave from the governor, under pain of forfeiting the money or beaver so intended to be transported." Yet, undesirables were often returned whence they came, as for instance, in

1634 Abigail Gifford who was sent to the colonies to rid the parish of her presence, was returned to that parish in England.

Stratford was settled in 1639 by the followers of Rev. Adam Blackman of the Church of England, and was the only colony in Connecticut not under the Puritan rule. Several from the plantations joined this settlement. Probably the most original of these was a couple named Birdsye from Milford, who were caught kissing each other on the Lord's Day, and consequently condemned to the stocks. They both escaped by swimming the river to Stratford where the laws were not so severe. It was believed at that time that Stratford was infested with the ghosts of Indian devils, who held pow-wows, entered the timbers of which the meeting house was built, and even Rev. Visey, a clergyman sent from New York, was unable to entirely rid the town of these pests when he read the Litany. Stratford has the honor of having had the first Episcopal church erected in Connecticut. It was built in 1743.

Settlements were rapidly being made in other sections of the country. Lord Baltimore had founded Maryland in 1633, and the following year it was in hostile dispute with the Virginia colony. The Swedes had settled in Delaware, where a whole colony had been wiped out by the Indians. New Amsterdam had erected its first church edifice way down on Pearl Street. Anne Hutchinson, though only in Massachusetts a short time, had already organized her women's society, since women were not allowed to speak at the weekly meetings. It was growing in numbers under the watchful, resenting and jealous eyes of the preachers. Rev. Wheelwright by his liberal views set forth in his sermons, was beginning to cause dissension in the community.

Philemon Permort's Latin School was opened in Boston. This evidently inspired the General Court to give four hundred pounds for the establishment of a school or college at Newtown, now Cambridge, which was the beginning of the famous university of Harvard.

Since the naming of the days and months of the year was not mentioned in the Scriptures, it savored of Romanism, therefore they were to go by numbers, such as Sunday, the first day. Johnson in his "Wonder Working Providence" explains it thus—"of purpose to prevent the heathenish and popish observations of the days, months and years that they may be forgotten among the people of the Lord." This custom is still used by the orthodox Quakers.

Sir Henry Vane, who arrived in 1635, was elected governor of the Massachusetts colony the following year. He was a mere youth of twenty-four years, but generous, liberal and much loved by all the colonists, except by the over-zealous preachers and the native governors.

Gorges' wonderful boat, of which there had been so much talk, and which was to bring him and his followers to New England to take possession of his claims, broke in two in England just after being launched, and that, with the loss of his health and money, ended that menace.

Rev. John Wilson, the first minister of Boston, was holding forth in strong form, damning the people in general, and as proof of his "tolerance," exclaimed when asked what one was to do with error, "Let them go to the Devil of Hell, from whence they came."

What would the labor unions of our day think of a law that was made in Charlestown in 1630 by the First Court of Assistants, "which settled the price of mechanical labor, mechanics to receive no more than two shillings a day, under a penalty of ten shillings to give and take."

It was at this time that the famous diarist Samuel Pepys and the still more famous architect, Sir Christopher Wren, were born in England. In this country Roger Williams was persccuted and exiled to Rhode Island on account of his religion, where he carried out his Christian policy, and bought the land from the Indians on which the city of Providence was to be built. In his letter to Mason that he wrote years after, telling when he was driven from his home some thirty-five years before, that he had neither bed nor shelter, but still speaks of "that ever honored governor Mr. Winthrop" in spite of his exile and treatment. He also mentions Winslow's kindness in visiting him later, who, realizing the poverty of the Williams family, placed a gold piece in Mrs. Williams' hand.

The confederacy of the Massachusetts Bay, Plymouth, Connecticut and New Haven colonies which was formed in 1643, caused Williams to go to England to have Rhode Island recognized and properly chartered. On that trip he wrote his "A Key into the Language of America, or, An Help to the Language of the natives in that part of America called New England." In this volume as well as in his daily intercourse with the American Indian, he speaks of their virtues. In one chapter, he wrote, "It is a strange truth that a man shall generally find more free entertainment and refreshing amongst these barbarians, than amongst thousands that call themselves Christians."

And in another place he lapses into poetry where he writes—

> *"God's providence is rich to his,*
> *Let none distrustful be;*
> *The wilderness, in great distress,*
> *These ravens have fed me."*

The struggle between the Puritans of England and the government was becoming very bitter, and though Parliament had but little time to trouble with the American colonies, they "passed orders in 1634 to the custom officers at the seaports, prohibiting the promiscuous passing of His Majesty's subjects to the American plantations. No subsidy men were to pass without a license, nor other persons without the attestament of two justices; while the statutes already proved that none should go forth without taking the oath of Allegiance."

Bishop Laud was gaining greater influence over the King and was given unlimited power over the Puritans which he used in persecuting them. He was also introducing into the service of the Church of England, a ritual that the public at large, as well as the Separatists, Puritans and Nonconformists, considered popish. These new ceremonies were similar to those in the Roman Catholic churches. The following incident illustrates, in a way, the feeling of many regarding Laud's innovations. When he asked the daughter of the Earl of Devonshire why she had turned Catholic, she replied, " 'Tis chiefly because I hate to travel in a crowd, as I perceive your grace and many others are making haste to Rome, and therefore to prevent my being crowded, I have gone on before you."

Louis XIII was king of France. Cardinal Richelieu came into power in 1624 and was the actual ruler of the kingdom for the next twenty years. It was said that he was "neither meddlesome, nor cruel, but that he was stern and pitiless." One of the first beneficent laws he brought about, though difficult to enforce, was to prohibit dueling. Richelieu founded the French Academy, where the Dictionary was soon begun. Marie de' Medici was the queen-mother and Anne of Austria was Louis' wife. Literature flourished in the French capital. The Hotel Rambouillet was already famous as the rendezvous of wits and the literati. This period produced René, Descartes and Corneille.

England, at this time, lacked the great literary geniuses of Shakespeare's generation, but among those who were locally conspicuous was Richard Lovelace and Samuel Butler. The latter wrote the satire "Hudibras" on Puritans and puritanism, but all the lesser ones are comparatively lost in the brilliant light of the gifted John Milton.

The Thirty Years' War was still going on, and fanaticism had full sway throughout the world. Urban VIII occupied the Papal throne, and Ferdinand II ruled Florence, while Galileo, one of the greatest scientists the world ever produced, was languishing in prison, another victim of ignorance and bigotry.

CHAPTER IV

THE energy and force which marks the American of today, was a leading characteristic of the colonists in spreading their settlements over New England. It seems almost incredible when looking back at the time in which they lived, with the obstacles they had to overcome, that they could have accomplished what they did within so short a time. The cabins they built at the beginning of a settlement, were gradually replaced by structures of fine architectural designs, and their wainscoted walls with beautiful paneling are still the admiration of the present age. It is interesting to note that Winthrop censured a man in 1632 for his extravagance in "wainscoting and adorning" his house, which he said was done at too great a cost for a house at the beginning of a settlement, and that also, it set a bad example.

Window glass was at first difficult to obtain, and oil paper was used for that purpose, but soon it was possible to import leaded glass windows, usually of the lozenge design. Furniture was scarce, in spite of the thousands of pieces that were said to have been brought over in the *Mayflower.* Some writer recently said that if these statements were true, it would seem that our forefathers did nothing but erect warehouses in which to store antiques for their descendants. Stools and benches, and later rush bottom chairs with carved woodwork, long dining tables, the occupants sitting on one side which facilitated waiting on them, together with cupboards and chests made up the furnishings of the house. Beds were but poor affairs, generally made by the owner. Light from fireplaces was supplemented by pine knots. Betty lamps and later, candles, were the only means of illumination. The houses were heated by open fireplaces, which served also for cooking. Many years later Dutch and China stoves were imported. Only a small amount of silver articles was to be found in the colonies, as wooden spoons and pewter were in general use. Forks were scarce, and came into use gradually. They were no longer considered effeminate or looked upon by the preachers as an "ungodly substitute for fingers." Table cloths and napkins were in every household, as the thoughtful housewives managed to store them in the chests which they brought over from England. The hours were timed by sundials, moonbeams and the hour glass, though a few of the colonists could sport a clock or a watch. Boston could boast of a town clock as early as 1657.

Mason was evidently not superstitious, at least regarding the number 13, as that was the number of the town lot that he chose in the new settlement at Windsor. It was situated on the road to the Rivulet ferry, and although he removed to Saybrook within a few years, he did not sell his Windsor property until 1653, when it was purchased by Henry Clark. No description exists, so far as known, of the first houses erected in Windsor, but presumably the one built by Mason was, like the others, on the style of the Fyler house, and of a very modest type, and much less imposing than the one he erected when he moved to Norwich. His first child Isabel was one of the first children to be born in the new town.

The Captain had but little time to give to cultivating domestic interests, since from the first the Pequot Indians had shown a restlessness that did not insure safety for the inhabitants. They feared the treachery of the red men, so that Mason took every precaution that was possible to fortify the town to prevent a sudden attack. It was held by the colonists in general "that in the case of hostile Indians, no good can come of attempts to conciliate, unless respect is first imposed by a sufficient castigation." Seemingly no such attempts had been made with the Indians by the whites in that vicinity.

The Indian tribes were more numerous in the Connecticut Valley than in all the rest of New England. Winthrop estimated that in 1633 they numbered between three and four thousand warriors, and that in the whole state there were probably only twenty thousand. The Pequots were the largest tribe in the northern colonies, and noted as being the most warlike. The other tribes, besides numerous small branches under various names, were the Narragansetts, Mohegans and Nahanticks, while at the west were the powerful Mohawks or Iroquois.

It is believed by students that the different tribes were originally one, and that all belonged to the Delaware or Algonquin race. That from time to time, groups had broken away from the parent clan and established their own independence. One of the best proofs of this was that the language of the several different clans was so similar that they could readily understand one another.

Also, the sons of a sachem would leave with some followers and start a new tributary, which, in the passing years, would become an independent tribe. It was difficult for the student to trace the relationship between subdivisions which had probably taken place a century or more before.

The English found that the Indians, like all primitive races, were grateful for kindness, but quick to take offence, and very revengeful. They never forgot nor forgave an injury. They wore but little clothing, often went naked, even in the coldest weather, being little affected either by extreme heat or cold, having been hardened by their early training to endure all hardships and even torture without a groan. Even the Spartans of Greece could not be compared with the American Indian in regard to endurance of physical pain. Williams in his account of the aborigines said, "I have known them run eighty to one hundred miles in a summer's day, and back again within two days." When under torture by their enemies they would heckle their tormentors to greater efforts, calling out to them "that their tortures were as sweet as Englishmen's sugar."

The Indians at the time of the early settlements, and before they came in contact with the whites, were perfect physical specimens. Tall, straight, well proportioned like statues of bright bronze. Cripples, unless the result of an injury in war, or an accident, were rarely seen. They were a healthy race, ate when and where food could be found. Very improvident, lived for the moment, and never worried. The men hunted, fished and loafed, while the women worked and drudged. Trial marriages were common, and if the couple found themselves unsuited, they separated, to try again. When the right partner was found, the marriage was performed by a sachem of their tribe. The men of wealth, especially the sachems, always had several concubines, so that from the English standard their morals were of a low degree. The sachem, or chief, was an absolute monarch, judge and executioner, obtaining his throne by inheritance only. But he always had advisers called "paniese," and no great question was decided without holding a consultation with them. In a few cases if there were no male heirs, the crown fell to a daughter of the late sachem, as the squaw queen Menunkatuck of a tribe at Guildford. The Indians reverenced the dead, buried them with ceremony amidst much wailing and noise, and kept certain plots as burying grounds. They were very particular regarding the boundaries of their lands, the rivers and lakes often forming the boundary lines.

All of the small tribes feared the powerful Pequots, who continually made war on them. The Pequots, whose name it is said translated into English meant "destroyer," claimed as their territory all the land along the coast of Long Island Sound, while their principal forts were located at New London, then known as Pequot and Mystic. Their chief, Sassacus, had twenty-six sachems under him, and about eight hundred warriors at his command at the forts. He was always at war with one or more tribes, and always with the Narragansetts who lived in the territory surrounding Stonington, numbering about three thousand. The Narragansetts was the one tribe that the Pequots had never conquered, and now that Canonicus was old and feeble, he gave the control over the tribe to his nephew

Miantonimo, who had succeeded in keeping the Pequots at bay. Mason said that Miantonimo and his tribe had great fear of Sassacus, saying that "Sassacus is all God; no man can kill him." Ellis states that "probably the fairest estimate of the native nobility and courage of the Indians, sometimes magnified by overwrought descriptions, would be gathered from this common reverence and dread of any one, who displayed any remarkable prowess."

The Indians probably never suspected when the first whites came to the country that their number would ever be large, or that they would fear them as being conquerors of the land. Histories usually stress only the wars between peoples and nations—so it is well to understand that there were friendly interchanges and intervals of peaceful living, though the settlers had to be ever vigilant. The fascination of trade with the planters bringing articles they had never seen before, but which they coveted, and the vanity the finery aroused with which they bedecked themselves, besides the axes, and other weapons they obtained, made them anxious to continue trading with these white gods of gun-powder fame. Furs were easily gotten by the savages and were much sought after by the planters, so that the exchange was of mutual benefit. The smaller tribes always encouraged the whites to settle in their territories as they protected them from the Pequots and other powerful clans.

Sassacus, the wily chief of the Pequots, like King Philip, Tecumseh, Black Hawk, Pontiac and other chiefs later, was the first to realize that the English, with their guns, would eventually drive the Indians from their land, or annihilate them in war. His jealousy, together with his fear for the future of his people, aroused his enmity which was to lead to war with the planters, and the destruction of his race.

If the English had always proved worthy of the confidence the Indians usually had in them, much trouble might have been avoided. This trust was shaken when Captain Thomas Hunt enticed twenty Indians on his boat with promises of trade and presents, then made them captives, and sold them as slaves in Spain. News of this treachery of the white man was soon known throughout New England by the different tribes, and instilled into the minds of the red men a hate and fear of the English which was never entirely overcome. In the early days of the colonies, a lad named John Billings was lost in the woods, but found later and kept by the Indians. Two of the settlers were sent to bring him to his people, and in writing of their experience of this trip they recounted what they had learned of one unpardonable result of Hunt's treachery. They wrote—"One thing was very grievous unto us at this place. There was an old woman, whom we judged to be no less than an hundred years old, which came to see us because shee never saw English, yet behold us without breaking forth into great passion, weeping and crying excessively; We demanding the reason of it, they told us, she had three sons who when master Hunt was in these parts went aboard his ship to trade with him, and he carried them away into Spain, by which means shee was deprived of the comfort of her children in her old age. . . . So we gave her some small triffles, which some what appeased her."

The slaying in cold blood of the two chiefs, Peeksnot

and Wiluwamat at Wessagusset by Miles Standish, was another proof that the white man could not be trusted. This fear included both the English and the Dutch. The latter had killed the old sachem Totabam. He was the chief of a small branch of the Pequots who had rebelled against the tyranny of the great Sassacus, and was murdered by the Dutch when on a peaceful trading expedition. This murder was the cause of the followers of Taboban going to Winthrop in 1634 to invite the English to settle in their midst in the Connecticut Valley, hoping they would protect them from both the Dutch and the Pequots.

Much of the cruelty of the whites toward the Indians was no doubt due to the fact that the settlers looked upon the natives as "children of Satan," and the preachers, whose word was law, called them that from the pulpits, as well as other damning terms. To the Puritans, as well as to all others who were orthodox, Satan was a real personality. He could communicate with mortals, do them many bad turns, and even give them unlimited power, as in the case of witches, if they would sign a contract with him. Increase Mather, during King Philip's war, prayed in the pulpit every Sunday for that powerful chief's death, and his son, Cotton Mather, many years later wrote, as an appendix to the title of his work, "A Book of the Wars of the Lord," that among the adversaries of the church were "the Devil, Quakers and Indians." It can easily be seen that the Indians were to the settlers real and special emissaries of Satan. When they were defeated in battle, it was a sure proof that the Devil was losing power. Therefore the sooner they were exterminated, the better for the country. The good churchgoers were even

known to sing hymns during the execution of these unfortunates. It is not surprising, therefore, with such feel-
ings against the natives, whose land they wished, and
claimed, together with the treacherous manner in which
they treated them, that the Indians no longer trusted the
settlers, or put much faith in their promises. They began
to regard them as intruders on their hunting grounds and
their natural prey. With such sentiments held by both
factions, the inevitable happened.

The authorities at Boston had been much annoyed on
several occasions by John Stone, a sea captain from Virginia, who, when in the Massachusetts capital, had broken
many of the conventions of respectable society, by his immoralities. His actions were so objectionable to the Puritans, that he was banished on two different occasions. The
last time this occurred was in September, 1633. Some time
later, he, with Captain Norton, sailed to the Connecticut
River, to trade with the Indians and Dutch. Not knowing
the country, he engaged two Indians as guides, and allowed
eight others to board the boat. Night came on before
they had made much headway, and fearing to proceed
farther in the dark, they anchored the vessel to wait until
daylight. This proved to be the last of Stone's adventures,
as he, with the rest of his crew, was murdered during the
night by the Indians. Later reports gave more details of
the massacre, and told how Captain Norton had been able
to get to the "cook-room," where he shot at the Indians
through the window. He loaded his gun from an open
pan of powder which was accidentally ignited. This
blinded him so badly that he was helpless and was killed.

The first knowledge the authorities at Boston had of

this tragedy was not until some time later, when the
Pequots, who evidently feared the action that the Court
would take when the crime became known, sent a messenger to the governor, with presents, asking for the friendship of the whites.   Ludlow was deputy governor at the
time, and he informed the man that the Pequots "must
send a worthier representative before Governor Dudley
would consider the matter."   The following month two
Indians sent by Sassacus, arrived, also bringing presents
and promises.   They were taken before the magistrates to
give their version of the tragedy.   They informed the
Pequots "that it is not the manner of the English to take
revenge of their injuries until parties that are guilty have
been called to answer fairly for themselves."   They were
also told that unless they could clear themselves of the
charges, that otherwise no peace could be signed, and that
they would, if they were found guilty, "revenge the blood
of our countrymen as occasion shall serve."   The Indians
told their story, and claimed that Stone had ill-treated
the Indians on the boat.   That he had bound the two
guides, and had forced them to pilot him up the river.
The Indians had planned, after murdering the crew, to
take the vessel, but that it suddenly blew up.   They also
said that the Dutch had killed the chief of the tribe who
had committed the massacre, and that all of the others
who had taken part in the affair, save two, had since died
of smallpox.   Winthrop records that "this was related with
such confidence and gravity, as having no means to contradict it, we inclined to believe it."   A fact, too, that
aided them in this decision, was that Oldham, and his
party, who had recently traded with this tribe, had been

well received and kindly treated, while Stone's relations with the natives were known to be cruel.

A treaty was finally signed in which it was stipulated and agreed that the two surviving Indians who took part in the massacre should be delivered to the English, and the Court agreed to begin once more trading with the Indians in that territory. The Pequots were anxious at the time to become friends with the English, as they were on bad terms with the Dutch, and also with the Narragansetts, and between the two they might meet with terrible losses should they be engaged in active warfare. The colonists thought that they had brought about peaceful relations between the two tribes when it was learned that a party of Narragansetts under two of their chiefs, was in the neighborhood. The authorities brought the representatives of the two tribes to a meeting when they signed a treaty, and made promises for a perpetual peace. Savage states in his note on Winthrop's "History of New England" that this endeavor is a demonstration on the part of the founders of New England of their pacific principles in their relations with the Indians, and we agree with his statement that "such mediation is more useful than victory, and more honorable than conquest." Unfortunately the Indians were not of this opinion, and the warlike attitude of both tribes was at once continued, and the treaty they had signed in the presence of the whites was ignored.

Time passed, and while the Pequots made presents of skins and wampum to the settlers, they did not deliver the two men who had taken part in the murder of Stone and his men. Excuses were made, and they parried questions, and dillydallied, but no results came of it. It was known that the men who had killed Stone and his crew were not members of Sassacus' Pequots, and consequently not called real members of that tribe, but that they did, however, belong to a subsidiary branch under the control of the Pequots. It was also known that the loot obtained from Stone's vessel, had been divided with Sassacus and his people.

The bloody Pequot war which Major Mason was to end, began with sporadic attacks on the whites. Reports of atrocities committed by the Pequots were being reported from every quarter. At the Saybrook fort, Captain Gardiner was being continually annoyed by them. Then came the news of the murder of John Oldham in his boat off Block Island. He was a man who stood high in the community, although at one time he had been banished from the colony on account of religious differences, but had been allowed to return. Also, Oldham is credited as being first to really open the Connecticut valley to the English. His dealings with the Indians had always been conducted with honesty and kindness. Therefore, it was with great excitement and horror that Boston learned in the latter part of July, 1636, that Captain Oldham had been murdered in his pinnace by Narragansett Indians. This was supposed to be on account of his having attempted to make peace with the Pequots. It was said and believed, that the crime was not known at the time to the Narragansett chiefs, Canonicus and Miantonimo.

Oldham was on a trading expedition to the Narragansetts, when he was attacked and killed by a party of fourteen warriors. His head had been cut off and also his hands and feet. The crime was discovered by Captain John Gallup, the same who had assisted Mason in searching for the pirate Bull some time before. Gallup was cruising in his twenty-ton shallop, with a crew of one man and two small boys. The wind changed suddenly and bore him to Block Island, where he saw Oldham's pinnace, which seemed to him to be out of control. His curiosity, as well as suspicions were aroused, and as he neared Oldham's boat, he saw that there were several Indians on the deck, and that a canoe that had just left it, was making towards the shore, loaded with goods.

Gallup could get no response to his calls, and at once began bombarding the sloop, as he was fortunately armed with pistols and guns. At the first fire, the Indians went below the hatch. It was too dangerous for Gallup to board the pinnace with so many armed men aboard, but his experience of many years as a sailor served him well in this emergency. He rounded to, and sailed with full force and jammed the pinnace so that the Indians evidently thought it would capsize. Six of them came on deck at once and leaped into the sea, and were drowned. Gallup got another good start and jammed the pinnace again, then making it fast to his own boat with his anchor, he went on board. Four more of the Indians leaped overboard and they also were drowned. Two more of the Narragansetts came on deck, and after some trouble, Gallup succeeded in binding them and put them in the cabin, but knowing how clever the red men were in getting out of such meshes, he threw one of them into the sea. The other one was eventually sold as a slave. That left two more in the hold, where Gallup kept them. He then took the remaining goods of Oldham's, together with the bound Indian on to his boat, made the pinnace fast with a line, and started to tow it to Massachusetts. The wind this time was not in his favor, and he was obliged to cast it adrift.

Governor Vane no sooner heard of the fate of Oldham, than he sent representatives to Canonicus, to learn further particulars, and to find out which tribe was guilty. The authorities believed the men who had committed the atrocity were Narragansetts, and that they had gone to the Pequots for protection. In cases of this kind, though not friendly, they would help one another when it came to trouble with the foreigners. Miantonimo received word that the murderers must be given up. He went in search of the men himself and returned with the two English boys who had been with Oldham, promising to restore the stolen goods. The chief who was a clever politician made no efforts to find the murderers.

The planters, as well as the authorities, were aroused to a degree that demanded extreme measures be taken. Governor Vane, with the approval of the magistrates and the ministers, made that unfortunate decision of sending Endicott to the enemies' stronghold to wreak vengeance on the Indians. The order read—"To put to death the men of Block Island, but to spare the women and children, and to bring them away, and to take possession of the island; and from thence to go to the Pequots, to demand the murderers of Capt. Stone and other English, and one thousand fathoms of wampum for damage, ETc., and some of their children for hostages; if they should refuse they were to obtain by force." This only resulted in what is best described in Captain Gardiner's own words—"you come hither to raise these wasps about my ears, and then you will take wings and flee away." Gardiner realized what the campaign would bring about, and he knew he had not a force strong enough to protect the settlers in that vicinity should the Indians unite in an attack on the settlements.

Endicott with his ninety men, which included Captain Turner and Captain Underhill, and others with some knowedge of warfare, sailed in three pinnaces, "besides two shallops and two Indian guides. They went as volunteers, victualed, but unpaid." When the small navy neared Block Island the surf was running too high for them to land, and while waiting for better conditions in which to make a landing, they were pelted with arrows by the Indians on shore. Some of the volunteers finally succeeded in gaining land, where they were attacked again. Captain Turner and another of the party were struck, but owing to the thick collars they wore, the wounds were not serious, and Underhill adds—"myself received an arrow through my coat sleeve, a second against my helmet on the forehead; so if God in his providence had not moved the heart of my wife to persuade me to carry it along with me, (which I was unwilling to do), I had been slain. Give me leave to observe two things from hence; first, when the hour of death is not yet come, you see God useth weak means to keep his purpose unviolated; secondly, let no man despise advice and counsel of his wife, though she be a woman."

After the attack the Indians beat a hasty retreat, and made no further efforts to defend their camp. Endicott's party slept on shore that night, and the next morning burnt the wigwams, corn and all inflammable articles, both at the place of landing, and also one a little distance inland. The only articles the soldiers took away with them were some "well wrought mats and several delightful baskets."

Then they sailed to the Saybrook fort, where Gardiner, in spite of his opposition to the expedition, did the best in his power to help, allowing Endicott two shallops, a few men and empty bags, as he said they would probably be able to fetch away some corn, though it was not likely that they would take many of the enemy. Once more the Endicott party set forth, and this time to the Pequot River. When the Indians discovered their approach, they ran along the shore, "crying out, 'What cheer, Englishmen? What cheer? Are you angry? Will you kill us? Do you come to fight? What cheer, Englishmen? What cheer?' "

The boats sailed into the harbor where they anchored for the night, as the men were afraid to go ashore. On both sides of the river were large numbers of Indians who kept fires burning, and according to Underhill—"they made most doleful cries all the night, hallooing one to another, and giving the word from place to place to gather their forces together fearing the English were come to war against them."

The Pequots evidently believed that the English had not come on a peaceful mission, and were therefore reinforcing their fort. In the morning they sent a representative to the boat to ask the reason for this visit from the colonists. Endicott followed the instructions of the Court, demanded the murderers of Stone and Norton, a thousand fathoms of wampum, and some children as hostages. The Pequot who was of high caste, and a man of intelligence, told, as a pardonable excuse for the tragedy, how a vessel had come to their land before the arrival of the English. How the white captain of the boat had invited the sachem of the tribe on board, and then held him for a large ransom, which when paid, the captain killed him, and sent his murdered body to the shore. The son of the slain sachem had sought revenge for his father's death. When another vessel had sailed up the river, he had not distinguished the difference between the Dutch and the English, so he had slain Stone, but that was the only one murdered by the Indians. The others had been killed when the boat blew up. Endicott did not consider the explanation satisfactory, and again told the Indian, "We must have the heads of these men, who have slain ours, or else we will fight. We would speak with your sachem." Sassacus, the Pequot said, was on Long Island, and that the other chiefs were away, but would return shortly.

The soldiers went on shore after it had been agreed that the Indians would move some distance back. Winthrop wrote that if the Indians had planned to attack the English, that was their opportunity, "for all the shore was high, ragged rocks." Kutshamkin, the Indian interpreter that Endicott had brought with him, consulted first the Indians and then the English, stating the demands and refusals and apologies, but, as we say today, "getting nowhere," and this continued for hours. As the day passed there was no evidence that the sachems were going to return. In the meanwhile, the English noticed that the Indians were moving their women and children and portable household goods. It finally dawned on Endicott that he was being tricked. He thereupon told the Indians since they would come to no decision, or pledge, that they were come to fight, and that now they would fight. With that the savages fled, shooting a few arrows as they did so, but harming no one. The soldiers raided the settlement, and Underhill tells of their very regrettable actions which seems to have been the custom in most wars, and considered legitimate. "We suddenly set upon our march, and gave fire to as many as we could come near, firing their wigwams, spoiling their corn, and many other necessaries that they had buried in the ground, we raked up, which the soldiers had for booty. Thus we spent the day burning and spoiling the country. Towards night embarked ourselves."

One Indian was killed by Kutshamkin, the interpreter for the English, who had hidden in a thicket, slew his man, and scalped him. Gardiner attributes to this act the cause of the Pequot war. Kutshamkin sent the scalp to Canonicus, the powerful sachem of the Narragansetts, who boastfully sent it from sachem to sachem which aroused the wrath of the Pequots to a boiling point, and not only increased their hatred for their enemies, but for the English, who were slowly but surely taking possession of their land. In his narrative, Gardiner refers to this act as "Thus I have written in a book that all men and posterity might know how and why so many honest men had their blood shed, and some flayed alive, and others cut in pieces and roasted alive, only because Kichamokin, a Bay Indian, killed one Pequot." The hostility of the Pequots against the English was no longer concealed from the whites. The fire of destruction was ignited and gained in momentum until finally it destroyed this once-powerful tribe.

The following day Endicott and the men he had brought from Massachusetts embarked and sailed to Boston, leaving behind the men who had come from Saybrook, and who were obliged to wait in the harbor for a more favorable wind. They were in view of the fields of corn that had not been destroyed in the destruction of the day before. The bags that Gardiner had given them on leaving, saying if they did not load their barks with Pequots, to load them with corn, were still empty. The temptation seemed too strong to resist. The two men landed and hurried to the field, and began to gather the crop. They were successful at first, and after emptying their bags in the boat, they went back for more, but went once too often, for a band of infuriated Indians suddenly appeared and shot at them with their arrows. A skirmish followed. The whites escaped unhurt and did not learn whether or not they had wounded or killed any of the savages. Endicott's expedition had aroused the hatred that could only result in the annihilation either of the Indians or the whites. The outlook for the colonists was most grave.

Roger Williams wrote to Winthrop at this time and stated that "Cannounicus . . . was very sour and accused the English and myself for sending the plague amongst them, and threatening to kill him especially. . . . Miantubimow kept his barbarous court lately at my house, and with him I have far better dealing. He takes some pleasure to visit me, and sent me word of his coming over again some eight days hence."

The winter passed with the hearts of the inhabitants of the outlying settlements filled with fear. Several atrocities were committed by the savages. Then on April 23, the following year, 1637, the murderous attack on Wethersfield occurred.

The Massachusetts Bay authorities always took a superior attitude toward the other colonies, especially Connecticut, and seldom called them in consultation regarding Indian or other troubles. This probably explains, as one writer said, why Mason was not asked to give his views on this expedition. If he had been consulted historians might have had a different story to relate as with his long experience in dealing with the natives, he had the foresight not to complicate conditions for the future government of the land.

CHAPTER V

IN the short time since the settlement of Windsor, Captain Mason had become known among the Indians as a man to be respected for his sense of justice and fair dealing. They also knew him to be a brave warrior, and his presence alone was proved on many occasions sufficient to protect the colony in which he lived. He had not only won this distinction among the neighboring tribes, but he had formed a strong friendship with Uncas, the chief sachem of the Mohegans.

Uncas was a genius in many respects, being clever, a politician, and at times he showed the tact of a diplomat. He was cunning, unscrupulous, and yet in all of his dealings with Mason, he was never known to deceive him, and was loyal to the last. He was descended from the royal line of the Pequots as was his wife. She was the daughter of Totabam, the old chief of a tributary branch of the Pequots, who was murdered by the Dutch.

Uncas was a petty sachem under Sassacus, but disagreeing with him in some matters, rebelled and was banished from the country of the Pequots. This had happened just previous to the first settlements in Connecticut by the English. Uncas' unusual personality was demonstrated by his being adopted by the Mohegans, and within a short time to be elected as their chief; the sovereignty was to descend to his son. It can be seen what such an alliance meant to Mason and to the colonies.

The failure and retreat of the Endicott expedition encouraged the boldness and daring of the Pequots, who
evidently believed themselves the victors, since the whites
had not gained their points, and had sailed away without
venturing to continue their attack in the Indian country.

A few days after Endicott's force had left, Gardiner
sent out a party of five men a short distance up the river
from the fort at Saybrook, to harvest the hay. It was an
opportunity for a party of Pequots who were lurking about
and who had hidden in the high grass, to attack them.
They captured one of the men, named Butterfield, who
was later burnt at the stake. The place has since been
known as Butterfield Meadow in his memory. The rest
of the party escaped to the boat, only one of them being
wounded by an arrow which fortunately did not prove
fatal. Two weeks later Gardiner sent out six men to
gather in the crops at a strong house that had been erected
two miles away. He warned them before leaving that
they were not to hunt, take any risks, or leave the place
to where they were directed. When they saw a flock of
ducks near by, they ventured far enough to get within
firing distance. Immediately a large band of Indians
rushed out and captured three of the whites, two of whom
they ripped their bodies up "from the bottom of their bel-
lies to their throates," hanging the halves on trees, while
the third, old Mr. Mitchell, was taken away and later
burnt alive. Again in February the Indians made another
assault, when Gardiner and some of his men were burning
brush near the fort. One of the men was killed, Gardiner
and a few of his companions wounded, while two of the
soldiers ran away. Such unsoldierly conduct of the latter

so enraged the Lieutenant that when the men came back
to the fort he offered "to let the cowards draw lots which
should be hanged first, for the articles did hang upon the
hall for them to read." The sentence was mitigated by the
persuasion of Chaplain Higginson.

Gardiner took advantage of the attack to take the arrow
that killed the man, and sent it to Governor Vane and
the magistrates, to contradict their assertions that an
arrow had no force. Also to complain of their indifference
to his position and their neglecting to provide sufficient
protection. Another ambush was made when Joseph Tilly
sailed down the Connecticut in a small boat and anchored
a few miles above the fort. He took one of his crew with
him, and the two went ashore to hunt. The firing of the
rifles brought a band of Pequot warriors about them.
They killed Tilly's companion, but Tilly they saved to
suffer a most terrible fate. His hands and feet were cut
off, and then they continued to torture him until he died.
Not content to torture and kill their victims, they mocked
them when they groaned, decorated themselves in their
clothing, and would parade before the English thus clothed
to add to the terrors of Indian warfare.

Conditions became graver every day as the occupants
of the fort were practically in a state of siege. They were
surrounded by the enemy, always hiding, and were compelled to keep watch day and night. It was impossible
for them to cultivate the fields, or to gather sufficient
fodder for the live stock, and many of the cattle died
before spring from starvation. The waters of the ocean
and the Connecticut flowed at their door, but they were
unable to fish, or to hunt the game that abounded in the

surrounding woods. Thus the winter passed. Starvation faced the inmates of the garrison. It was then that Mason learned of the ambush, and with twenty of his men, went to Gardiner's relief. It was impossible for him to take a larger force from the infant colony, as Windsor needed all of the stronger members of the place for their own protection from the surrounding savages, as they, in turn, feared an attack at any time. Mason states in the preface of his history that "after his coming (to Saybrook), there did not one Pequot appear in view for one Month Space which was the time he there remained." This was not bravado, but a statement of the case, which was also mentioned by other authorities.

The Court at Hartford joined Gardiner in demanding reinforcements for the Saybrook fort. They also expressed criticism of the Endicott expedition, and demanded to know the intentions of the authorities in future regarding the Indian question. These petitions resulted in the Massachusetts Bay Colony sending Captain Underhill to the fort with twenty men, which relieved Mason, who was then able to return to Windsor, where he was much needed.

During that winter there were said to be twenty-four men, women and children at the fort, as well as some additional soldiers. The cold winter and early spring months passed, when on the 23rd of April, 1637, the conditions were brought to a climax by the Wethersfield massacre. Two hundred Pequots had sailed up the Connecticut River the previous night in their canoes, and concealed themselves in a small branch of the stream, where they waited until morning.

The inhabitants of Wethersfield were out in the fields preparing for the spring planting, men, women and children, little dreaming of the tragedy that was about to befall them. The day was pleasant and warm, and seemingly every thing promised well for a season of good crops. Suddenly, and without any warning, the red warriors appeared in their war paint, shouting their terrifying, bloodcurdling warwhoops. The result was the death of six men, three women, twenty cows, and the capture of two girls; the older was sixteen years of age.

The Indians after finishing their bloody task, sailed down the river in great glee, and when they passed the fort, they waved the clothing of the victims they had murdered, to attract the attention of the soldiers. Mason and Gardiner realized that the Indians were on the warpath and returning from some murderous expedition, and taking a chance shot at them "with the Piece of Ordinance," Mason said, "Which beat off the Beak Head of one of the Canoes wherein our two Captives were." The Indians hastily pushed their canoes over the sand bar at the mouth of the river and disappeared. The Captain states they were all dejected at the fort, and were enraged when they learned of the outrage that the Indians had committed. The canoes of the Indians at that time were very large, often having a capacity for eighty warriors, so that only a few were required to convey an Indian army to a seat of war.

At the urgent request of Gardiner, a Dutch captain went after the two girls taken by the Pequots. He offered a large ransom for their return, which was refused. There

were several Pequots on his boat, and the Captain decided
to keep them for hostages, when several jumped overboard, but he still had six, which resulted in an exchange.
The girls had been well treated, though practically
stripped of their clothing. Monotto's squaw had looked
after the maidens, and it was due to her care that no
violence was shown them. Her intercessions and care
were not forgotten by Winthrop, when later she was taken
prisoner with members of her tribe. The Pequots had
asked the girls when in their camp, if they could make
gun powder, and seemed to believe that they could. It
was likely with that idea that they had been taken prisoners. It was thanks to the consideration of the sailors
on the Dutch boat, who gave the girls coats, that their
nakedness was covered.

Some authorities state that the initiative in rescuing the
girls was made by the Dutch governor, who claimed as
his reward that he should be the first to have the privilege
of seeing them on their return. This statement seems in
a way verified, by the fact that the girls paid him a visit,
as he requested. Mason mentions this very friendly act
of the Dutch. He questioned the girls regarding conditions at the Pequot fort, and learned many important
facts, among others, that the Indians had sixteen guns.
The eldest girl said that she never lost faith in the power
of God to rescue her, and prayed all the time she was a
prisoner. Winthrop first learned of this incident from
a messenger sent by Miantonimo, who said that Mason
with a party of Englishmen had surprised and slain eight
Pequots on the river, and had taken seven squaws. Quite

a different version from the correct one, and which must
have caused considerable agitation among the magistrates
at Boston.

Monday, the first of May, the Court convened at Hartford. The authorities realized that by waiting any longer
before striking a fatal blow against the Indians, meant the
extermination of the colonists. They could see that Sassacus was planning to annihilate the settlers. Perhaps a
few at a time, which would not incur the dangers of actual
war, but which would drive those who escaped from the
country. Their chief was wise enough to believe that if
he could get the Narragansetts to unite with the Pequots,
there would be no difficulty to rid their hunting grounds
from the intruders, even though it might mean a declaration of war. Accordingly he sent his ambassadors to
Miantonimo, to persuade him to his cause. The Pequot
arguments were convincing to the great chief, and had it
not been for the good work of Roger Williams, they would
have succeeded in forming a powerful army.

Boston learned of this new menace, and sent to Roger
Williams for his aid in counteracting the effect of Sassacus'
emissaries, for he had won the confidence of the Narragansetts, by his fair and just dealings, so that his influence
was invaluable to the English. It must not be forgotten
that the authorities of Massachusetts had banished Williams owing to his religious beliefs. They claimed that
Williams looked upon himself "as one who had received
a clearer illumination and apprehension of the state of
Christ kingdom, and the purity of all Communion than all
Christendum besides." The colonists thought him a "very
self conceited, unquiet, turbulent, and uncharitable

spirit." One would think that it should have been with humiliation that they sought his aid in this emergency. Williams proved then, as he did in many other instances, his belief in practicing the Golden Rule, of loving his neighbor as himself, and in carrying out his policy of kindness. The experiences of his mission are best told in the letter that he wrote to Mason many years later when they were both facing the sunset of life. He began his communication, written under date of 1670, to his "honoured deare and ancient friend," and said in part, "When I was unkindly and unchristianly, as I believe, driven from my house and land and wife and children (in the midst of a New England winter, now about 35 years past). . . . When the next year after my banishment, the Lord drew the bow of the Perquot warr against the country in which, Sir, the Lord made yourselfe, with others, a blessed instrument of peace to all New England, I had my share of service to the whole land in that Pequot business, inferiour to very few that acted." Then he refers to the letters from the "Councill at Boston requesting me to use my utmost and speediest endeavours to break and hinder the league harboured by the Pequots. . . . The Lord helped me immediately to put my life into my hand, and scarce acquainting my wife, to ship myself all alone in a poore canow, and to cut through a stormie wind with great seas, every minute in hazard of life, to the Sachem house.

"Three dayes and nights my busines forced me to lodge and mix with the bloudie Pequot ambassadours, whose hands and arms, methought, reaked with the bloud of my countriemen, murther'd and massacred by them on Conneticut river and from whome I could not but nightly looke for their bloudie knives at my owne throate allso. When God wond'rously preserved me and help't me to break to pieces the Pequots negociation and designe." It was owing to Williams' diplomacy on this mission that the colonies were saved from the menace of the league of most of the Indian tribes.

Reports of the massacres in which the Indians tortured their victims were continually coming in from every side. It was said that over thirty English had been slain in the Connecticut valley, "that they had tortured and insulted their captives in a most barbarous manner. In some they cut large gashes in their flesh, then poured live embers and coals into the wounds," and when the poor sufferers cried out in their last agonies to "their Redeemer," the savages would shout and dance in glee.

These acts by the savages created a fear and enraged the English into a desire for vengeance. They began at once to take practical steps toward that end.

While atrocities were taking place in New England, how were the civilized and Christian authorities in the Old World conducting their criminal cases?

The rack was not abolished until 1640 and the Inquisition, not until 1821. Burning at the stake, and innumerable instruments of torture of the most fiendish conception, were not only employed, but in most cases organized or sanctioned by the church, as most of the so-called crimes arose from religious causes. We, who are told of the horrors of the settlers being roasted alive, forget that thousands suffered that death all through Europe as late as the latter part of the seventeenth century, at the time of the witchcraft panic that spread over Europe, as well as

America. It was during the middle of that century that Damiens of unsound mind, who had inflicted a slight wound with a penknife on Louis XV, was tortured and executed under the government of the "Most Christian King of France and Navarre" in the following manner, as vouched for by Casanova. His right hand which had held the knife, was consumed in burning oil, lead and resin were poured into the wounds, while at last he was torn asunder by four horses. This description states that not only the populace surrounded the scaffold, but the lords and ladies of the Court.

To return to the troubles in the Connecticut valley. At the session of the Court at Hartford in March, 1637, some questions were brought up regarding the manner in which Pynchon had imprisoned and whipped some Indians, which was regarded by many as one of the reasons that had led to the massacres previously mentioned. At a Court that convened April 18, 1637, "for a special occasion of prosecuting the war against the Pequots, it was agreed and ordered, that the war having been undertaken upon just grounds, should be seriously prosecuted, and for this end there shall be one hundred and sixty men provided to be chosen within a week, out of the several towns." Hartford was to furnish forty-two, Windsor thirty, and Wethersfield, eighteen. Word was sent at once to the Massachusetts and Plymouth colonies, who notified Connecticut that they would send an army of two hundred men from Massachusetts and fifty from Plymouth. Unfortunately, none of these men arrived until after Mason's great victory.

CHAPTER VI

THERE was great excitement in the three settlements, as they made their preparations for the war. In Boston, where the authorities had at last awakened to the seriousness of conditions, they abandoned for the time, the idea of the synod of the preachers, and the prosecution of Anne Hutchinson and some of her followers. War was in the air, and was the dominant thought in the minds of all.

It can be well understood what fear filled the hearts of the inhabitants of the three towns along the Connecticut. Practically all of the able bodied men were enlisted to go to the scene of action. What would be their fate in this conflict with the vicious savages, no one knew! The soldiers were leaving their families in the care of a few armed men, a number inadequate to protect the settlements in case of an attack. The towns were all surrounded by dense forests sufficient to conceal hordes of red men, whose warfare always consisted in ambushing the enemy.

The Court at Hartford had appointed Captain Mason commander of the troops, with Lieutenant Seely, second in command, and the Rev. Mr. Stone as chaplain. The authorities believed in having their men well "victualed," accordingly they gave orders for the Captain to have "good beer, three or four gallons of strong water and two gallons of sacks." In addition to this they were to be supplied with corn both whole and ground, "biskett, firkins of sweet and firkins of bitter, Oatmeal, Pease, fish, butter, Indian beans, Pork, rice and cheese." All of this at a time when the colonies were poor and food was scarce. Furthermore, every man was to carry a "length of natch with Brimstone matches with him to kindle the fire withal." They must have presented an odd appearance even in that day, as the armour of corselets, muskets, bandoleers, rest and swords, were of a miscellaneous kind. It was also ordered "that Hartford shall send fourteen armor in this design; Windsor six"; This "armor" was a padded garment, which was a protection against the Indian arrows. Captain Mason's pay was 40s per day, of a six day week, since it would be sacrilege to pay for fighting on Sunday. The lieutenant and sergeant were to receive half that amount, while the common soldiers were to be rewarded with only 1s 3d.

The time was too short for the Captain to give his little army any practical training as he started with his ninety men and seventy Indian allies on their hazardous venture ten days after the appointment by the Court. They sailed down the Connecticut in a "pink, a pinnace, and a shallop," accompanied by Uncas and his warriors. The trip was slow and tedious. The boats often became stalled on sand bars, much to the annoyance of the Indians who could not adjust themselves to this sluggish way of travel, so slow in comparison with their own swift canoes. At their request, Mason allowed them to go ashore, as they promised to meet the army at the Saybrook fort. The English never felt sure of the loyalty of the red men, and it was with great misgivings that they saw Uncas and his men disappear into the forest. Would they see them again? Would they go to the Pequots and betray their plans? Perhaps at the time Mason had his fears in this respect, though he never voiced them.

It was joyful news that Captain Underhill brought to the soldiers when he rowed up the river to meet them. He said that when he made his boat fast, and went on deck, Chaplain Stone was in the midst of a prayer in which he was beseeching the Lord for the fidelity of their Indian allies. Underhill told him at the close of his petition that his wish had already been granted. Then he went on to tell how Uncas and his Mohegans met a party of Pequots on their way to the fort, and slew several of them, and took one prisoner. This act convinced the English that the Mohegans could be relied upon.

The army arrived at Saybrook on Wednesday the 17th of May and were cordially welcomed by Gardiner, but when he saw how small and poorly equipped the contingent was, both he and Underhill thought it absurd for them to venture an attack in the enemies' country. Gardiner says in his account, "when captain Underhill and I had seen their commission, we both said they were not fitted for such a design, and we said to major Mason, we wondered he would venture himself, being no better fitted, and he said the magistrates could not or would not send better. Then we said that none of our men should go with them, unless we, that were bred soldiers from our youth could see some likelyhood to do better than the Bay men with their strong commission last year," which referred to the Endicott expedition.

Even though Underhill's pessimistic opinion when he first saw Mason's army, caused severe criticism, yet he asked Lieutenant Gardiner, who was the commander of the fort, the privilege to join it, with nineteen of his men from Massachusetts. This was granted, and with this addition of trained men, Mason was able to send twenty of his own men back to the settlements to protect their homes.

The Captain's army remained at the fort until Friday, and during that time an incident occurred that reflected discredit on the English. Several versions of this tragedy have been given, as well as excuses for it, and the facts as far as it is possible to learn are as follows. A party of Uncas' Mohegans in roving about the vicinity of the fort encountered a band of Pequots, five of whom they killed, and later placed their heads upon the fort, as a warning to all enemies. This was a custom at the time in England, as well as throughout Europe. One Pequot escaped, and one was captured. This proved to be Kiswas, who had lived about the fort some time. He had learned English so that he became a valuable spy for the enemy, keeping Sassacus informed of all the movements and plans of the authorities. Gardiner had previously learned of Kiswas' traitorous acts, but not until he had gotten safely away. When he was captured, Uncas insisted with Indian logic and custom, that the spy should be put to the torture as a lesson to the Pequots.

Underhill put a stop to the poor wretch's suffering by shooting him through the head. The Mohegans had danced with glee about the stake, and are said to have later eaten some of the victim's flesh, stating, "it was the sweetest morsel they had ever tasted."

The two days that Mason remained at Saybrook, he consulted with the others regarding the best way to proceed. He, as well as the others, had but little knowledge of the

Pequot country. Underhill had been as far as the mouth of the Pequot River, but could give no information regarding the surrounding territory. It was known that the Pequots kept guards constantly on duty at their fortifications, and along the river, so that it would be impossible to make a surprise attack from the west. They also learned from the two girl captives, that the Pequots had sixteen guns, and were equipped with plenty of ammunition. Mason advocated sailing to the country of the Narragansetts. He argued that to march across land would be learned by the Pequot's spies. To sail past the Pequot River, and then march back, the Captain said, was the only way that a surprise attack could be made. The other officers were not convinced of the logic of Mason's arguments. They reasoned that the only way to proceed was to sail to the Pequot River, as the commission directed, and which instructions had been confirmed by a letter to them at Saybrook, and Mason was liberal enough to state that "there was strong ground for this opinion. The majority wished to follow the rules laid out by the authorities, and attack the nearest and quickest way. This they believed would be the safest manner in which to destroy the enemy, and could be done at once.

Mason's diplomacy and tact were well illustrated at this critical time, as well as upon many other occasions. He realized that the way of attack as directed by the magistrates, was too hazardous to attempt, and yet, even though he was the commanding officer, he had to have some higher authority to sanction his views. He did the wise, and as we would say in our time, the cleverest thing possible. He consulted Chaplain Stone, asking him that he might

ask the Lord, during the night, "to direct how in what
manner we should demean ourselves in that respect."
Mason visited the Chaplain who was staying on one of
the shallops, while the Captain lived on shore. We may
be sure that when the Captain asked the Chaplain for instructions from the Lord, that he very carefully pointed
out the whys and wherefores of his own views. It was
therefore not with surprise, but with great satisfaction,
when the Chaplain visited him the next morning, to be
told that he had followed Mason's wishes, and that his
views were the right ones. Then the contingent arranged
to sail the following morning.

In his history of this war, Mason stops at this point to
moralize, and to point out, how justly the commander of
an army can go contrary to directions by the government.
"For," as he wrote, "it is not possible for the wisest and
ablest Senator to foresee all Accidents and Occurents that
fall out in the Management and Pursuit of a War"; even
though "he might be trained in Military Affairs." The
Captain did not wish to encourage soldiers to go contrary
to directions, however, "for so doing," he says, "they run
a double Hazard. There was a great Commander in
Belgia who did the States great Service in taking a City,
but by going beyond his Commission lost his life. His
name was Grubbendunk."

The reference was to the Belgian general who was governor of Bois-le-Duc during the several sieges of that town,
and which he lost in 1630 at the time Mason was in the
attacking army. It was due, no doubt, to Mason's early
training in the English army in the Low Countries, that
gave him that insight to conditions and the courage to

"put over" his convictions which were contrary to those of the majority.

The army sailed for the Narragansett country Friday morning. They passed the Pequot River at some distance from its mouth, but in view of the Indians, so that they could even hear their shouts. The Indians believed the English were already beaten by fear of the powerful Pequots and had abandoned their idea of war, and were returning to Boston for greater protection. Mason's maneuvers had succeeded, though at the time he could only guess what the enemy's convictions were of this movement. Mason was a master of strategy, and no doubt he realized how this action would be interpreted by Sassacus and his warriors.

The little fleet did not reach Narragansett bay, a distance of fifty miles, until Saturday evening, and as the Sabbath began at sundown they anchored and prepared to remain on board until Monday. Chaplain Stone held divine services on the boats, and the day passed without any other incident. The army was disappointed on awakening early Monday morning to find a strong northwest wind blowing, and which kept up and prevented their landing until Tuesday evening. Mason, with a few of his men, landed at Tower Hill, the best harbor in the vicinity north of Point Judith. He went at once to the Indian town to see Canonicus, chief of the Narragansetts, to explain the cause of their being in his territory without previous notice. The old chief sent immediately for his nephew Miantonimo, who came the following day. Mason then went into detail regarding the expedition, apologizing profusely, as the true diplomat that he was, for his seeming neglect in not sending a representative in advance telling of their coming. He explained to the two chiefs why the English were warring on the Pequots, who were the enemies of the Narragansetts as much as they were of the English. How the common enemy had massacred the colonists without cause, and had tortured their captives in a most fiendish manner. He ended his talk, asking for the privilege of passing through his country to the land of the dreaded Pequots. Canonicus readily agreed, but expressed his doubts as to the success of the campaign when he noted the small army which was planning to attack an enemy many times its size, and added "the enemy who were very great Captains and men skilled in War."

Before daylight the same morning, Mason was awakened by a messenger from Captain Patrick who had arrived at the plantation of Roger Williams, stating he had forty men with him, as they had been sent in advance of the main army of the Massachusett's contingent. He hoped that Mason would wait until he could catch up with him, though he did not state when that would be. This was reassuring news, that the Captain could eventually count on reinforcements if needed, yet he realized the importance of making a quick attack before the enemy could gain any knowledge of the impending assault. Therefore, early Wednesday morning he selected a few of his men to man the boats, and sail back to Pequot harbor in order to meet the army, after the battle. This left only seventy-seven whites, sixty or more Mohegans, and about two hundred Narragansetts who had asked to join the expedition, besides some stragglers. Having given his instructions to the crew on the boats, he went to his men on shore and

gave the order to march. Shortly after, the army was on
its way. The weather was extremely hot, and only narrow
Indian paths over which to travel, but in spite of these
drawbacks, they made from eighteen to twenty miles the
first day. Toward evening they arrived at another Narragansett fort, called Nehantics, which was situated near the
Pequot country.

Here the English were not welcome, even though they
had a pass from Canonicus, and these Indians were his
subjects. This was owing, perhaps, to the fact that many
of these members of the Narragansetts were related by
marriage to Pequots. At any rate, they forbade any of
Mason's army entering the fort, and Mason, in turn, gave
orders that no one should enter or leave the fort "upon
peril of their lives," which proved effective as no attempt
was made to disobey these instructions. The English
camped there for the night. The next morning a large
party of Miantonimo's warriors came to Mason wishing to
join his forces. They "suddenly gathering into a Ring,
one by one, making solemn Protestations how galliantly
they would demean themselves, and how many men they
would kill." Evidently the Captain was not impressed
with their bravado or the sincerity of their promises. With
this addition his army now numbered about five hundred
men.

They set out again Thursday morning feeling refreshed
after the night's rest, but the increased intensity of the
heat, together with want of proper food, and the fatigue
of the march, overcame several of the soldiers, who fainted.
It was found necessary to halt after a march of twelve
miles. They fortunately found a desirable place to rest

on the banks of the Pawcatuck, now Stonington River. They were told by the Narragansetts that this site was a favorite place for the Pequots to fish, but none appeared at that time. While resting, some of Miantonimo's men appeared to be nervous and showed great fear, so that many of them left and returned to their fort. Formerly they had insulted the English by telling them that they would not dare to attack the Pequots, and that they would even run away at sight of them, while the Narragansetts would do the fighting, and show the English how to act in war. These Indians could not believe that the whites would actually dare to attack such powerful warriors as those Sassacus had under his command, though Mason had told them that they would fight the Pequots even thought it meant their death. "I then inquired of Onkos," Mason writes, "what he thought the Indians would do? Who said, The Narragansetts would all leave us, but as for Himself, He would never leave us; and so it proved; For which Expression and some other Speeches of his, I shall never forget him. Indeed he was a great Friend, and did great Service."

After a short halt the men took up their arms and began again making their way over the Indian path, but at the end of three miles, they came to a newly planted corn field which proved they were getting closer to the enemy's quarters. They supposed they were near the Pequot fort as they had been thus informed by the Indian spies. These runners also gave them further information, saying that the Pequots had two forts, about two miles apart. Upon learning this, the officers thought they would attack both forts at the same time, but the fatigue of the men had told too much on their strength to permit entertaining such an assault, and the idea was abandoned. Again they took up their arms and were on the march which they kept up until night. The only sound was the tread of their feet, or the breaking of branches and twigs. Silence was necessary, as they never knew when some member of Sassacus's band might be lurking about. Another danger that must have haunted them, was that an Indian runner from the fort they had just left, and which had proved so inhospitable to them, might have preceded them by a short and more direct route to notify the Pequots of their approach. In the meantime more of the Indian allies who had so valiantly boasted of their prowess, and at first led the battalion, were dropping farther and farther to the rear.

The place that Mason selected for the final encampment was near the head of Mystic River, and now known as Porter's Rocks. "It lay between two bare granite rocks, with sides almost perpendicular, forming with some smaller rocks two thirds of a circle . . . and was only accessible through a narrow entrance." It formed a most secure hiding place, and Mason said, "the rocks were their pillows, yet rest was pleasant" after their long day's march through the intense heat. It was a moonlight night and so bright that when they awoke before daylight, they thought that it was already day, which would have defeated their plans, and perhaps their victory. They were soon reassured, and given renewed promise of success, when their Indian spies brought the news that the enemy had kept up their singing and shouting until way into the

night, rejoicing in the belief that the English had returned
to Boston in great fear.

It took but a few minutes for the men to buckle on their
armour and adjust their accoutrements, when, after a short
prayer by Stone, they began the ascent up the rolling country led by the Indian guides.   They advanced about two
miles, when the Captain called a halt, for he had become
suspicious, as there were no signs of the Pequot forts,
though a newly planted corn field again indicated the
nearness of an Indian camp.   Uncas and Wequash, a member of his tribe, told Mason that they were at the bottom
of the hill on top of which the fort was located.   Then
Mason asked what had become of the Narragansetts, who
were so vain in their boastings, "behind" Uncas replied,
"exceedingly afraid."   At which the Captain said he
should tell "the rest of their Fellows, That they should by
no means Fly, but stand at what distance they pleased, and
see whether English Men would now fight or not."

Mason consulted with Captain Underhill, and as they
had learned that there were two entrances to the stockade,
it was decided for each of them to take his regiment and
enter the fort at opposite ends at the same time.   Once
more they began their march, and this time up the hill,
going as carefully as it was possible, in order not to awaken
the enemy, and to take the place by surprise.   There were
still two hours before daylight, and after the carousing of
the Pequots all night, it was not probable that they had
the slightest suspicion of the approach of the English.

The fort covered an area of about two acres, and was
surrounded by a palisade of trunks of trees, buried in

the ground about three feet, and about twelve feet exposed. They were bound together at the top, and sufficient space was left between the tree trunks to enable the Indians to shoot their arrows. This was one of the strongest forts of Sassacus, the great chief of the Pequots, who was dreaded and feared by all the Indian tribes east of the Hudson.

Nearing the top of the hill, all seemed well for a quick attack before the Pequots would be aware of their presence. Then suddenly a dog in the stockade barked. An Indian awoke, and seeing the English outside the walls, he shouted "Owanux! Owanux" (Englishmen! Englishmen!) and ran through the streets of the stockade to rouse the sleepers. The Pequots were dazed, as they awakened from a sound sleep, and hearing a bewildering cry of danger, they seemed incapable of grasping the significance of the warning.

Mason gave orders to fire into the fort, and at the same time he hurried to the entrance at the northeast side, while Underhill and his men went to the opposite end as they had planned. Mason pushed his way over the branches that covered the entrance, and was followed by Lieutenant Seely and several men. They found themselves in one of the two streets of the camp, on either side of which were the wigwams. In the meantime Underhill and his men had forced their way into the camp from the other end, acting simultaneously, and took the enemy completely by surprise; as Underhill says in his history, "We could not but admire at the providence of God in it; that soldiers so unexpert in the use of their arms, should give so complete a volley, as though the finger of

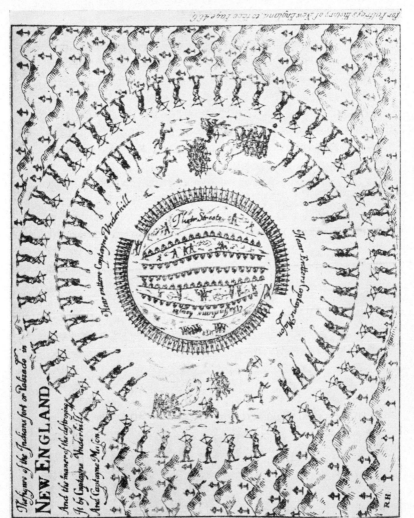

CAPTAIN UNDERHILL'S DRAWING OF THE STOCKADE

God had touched both match and flint." The confusion
of the Indians was so great that they were in a panic,
running madly down the streets hoping to escape, only
to be attacked at both ends of the fort by the English
with their swords and guns. Both entrances had been
blocked by the soldiers, and escape was impossible, though
many attempted to battle their way out, only to be killed,
while some sought shelter in the wigwams, hiding beneath
the bed mats.

It had been the original idea of Mason's to destroy the
Indians, and save the plunder, but this plan had to be
abandoned. Entering a wigwam, and finding the Indians
hiding beneath the mats, he was immediately set upon,
but he fought them off with his sword. Returning to the
lane, he pursued several Indians, who ran down the street
towards the other entrance, only to be shot down by Pat-
terson, Barber, and other soldiers. "Then," Mason said,
"the Captain facing about, marched a slow pace up the
lane he came down, perceiving himself very much out of
breath," and coming up to some soldiers, told them that
they would never kill them in that manner. "We must
burn them!"

He went at once into the wigwam where he had been
before and brought out a firebrand. At that moment an
Indian had drawn his bow, which was pointed at Mason's
head. In another moment it would have ended the
leader's life, had not a soldier named Daniel Heydon cut
the bowstring with his sword. This sword is now in the
Connecticut Historical Society's rooms at Hartford.

Mason fired one of the wigwams. The flames spread
with speed over the combustible material of which they

were made. It created a gas, and that, together with the draft, seemed to set the very air on fire. The poor savages ran about in frantic terror in their efforts to escape. Some, it was said, in their panic, ran into the flames. Once the wigwams were ignited, the English withdrew and with their Indian allies surrounded the palisade, shooting any of the Pequots who attempted to escape. The scene was one of horror, and added to the shrieks and groans of the wounded and dying, were the shouts of glee from the Indian allies, until it must have seemed that hell itself was let loose. It is recorded that a last attempt to escape was made by about forty Pequot braves, who had climbed to the top of the palisades with the flames sweeping over them, only to be shot and fall back into the fire. In spite of the bewilderment of the Indians when they awoke, they had put up a strenuous fight, hiding behind the wigwams and shouting at the invaders, but all to no purpose. The odds were against them from the first, and nearly all perished in the fort they had built for their protection.

It was learned later that many of the warriors from the other Pequot fort had come the night before to join in the celebration in what they believed was the retreat of the English. It was also learned from the surviving Pequots that nearly seven hundred of their tribe were destroyed. Seven were said to have escaped, and seven were taken prisoners.

The victory was won, and the fort but a heap of ruins within two hours after the English had fired their first shot, but Mason well knew that all was not over. Two of his men were killed, and twenty were wounded, and these had to be carried several miles over a wild country to the bay, where he hoped the vessels would be waiting. The English had made but little progress, when they were surprised by a shock of arrows coming from the near-by trees. The Pequots from the other fort were pursuing the army, and as they knew the country, while the English were strangers, they at first met with some success. Mason bribed the Indian allies to carry the wounded to the boats, while he led the attack against the enemy. In the meanwhile the Narragansetts who had remained, about fifty in all, fled at the sight of the Pequots. Mason had to send a party of soldiers to their rescue as they were in a perilous position. Underhill had to persuade them, he said, to make a counter attack, which they did in such a desultory way, "that they might fight seven years, and not kill seven men." When a Pequot was killed, the Mohegans would venture, if possible, to bring back a scalp or head. The English were still in a very serious situation. They were exhausted from their forced march of the several days previous, and they were still some distance from the harbor. Worst of all, their ammunition was giving out. Several of them were wounded in these skirmishes. It must have been with hearts filled with gratitude therefore, when the soldiers saw that the vessels had arrived and were anchored in the harbor. The army had not been molested by the Pequots during the last two miles to the bay, and they had marched "with colors flying," but without the drum, as that had been left where they camped the night before. The soldiers shouted with joy as they approached the shore, and the men on the boats cheered in their turn.

The life of a commander is not all glory or a path of

ease, as will be seen by the following incident, and that much of Mason's anticipated joy must have been dampened by the wrangling of the officers. Captain Patrick and his regiment of forty men had gone to Narragansett from Providence, in time to embark on the vessels that were to sail to Pequot harbor. He came on shore, when the soldiers arrived, as he told Mason, "to rescue" them, though as Mason adds, "there did not appear any the least sign of such a thing," as the fighting was all over. Patrick stubbornly refused to have his men leave the shallop, though he had no right to it, and it was some time before Mason succeeded in having him do so. The wounded were then placed on the boats. This settled, Patrick then had a dispute with Underhill as to which should have the use of Underhill's boat in which Underhill had an interest. The outcome was that Underhill sailed away with his contingent and the wounded, while Patrick came ashore and marched with Mason and his tired, twenty men to Saybrook. There was evidently not much friendliness between the two captains, as Mason told Patrick in plain, soldierly bluntness, that "he did not desire or delight in his company." Nevertheless, Patrick marched with him. The only incident that happened on their way to Saybrook was running across a tribe of Nehantics, a tributary of the Pequots, who fled to a nearby swamp, and were not followed by the English.

The soldiers, footsore and weary, reached the eastern shore of the Connecticut opposite Saybrook late Saturday afternoon, where they were welcomed and "nobly entertained by Lieutenant Gardiner with many great guns." It must have been disappointing to the men that they were

obliged to remain there all night, not being able to cross
the river until the next morning which was Sunday. They
reached Saybrook in time, however, to attend services.

The picture of rejoicing of the inhabitants of the town
can be imagined, and even though it was the Sabbath, it
is probable that some of the strict Puritan laws may have
been stretched a bit upon this momentous occasion. The
colonists felt for the first time that they were practically
free from the menace of an Indian massacre. They gave
thanks for their deliverance which they believed had been
brought about by Providence.

All of this had taken place within three weeks and three
days since the decision of the Court. The little army had
tramped through trackless forest, sixty miles in all, in four
days, in a heat almost unbearable, so that some of the men
had fainted. The victory was a complete one, and one of
the most remarkable in the history of warfare in the
colonies settled by the English. It must not be forgotten
that the settlements along the great river did not number
all told eight hundred, and that less than two hundred
were able to bear arms to fight the battle, and protect the
homes. Also, that Connecticut in its quick decision, led
by Mason, to settle the matter at once, and not wait for
assistance from the ever vacillating magistrates of Massachusetts, made peace possible for the further settlement of
the country. Another fact that must not be forgotten, that
while Connecticut always made quick decisions and carried them out, Massachusetts dilly-dallied, as she did with
the murderers of Captain Stone for over three years, and
then, the criminals were not executed. Sassacus was no
longer the terror of the other Indian tribes. Mason was

the man they now feared, as Prince said, "he soon became the equal dread of the most numerous nations, from Massachusetts to the Hudson river."

Terrible as the slaughter was, there was no other way out of the threatening situation. Either the settlers had to defeat the Pequots and annihilate their race, or to be tortured and murdered by the savages. It was kill or be killed. Regardless of the rights of possessing the territory, the planters had a situation that had to be met at once. As Isaac H. Bromley said in his oration at the dedication of the Mason statue at Mystic in 1889, when touching on this subject—"It is well to remember, too, that from the beginnings of history, all progress has been in the wake of war, and every forward step in our boasted Christian civilization has been in its bloody footprints. And this was war in its worst form; a war of extermination on the one side, or self preservation on the other."

George E. Ellis in his "Life of John Mason" when referring to the Pequot War said, "Of this battle Mason was the hero. His judgment, intrepidity, and valor are apparent through the whole conduct of the expedition which he commanded." And Dr. Dwight added to his article on this subject that "few efforts made by man have been more strongly marked with wisdom in the project, or with superior courage and conduct in the execution. Every step appears to have been directed by the spirit and prudence which mankind have with one voice regarded with admiration and applause in the statesman and the hero."

Captain Underhill in his history of the war wrote—"It may be demanded why should you be so furious (As some one has said) Should not Christians have more mercy and

compassion? But I would refer you to David's war. . . .
We had sufficient light from the Word of God."

According to Winthrop, one of the best results of the
Pequot War was the suggestion for the confederation of
the four New England colonies, the first motion for which
was made in Boston, August 31, 1637.

The statement Mason wrote at the conclusion of his
history of the war, indexes the man as well as the times in
which he lived. "Thus we may see," he said, "how the
Face of God is set against them that do Evil, to cut off the
Remembrance of them from the Earth. Our Tongue shall
talk of thy Righteousness all the Day long; for they are
confounded, they are brought to shame that sought Hurt!
. . . Thus the Lord was pleased to smite our Enemies in
the hinder Parts, and to give us their land for an Inheritance; Who remembered us in our low Estate, and redeemed us out of our Enemies' Hands. Let us therefore
praise the Lord for his Goodness and his Wonderful
Works to the Children of Men!"

CHAPTER VII

THE Narragansetts were sent back safely to their country by an escort of English, and Mason's soldiers returned to their homes, where the Captain said they were "Entertained with great Triumph and Rejoicing, and Praising God for his goodness."

The authorities both at Boston and Hartford realized that the colonies were not safe from the remaining Pequots, who would seek revenge for their overwhelming defeat, and at once sent about to muster another army. There was not so much to fear in and about Boston, as the settlements in that section had grown so large that there was but little distance between the several towns, such as Newton, Watertown and Charlestown. In Connecticut, conditions were far different. The scattered settlements only numbered a few hundred souls in all, and the growth had been slow owing to the Indian warfare. Consequently within a month after the Mystic fight, Massachusetts had organized a new army to go to the Pequot country to join one from Connecticut, with instructions to destroy the remaining members of the once powerful Pequot tribe. It is to be added, that with the exception of the twenty men with Underhill, no other soldiers had gone to the seat of action from Boston. Their tardiness, the authorities explained, was because it was learned "that some of the officers, as well as some of the private soldiers, were still under a covenant of works; and that the blessing of God could not be implored, or expected to crown the arms of such unhallowed men with success." This excuse was evidently prompted by much personal feeling so that the blame could easily be shifted. "The alarm was general and many arrangements necessary in order to cast out the unclean and render this little band sufficiently pure to fight the battle of a people who entertained high ideas of their own sanctity."

The accounts of the war written either at the time or by those who participated in it, give full credit to the men who fought and won the battle. The first to be printed, was by Philip Vincent, who, though he did not take part in the war, was evidently in that vicinity at the time. His account was published in London in 1638, and Captain Underhill's appeared the following year, while Mason's and Gardiner's were not written until some years later.

The Massachusetts' contingent of the new army numbered over a hundred men with Captain Israel Stoughton in command, and Captains Trask and Patrick in his company, with Rev. John Wilson as chaplain. They sailed to the Pequot River, where they were joined by an army of Narragansetts. The army marched at once into the Pequot country, and soon came upon a body of the enemy which they were able to hem in on a point of land running into the river. They killed several, and made a large number of prisoners. Of these last, about thirty were warriors whom they placed on a vessel under Captain Gallup, sailed out to the Sound some distance, and dispatched them. Winthrop's account mentions the slaying of the captives in this manner, but adds that twenty-two were "put to death" and that the remaining prisoners were divided between the Narragansetts and Massachusetts Indians, while the remainder were sent to Boston. This account also states that a Pequot warrior who was captured on the water was given to "Mr. Cutting to carry into England." This expedition was commanded by Stoughton, who later sat as one of the judges at the Salem witchcraft trials. The captives were kept as slaves. They often ran away, but when caught and returned to their masters by friendly Indians, were branded on the shoulder. A number of Pequot squaws that had escaped from slavery in Boston were taken and sent back to their owners by Miantonimo the Narragansett chief. Among other troubles the whites had with their Indian slaves was the fear the Indians had of Hobbanock, the name they gave to one of their devils, who, they claimed, kept counciling them to have nothing to do with the English, nor learn their ways, but to leave them.

Mason arrived with his company of forty men on June 26, with Mr. Ludlow as adviser. After some consultation among the officers, when it was learned that the principal body of Pequots were fleeing along the coast towards the Dutch settlements, it was decided to pursue them both by water and also along the coast on foot. They knew that the Indians were handicapped by their old men and women, and probably by others who had been wounded in the several attacks. They also were aware that the Indians' supply of food must have been small, as they had but little time to prepare for their flight. The English probably suspected that the fugitives would be obliged to subsist mostly on clams they could dig up on the beach, and berries they could pick along the way, or game they could shoot.

Uncas, with some of his Mohegans, had gone in advance, and meeting three Pequots, one of whom was a sachem, beheaded them, placed the skull of the chief in the crotch of a tree where it remained for many years, giving the place the name of Sachem's Head, now a part of Guildford. On July 13, the English were successful in taking a straggling Pequot prisoner. He was promised his life if he would betray the location of his people. He turned traitor, and led the army to the site of the Pequot's encampment, which was located near the present town of Southport. At the sight of the army, the Indians ran to the top of the hill, pursued by the English, and once there, the soldiers discovered some wigwams, and beyond a swamp, into which the Indians disappeared. Within a few minutes, Sergeants Palmer and Jeffries together with Ensign Davenport, reached the wigwams, where they were set upon by Pequots, some of whom were wounded and a few slain. The English did not escape unhurt.

The swamp was surrounded, so that the enemy was completely hemmed in. They did make futile attempts at shooting the whites, but only a few of the soldiers were wounded. The question of procedure was puzzling to the whites. Patrick suggested that they should "cut down the swamp," as in their flight, the Indians had left their hatchets. Trask approved of this method, while others thought it best to fill up the passages with timber and brush, making it more difficult for the enemy to escape. Many other suggestions were made, all of which, Mason said, "were very grievous to some of us," and concluded that the Indians would make an escape in the Night. It was only three in the afternoon, so that the army had time to work out Mason's idea, which was to cut through the narrow part of the swamp. The work was carried out by Sergeant Davis. One wonders, however, how he escaped the Indian arrows when performing this heroic deed.

In the meanwhile Patrick could not give up the idea that it would be to the advantage of the English, if they would make a sudden attack as the Indians were still in a panic. Suiting his actions to his words, he, with three others, were rash enough to attempt to enter the swamp where they were immediately challenged by the Indians. He succeeded in killing one of the Pequots with his pike, when a sudden cry of "Lieutenant, they kill me," from one of his soldiers, caused him to hurry to his aid, as the man was being set on by "four stout Rogues," and he adds, "the Lord helped me soon to make three of them repent." The fourth Indian was more difficult to overcome, so that at first Patrick could not use his pike, for fear of wounding the soldier, but at last the "Lord gave him his wound in his belly, and so lost his prey."

Thomas Stanton, the Indian interpreter, offered to go to the Pequots and see if a treaty could not be arranged, as the English wished to avoid killing the women and children when an attack was made. The officers protested against Stanton's undertaking such a risky mission. He proved his valor by going into the camp and succeeded so well in his work, that he returned with nearly two hundred Pequots, mostly elderly men, women and children.

The Site of the Great Swamp Fight

The warriors decided to remain and take their chances of escape, as they said they would rather die than be captured.

Early in the night a band of Pequots attempted to force their way out at the section that was guarded by Patrick, who was immediately reinforced by Trask's company, but the Indians were beaten back by the small shot of the English. They were driven back several times, but later, when a heavy fog settled over the land, together with the darkness of the night, it was possible for about seventy of them to escape. A search of the swamp was made the next morning, when it was found that only a few of the enemy had been slain.

The fugitives, led by Sassacus and Monotto, made their way to the Hudson River to join the Mohawks, only to be slain by them. The scalps of the two chiefs were sent to Connecticut, and later parts of them, with scalps of five other sachems, were carried to Boston by the Rev. John Wilson, who had served as chaplain to the expedition, and who had been recalled to help settle the Antinomian quarrel. The settlers encouraged the Narragansetts and Mohegans to destroy lurking Pequots, and from time to time, they brought in their heads and scalps to the authorities, sometimes one or two a day.

Among the captives were the wife and child of Monotto. She was remarked as being very modest, and possessed of unusual good sense. It was due to her care of the captured girls at the massacre of Wethersfield, that they were not harmed. This noble act was remembered by Governor Winthrop, who took special care for their protection, and granted the woman's request that neither she nor her offspring should be dishonored. In all, the army had one hundred and eighty captives. It was decided to divide them among the different colonists to be used as domestic slaves.

A letter written at this time to John Winthrop by Captain Stoughton is quite enlightening in more ways than one. He went on to describe the personal advantages of a certain squaw that he would like to own. How fair she was, in fact the fairest; how large she was; better evidently in every way than the other squaws. He had given her a coat, as presumably she possessed no clothing. So, if it met with the approval of the Governor, he would like her for a servant. Then there was another member of his company who desired a little squaw, to whom the man in question had given a coat, if this met with the "liking" of his excellency. Then Lieutenant Davenport had picked out a tall squaw, who had three stripes on her stomach— "three III," which the lieutenant evidently admired. And there were still others who had made their choice, as for instance, the letter the Rev. Mr. Peter addressed to the governor, in which he said, that—"Mr. Endicott and myself salute you in the Lord Jesus. Wee have heard of a dividence of women and children in the bay, and would bee glad of a share viz. a young woman or girle and a boy if you think good. I wrote to you for some boys for Bermudas, which I think is considerable." So it seems that even the preachers took advantage of these unfortunate victims who had surrendered rather than be shot in the battle that they believed would follow their retreat in the swamp.

Roger Williams as usual used every persuasion to induce the authorities to be merciful in their dealings with the prisoners. He pleaded in vain, though in his arguments he said "since the Most High delights in mercy, and great revenge hath beene allready taken why could it not be that these unfortunates could be given to the friendly Indians."

The Indians made poor servants and slaves, as Mason said, they could not endure the yoke. They never were a menial race, but on the contrary a proud, arrogant and bold one. Many of the prisoners at different times were sold and taken to the West Indies or Bermudas. Such a fate befell a grandchild of Massasoit, the sachem who had given warning of the intended massacre to the Plymouth colony during the first years of the settlement. A like fate also befell King Philip's wife at the end of the war named for that chief. In 1703 it became legal to sell males over ten as well as females, whether Negro or Indian. The captives sent abroad were doomed to a life of servitude and hardships, while those in New England always had hope. There was always the possibility of escape in which they were often successful, even though branded. Later, when newspapers were printed, runaway Indians as well as Negro slaves were advertised with a reward for their return. In speaking of Indian servants, one writer said that it was anything but pleasant to have an Indian woman in the kitchen to do the work, who could not understand a word that was spoken to her, who rebelled at her enforced slavery, and might scalp the whole family at any time during the absence of the master.

The servant question was one of the most trying for the mothers of the families from the earliest years of the settlements. Many of the wealthy emigrants brought their retainers with them from England. Others were obtained by paying the passage of some ambitious, but poor emigrant who would sell his services for a contracted number of years. This arrangement often proved more than unsatisfactory. Once here, the indentured servant would sometimes become so obnoxious in his treatment of the family to which he was bound, that his services were no longer endured, much less his presence in the household, while many ran away to some other colony, disguised and under assumed names.

The birth of a child under these conditions was a much-desired blessing. Every child, if he lived, meant an additional worker, and without pay. Josselyn wrote that it was the land for children, as they could more than pay for their keep, as well as earning money for their parents. He said nothing as to the grim, sad life of the child. It easily explains why the offspring of the families often totaled eighteen or twenty and sometimes more. With all this number, there seemed no difficulty in finding original names to give them, as for example, the names of the children of Roger Clap were Experience, Waitstill, Preserved, Hopestill, Wait, Thanks, Desire, Unite, Supply. Other parents hit on such euphonious sounds as Sharach, Jephtab, Abmadab, Aquilla and Zorobabel. Lieutenant Davenport named a daughter Truecross, while a tradition states that a member of a family by the surname of Fish, had three successive generations with a child named Preserved. However, the prize in this respect should go to a family named Perkins who probably did not dream when they named their son, that he would one day be a physi-

cian, or they would not have dubbed him Bilious. All of
the foregoing seems to prove that the English in their new
homes were not as limited in their choice of names as
those on the other side of the water. For instance there
might be three Johns in the family, as John the Elder,
John the Middle and John the Younger.

The birth of a child came as often as nature permitted.
One woman had fourteen children during nineteen years.
Samuel Bass at his death had one hundred and sixty-two
descendants, while William Rawson had twenty-one children by a single wife. These verses by a local writer gives
the following regarding Mrs. Sarah Thyer and her children—

> *"Also she was a fruitful vine,*
> *The truth I may relate—*
> *Fourteen was of her body born,*
> *And lived to man's estate.*

> *"From these did spring a numberous race,*
> *One hundred thirty-two;*
> *Sixty and six each sex alike,*
> *As I declare to you.*

> *"And one thing more remarkable,*
> *Which here I shall record;*
> *Some fourteen children with her,*
> *At the table of her Lord."*

Some families were not so fortunate as to have a large
number of children and help became so scarce that chil-

dren of the best families went out to service. In such cases they were regarded as members of the family and were treated as such. This dearth of servants led to keeping negro slaves who proved to be much better servants than the Indians. The first record of a negro slave in the New England colonies is as early as 1630, where one was owned by Mr. Maverick of Noddles Island. He had the idea, which later proved successful in some of the southern states, to raise slaves, but his venture proved a failure. At first negroes were brought from other colonies, but after a while the New Englanders went extensively into the slave trade. Many families of today could trace the foundations of their wealth to the African slave trade carried on by their New England forefathers. Slaves were bought and sold in the public market and inventoried as property. This condition existed until near the end of the eighteenth century, when in 1787 it was prohibited by law. One of the strongest early Abolitionists was Mrs. Adams, wife of the President of the United States. It can be said in defense of the colonists of New England, that they did not hold their slaves in "hard bondage" as in some of the southern states, but were used mostly as domestic servants. It was not an uncommon thing for slaves in those states to be given their freedom, and often, in addition a lot and house in which to live, as in the Perkins family of Norwich.

To return to the year 1637, again there was rejoicing in the Connecticut valley, as the soldiers returned to their homes. They regarded their victory over the Indians as the guidance and blessing of the Lord, over a God-fearing people, and accordingly praised Him for His goodness.

Mason in an addition to his history, "by way of coment," in mentioning some "special Providence that God was pleased to vouchsafe" tells how two of his soldiers were shot in the neck, but saved by their knotted handkerchiefs. How Lieutenant Bull was saved by holding up as his only armour, a hard piece of cheese, which saved him from being pierced by an arrow. Regarding this incident, Mason said, "A little armour would serve if a Man knew where to place it."

Soon after the swamp fight, the government of Connecticut made Mason the Major-General of the Connecticut forces, a commission he retained until shortly before his death. The General Court desired the Rev. Mr. Hooker of Hartford to deliver the staff to Mason, which probably Hooker [1] gave, not only with a formal address, but also with a sermon and prayer, as he presented him with the "Principal Ensign of material Power, to Lead the Armies and Fight the Battles of the Lord and his People."

The Major's duties as well as being chief commander of the militia, was to train the military men in each plantation in Connecticut, ten days in each year, for which he was to receive a salary of £40 annually, to be paid out of the treasury quarterly. All males of sixteen and over, with the exception of the Commissioners and church officials, were to report for drill, and fined when absent. This practically made every male in the colony a soldier.

Mason's military achievements, and the recognition of the same by the Connecticut colony, was most gratifying to

the Major, who was still a young man of thirty-seven.   In
the midst of this success in this eventful year, he had a
great bereavement.   His wife sickened and died, leaving
him with a young daughter.

CHAPTER VIII

THE inhabitants of the Connecticut colony had incurred a large public debt by the Pequot war. The following winter was unusually severe. Articles of food and clothing were difficult to procure at any price, and the planters were generally poorly supplied. The price of corn had risen to the extraordinary amount of twelve shillings a bushel, and was scarce at that price. They were obliged to use seed corn to feed the chickens, and give malt to the swine. The colonists were suffering from their first depression, as Connecticut was bankrupt. Their farm utensils were so poor that it was with difficulty that they could till the hard soil of the meadows. It was estimated at that time that there were only thirty ploughs in all New England. Hoes were the principal farm implements to cultivate the ground, which could make but little impression on the heavy growth of grass roots imbedded deep in the soil. A little idea can be had of the high cost of living when a cow or a horse cost thirty pounds. With all of these economic troubles a tax was imposed in all the settlements to pay for ammunition and fire arms that had been used in the war.

The conditions had reached such a state that the Court convened at Hartford in February, 1638, to see what could be done to alleviate the suffering, and William Pynchon, the colony's agent for purchasing supplies from the Indians, was consulted as to the outlook.

Pynchon was among the first settlers of Agawam, now Springfield, and being a great traveler, was acquainted with the friendly Indians in that vicinity. It was thought, therefore, that he was better able to purchase corn from them at a moderate price. He was known far and wide in the forests, through which he traveled on horseback, always accompanied by a mounted servant. Pynchon's handling of the corn question, however, was criticized. He was even accused, finally, of acquiring a monopoly of the trade, and of selling at an advanced price to the different towns along the Connecticut River. How much truth there was in these accusations is not known, for two separate courts gave conflicting decisions, but knowing the prominence and standing that he had previously, and subsequently, it is difficult to believe that he would enrich himself at such a time, at the expense of his fellow townsmen. He possessed the rights of the valuable fur trade in that section, from which he and Cornet Joseph Parsons became men of wealth. It must be remembered that the colonists had suffered in many ways from the war; that they were hungry, and rebelled at the prices paid for food. At such a time and under such conditions it required only a word or a suggestion to start a rumor of false dealings, and create accusations of dishonesty.

The rumors grew and became so serious that matters were brought to a head at the March Court. Pynchon had not been successful in acquiring the corn that he was supposed to have purchased from the upper river Indians, but the colonists believed that he held it for a higher price. At this juncture, Major Mason was brought into the controversy.

The policies of Pynchon and Mason were conflicting. Mason had been bred to arms from young manhood, while Pynchon was a student and a lawyer. Pynchon was thought to be vacillating in his treatment of the Indians, while Mason, who proved his honesty with the natives by his long and close friendship with the Mohegans, was stern in his dealings. He held them strictly to their promises, which he in turn kept with them, and the natives respected and feared him. It is probable that neither of the two men held very high opinions of the aborigines.

The conditions had become acute by the time of the March Court. Pynchon's promise of corn that should have been delivered some weeks previous, was still waited for with impatience. The Court then took the commission from Pynchon and gave it into the hands of Mason and Ludlow. This decision met with the approval not only of the Reverends Hooker and Stone, but with the people. This order was dated March, 1638.

On the twenty-first of that month, Mason, with a few armed troopers, and a Nonotuck Indian guide, called on Pynchon at his home in Springfield. Upon entering the house, Mason began the interview by saying—"I am come to trade some corne with the Indians, and I have traded some at Woronoco, (Westfield), and I had purposed to have you to Nonotack, (Northampton), but I mett with one of Nonotack, here at Agawam, and I would have traded some corn with him yester night, but he saith he dared not without ye leave, for saith he, he is afraid of you, as alsoe are the Indians on the Riverside, for say they, you required six peeces of cloth of them, whereas they were but two whole pieces stolen, and thirteen coates, but

I told him that I thought you were not angry, and that you neyther could, nor would have hurt to them. But I pray tell this Indian of Nonotack that you will not be angry with him, if he trade corne downe the river."

Pynchon replied that he knew of no reason why the Nonotuck Indian should fear him, and then proposed that the conference should be carried on privately, as it was dangerous to have the Indians know to what extremes the English were in lack of food.

"I care not who knows them," Mason answered.

Pynchon insisted that they should retire to the trading house where they could converse without being overheard. The party consisted of Mason and his associate, Thomas Dewey, while Pynchon had with him his trader, Richard Everett.

"Sir," Mason continued as they seated themselves in the trading house, "I have brought some cloth and wampam, to trade some corne with the Indians, & I desire you to deal with them for us, & to Binde them to a bargaine to bring it down."

Pynchon's answer was to the effect, that it was useless to bind the Indians to a bargain or pay them in advance, as they never kept their promises, and continuing, said, "Where upon some anger might follow, and then, if I had a hand in it, they may beare me a grudge; for I feare their treacherous dealing, we being remote & but weaker; therefore, I will neither *make nor meddle* to binde you to a bargaine, But I will do this. I will propound a rate of 8 sixes to carry downe their corne, and 6 sixes to bring it to my house, and propound a free trade, and give them choice, or before I have declared."

When Pynchon had finished, it is reported that Mason exclaimed angrily, "What hurt can it be to you? I pray, Sir, let me know what hurt it can be to you, for it is a dark riddle to me."

Finally Parson Moxon and Henry Smith were called to act as council, and arrived, as Mason finished speaking. Pynchon explained what had been said, and stated how Mason had paid some Indians in advance.

"An Indian promise," Moxon said, "is noe more than to have a pigg by the taile."

To which Smith agreed, and they went on to say, how the Indians haggled for better prices, claiming there was a shortage of corn, as much had been ruined by the snow, and that the water in the river was too high to bring it down. Also that the Indians would avoid coming to the settlements when they were in debt to the whites.

The matter seemed to be adjusted amicably, but it was evident that the feeling between the two principals was not very kindly, and this was emphasized by Mason's abrupt departure.

Three days later the General Court issued an order for Mr. Pynchon's presence at the next session, where he was brought to trial. He was found guilty of "deliberately" raising the price of corn, and that he refused to lend a canoe to an Indian under command of Mason, to deliver corn; that he kept the Indians in great fear of him, so that "he might be considered the great English sachem of the Connecticut Valley"; and finally, that he had "induced certain Mohawk runners to sell him some beaver skins which were sent by Mohawk chiefs to the Connecticut authorities as presents, and assurance of good will."

Mason and the Indian from Agawam were the witnesses for the Court, and Parson Moxon and Henry Smith to testify in his defense. The Court called Rev. Thomas Hooker and Rev. Samuel Stone for a decision which found Pynchon guilty. Pynchon and his witnesses contradicted Mason "point blank," and at the end of the trial he exclaimed, "Now, if these things may not Justly Question the purport of the Captain's oath, I leave to the Judgement of wise men."

During the trial, Pynchon said that he had sacrificed and deprived his own family in order to help his townsmen. He was tried the second time on the same charges, which were brought by members of the Windsor church, the object being, it was said, "to withdraw from him the right of Christian fellowship." He was again found guilty, but later he appealed his case, and was acquitted by the Roxbury church, and the Massachusetts' General Court, while the Connecticut General Court and the Windsor church held him guilty. He was, however, permitted to continue to keep his rights to the beaver trade. The planters realized that it was imperative to have peace, and keep up pleasant trading relations with the natives on whom they were so dependent at this time for corn. The Court gave orders that no cause of offense should be given to the Indians, and laws were enforced to prevent the settlers from insulting or abusing them.

During this year Mason was elected a member of the General Court, an honor that was to lead to higher ones later. The liberal constitution that had been enacted, owed much of its merit to the Rev. Hooker's influence, and as Trumbull said, "is one of the most free and happy constitutions of civil government which has ever been formed." There were two general Courts or Assemblies held respectively in April and September each year. The officials were elected by ballot at the spring session, including six magistrates, one of whom was chosen governor, providing, of course, that he was a church member. The law provided that no one could be a magistrate unless a freeman. The requirements to become a freeman in Connecticut were much more liberal than in many of the other colonies. If the candidate had been received as a member of the other towns in which he had lived, and would take the oath of allegiance to the Commonwealth, he was duly elected. Connecticut was always loyal in word and deed to the sovereignty of the King, previous to the Revolution, though the word "King" did not occur in the colonial constitution. However, any one forgetful of his allegiance was punished. A case in point was that of Captain Scott in 1664 at Southold, L. I., who was arrested on such a charge. At the trial at Hartford, he was condemned to pay £25 "for words tending to defamation of the King's Majesty."

Thomas Hooker's liberal and advanced ideas had a great influence in shaping the constitution of the Connecticut colony. He preached the sermon at the opening session of the General Court, May 31, 1638, in which he said "the foundation of authority is laid in the free consent of the people . . . that the choice of public magistrates belongs unto the people by God's own allowance . . . they who have the power to appoint officers and magistrates have the right also to set the bounds and limitations of the power and place unto which they call them." The constitution adopted the fourteenth of January following, is unlike the constitutions of the other colonies in many respects, and in particular that suffrage was not dependent upon church-membership.

John Fiske states that it is "the first written constitution known to history that created a government, and it marked the beginnings of American democracy, of which Thomas Hooker deserves more than any other man to be called the father." The towns of the colony were independent, forming a federation, yet recognized the sovereignty of the General Court.

The great difference between the laws governing Connecticut and Massachusetts is illustrated by the opinion of Revs. Cotton and Hooker. The former declared that democracy was not a fit government either for the church or the commonwealth, to which it is said most of the clergy agreed, and which especially met with the approval of Winthrop, who wrote in a letter to Hooker regarding the restriction of the suffrage that "the best part is always the least, and that of the best part the wiser part is always the lesser." To which Hooker replied that "in matters which concern the common good, a general council, chosen by all, to transact businesses which concern all, I conceive most suitable to rule and most safe for relief of the whole."

The sessions of the Court began at seven o'clock in the morning, or one hour after sunrise. The distance for many of the members was long and had to be traveled either by horseback, or on foot, consequently it is not surprising that it was not exceptional for members to be fined for being late. Such an incident befell Mason, April 5, 1638, when serving his first term. One wonders whether he had fallen a victim to a law that he himself helped to make, as did the two carpenters who built the first stocks in their respective towns, and were the first to occupy them. This was described by a chronicler of the times, "that one often had the honor to sit an hour in them himself, to warn others not to offend honor in like manner."

The stocks in early colonial days, were generally, if not always, placed in front of the meeting house, which was, at that time, on the main square of the town. The instruments of punishment were also placed there, such as the whipping post and the pillory. The meeting house was the center of the settlement. It was the only place where one could be sure of meeting one's friends, as the laws made it compulsory for every one to attend meeting, also the Thursday lectures, and other special religious services.

To be punished in front of the house of worship, was to be seen by all the inhabitants of the town, and it had, it was believed by the magistrates and church officials, a good moral effect. Sitting in the stocks, was, perhaps, one of the lesser punishments, except when it meant at the expiration of the stipulated time that the culprit was to be whipped. Whipping was a frequent form of punishment, and carried to a brutal degree. Another milder form was to be obliged to stand on a small platform four feet high, with a large printed sign, telling the offense the culprit had committed. For instance, if it were for speaking in a disrespectful manner of the preacher or religion, the card bore in large letters "A Wanton Gospeller." In looking through the colonial records it is difficult for us of a later generation to understand the strict, and often unreasonable laws. Cursing, for instance, was a heinous crime in these religious communities. One man for saying "curse ye woodchuck" was heavily fined. Another man was put in the billoes, for saying "dam ye cow." One can easily see that such blue laws led to spying and "getting even" with one's enemies.

Immorality was severely punished. In one case the offender was whipped at the cart's end in his own town, and forced to stand in the pillory during the Thursday lecture. He was then whipped again, and after eight days, was taken to a neighboring town, where the lash was again applied. Often in such cases, the offender was branded on the cheek or forehead. No distinction was made of sex. Both were subject to the same punishment. There was a case in the New London courts some years later, where the "Widow Bradley presented for a second offense, in having a child born out of wedlock, (was) sentenced to pay the usual fine of £5, and also to wear on her cap a paper whereon her offense is written." She had the alternative of that punishment or of paying a fine of £15. Fortunately some one went her bond. One woman was whipped, and then whipped again after a month. A man named Robert Bartlett, "for his gross misdemeanor in slandering a Mrs. Mary Fennicke" had to stand on the pillory during a lecture of five hours and imprisoned for half a year. The penalty for adultery was death.

The strict laws of the Sabbath were broken in a most unholy way by Captain Kemble of Boston when, on his return from a three years' voyage, he was seen greeting his wife with a kiss on the steps of his home. For this "lewed and unseemly behavior" he was condemned to sit two hours in the stocks.

Another equally absurd "crime" occurred in 1670 when John Lewis and Sarah Chapman were tried for "sitting together on the Lord's Day under an apple tree in Goodman Chapman's Orchard." Elizabeth Eddy was fined for wringing out clothes on Sunday. Aquila Chase and his wife were fined for gathering peas on the seventh day. A soldier was fined forty shillings "for wetting a piece of an old hat to put in his shoe." Driving a horse fast, running, making undue noises, visiting friends, or in any way enjoying oneself in a modest way was subject to fine or imprisonment, while in New Haven, "Profanation of the Lord's Day" was not only punished by a fine, but in case of "proudly, and with high hand against the authority of God—with death." Probably one of the worst punishments was to be excommunicated, which was as severe as in the Catholic Church in mediæval times. It meant to be completed ostracized. This verdict was always passed on the followers of Foxians, Hutchinsonians, Gortians, Anabaptists, Baptists, members of the Church of England, Quakers, and all others not of the orthodox church of the colonists.

It is amusing to note that even the preachers fell foul of these laws at a little later period. One of them was severely censured for having amassed a fortune of some eight hundred dollars, another for playing bowls, and still another for wearing stockings, "footed with another color," and he was also accused of having jumped over a fence which his parishioners called hardly a dignified proceeding for a leader of their flock. This latter accusation was proof that the preachers were losing their unlimited hold on the government.

The meeting house also served for the pleasanter things. It was the place to post all notices, and in this way, served as a newspaper, and no doubt but what many a scandal was hatched there. Every community must have something to gossip about, and there was little to thrill the weary, working hours of the settlements at that time. Marriage announcements, that the law required to be given in advance, were generally posted on the meeting house door. Often they were in rhyme, as the one of the well-known Captain Renold Marvin of Old Lyme, which read—

> "Renold Marvin and Phoebe Lee
> Do intend to marry.
> Though opposed her dad may be,
> They can no longer tarry."

One of the strangest customs of the times, and one most difficult to reconcile with the reverence the settlers had for their place of worship, was to nail wolves' heads on or at the side of the meeting house door. They were often put there while the blood dripped, so that the doorway was splashed. It was not an uncommon thing to see signs placed on the door of the meeting house of offers of fifteen shillings for any one who brought a live wolf to the house of worship, and ten shillings if dead. Another sign told that if the wolf killer wished the reward, he was to bring the wolf's head and "nail it to the meeting house and give notice thereof." One successful hunter was able to bring in seven heads of wolves at one time, which must have given the place more the appearance of a butcher shop than a house of worship.

The meeting house also served as a granary in the upper portions. William Pynchon was only allowed to store four hundred bushels in the roof chamber of the meeting house in Springfield, unless he reinforced the floors. Ammunition for the use of the settlements was also stored in the churches, and it was known that during services in electric storms, the worshipers, fearing the edifice might be struck by lightning and explode the powder, thought more of saving their bodies, than their souls. They rushed out of the building in a body, and the sudden exodus must have given the appearance of a hurried military retreat, since the law required all men to go armed to the services. There is also a record of another cause for a quick exit from the Sunday worship, when a small black and white fur-bearing animal, noted for its fragrance, was chased into the meeting house by dogs.

The meeting house was used often as a storage place for drying the freshly cut leaf of tobacco, which was to be sold to the "ungodly Dutch." This is another inconsistency of our Puritan ancestors in using the house of worship as a storage place for the "filthy weed," when the laws regarding the use of tobacco were so strict, and rigidly enforced. The English colonies allowed no person under twenty, nor any other "not accustomed himself to tobacco, was allowed to use it without having bought a certificate." It was not even permitted to be used in public in the form of snuff, nor in the fields, nor in the woods. One could use it in one's own house, and in company with one other, only "who useth and drinketh the same week with him at the time," though never at dinner hour.

To return to the relations existing between the whites

and the red men. On September 21, 1638, the General Court assembled at Hartford, to which Uncas and Miantonimo were summoned. A treaty was made by which it was agreed that the Pequots then under the control of the English, should be divided between the friendly tribes. Mason says that eighty were placed with Uncas, sachem of the Mohegans, the same number with Miantonimo, sachem of the Narragansetts, and twenty with Ninigret, which was to pay for a mare owned by Edward Pomroy, that was killed. A little later about twoscore went to Long Island.

The treaty stipulated that there should be a perpetual peace between the two tribes, and that the Pequots allotted to them were henceforth to be a part and known as members of the tribe by which they were adopted. All questions of law or disputes were to be submitted to the English for settlement. All murderers of the English should be delivered to the Court. It was especially stated and agreed, that no Pequot, or any other tribe of Indians should again live in the Pequot country. The Pequots agreed to pay an annual tribute to the Connecticut colony; "a fathom of wampum for every warrior, half that amount for a youth, and a handful for a papoose."

While all the parties seemed satisfied at the time the treaty was signed, it was not long before it was learned that some Pequots had ignored their promises and were once more living on their former land. The Court sent Mason with a band of forty men to go in pursuit of them and force them to return to the tribes to which they had been assigned. Uncas with a body of his warriors accompanied the English. Mason encountered three Pequots to

whom he gave a message to be taken to their tribe which
would acquaint them with the mission of the whites. He
told them they were to live up to their agreement and
to leave the country peaceably, or they would be driven
out. Promises were made by the Indians to deliver the
message to their chief, but that was the last seen of them.
Mason waited some time for the Indians to return, and
then gave orders for his men to sail up the river. They
appeared so suddenly and unexpectedly at the Pequot
camp that the savages were taken by surprise and beat a
hasty retreat. This gave Uncas and his men time to
plunder the wigwams, when a skirmish took place between
the two tribes. Seven prisoners were taken, and acted,
it is recorded, in such "an outrageous manner," that it
was decided to decapitate them, but one of Miantonimo's
brothers pleaded for their lives, which was granted on the
pledge of the Indians to surrender to the whites some
criminal Pequots—a promise the red men never kept.
The following morning on awakening, Mason and his men
were surprised to see a large body of the enemy on the
opposite shore of the river ready for attack. On seeing
the English preparing to fight, many of the Pequots fled,
or hid behind trees. Mason called to them to hear the
orders of the Court which he gave them, whereat the red
men assured the Major that they were the friends of the
whites, and would even fight for them. Mason told them
if they wished to fight to go up to the end of the stream
where there was a better opportunity for a battle. Their
reply was to the effect that they would not fight with white
men, as they were spirits, but with Uncas. The result of
the expedition was more bloodshed and some captives, but

this ended the war with the Pequots and gave peace from actual warfare to the colony for some years to come.

The historian Bancroft wrote regarding the result of the war—"The vigor and courage displayed by the settlers on the Connecticut in the first Indian war in New England, struck terror into the savages and secured a long period of peace."

Rev. Samuel Niles in his "History of the Wars in New England" when writing of the Pequot war, pays this tribute to Major Mason—"I aim at the victorious captain John Mason, of whose heroic conquests we have just been speaking. Though he was bred to arms, as before remarked, yet he did not equip himself with arms and weapons of war till it was absolutely necessary, and in defense of a small people, then in their beginnings, who otherwise, according to all rational probability, must quickly have been entirely cut off."

Even Roger Williams, whose love for the Narragansetts made him biased at times against Mason on account of the latter's friendship for the Mohegans, wrote as hereinbefore quoted—"When the Lord drew the bow of the Pequot war against the country . . . the Lord made yourself and others a blessed instrument of peace to all New England."

Benjamin Trumbull in his "History of Connecticut" gives the following testimonial to the conqueror of the Pequots—"He was tall and portly, full of material fire, and shunned no hardships or dangers in the defense and service of the colony. He was a gentleman not only of distinguished heroism, but of strict morals and great prudence."

Connecticut was much too poor to have an elaborate celebration over her victories, but Massachusetts appointed the 12th of that October for a day of Thanksgiving, as they had the preceding June after the Mystic fight. All the soldiers of that colony who had taken part in the war, were treated to a feast by the town and church officials. While showing so much appreciation to their own soldiers, the Bay colony did not recompense Mason "for his good services against the Pequots and otherwise," until 1639.

The outlying settlements could at least live in comparative peace, though they were not entirely without fear in spite of the seemingly friendly attitude of both the Mohegans and Narragansetts. It was thought that they could never be trusted to keep the peace. With these new conditions, the immigrants began to pour into this section of New England, which offered so much more in fertile soil than the bleak coast farther east.

New Haven was founded this year under the leadership of John Davenport, noted as a very prominent Nonconformist, and who had previously occupied an official position in the East India Company. The Massachusetts colony endeavored to persuade this band of emigrants to remain in the Bay colony, but they wished to have an independent settlement, and one in which the laws were founded on those of the Scriptures. New Haven remained an independent colony until years later.

During this year New England experienced an earthquake, which was looked upon as a sign and a criticism from the Lord, and foretold no good for the careless or unfaithful in not following strictly the teachings of the Scriptures.

CHAPTER IX

MAJOR MASON'S duties as Commander-in-Chief of the military forces of Connecticut, necessitated his visiting the several settlements. He evidently traveled much during this period, and on occasions visited Boston, and the neighboring towns. On one of these trips, when at Hingham, he became acquainted with Anne Peck, and perhaps fell in love at first sight, at any rate they were soon engaged. Josselyn tells us that in 1663, courting was permitted in public, that "On the South there is a small, but pleasant Common where the Gallants a little before sunset, walk with their Marmalet, madames, till the nine o'clock bell sings home to their respective habitations."

The consent of Anne's parents, which the law required, was evidently not difficult to obtain, as Major Mason was still a comparatively young man, fine looking, and one of the most prominent, and promising in the community. He must have been considered most desirable as a son-in-law.

The law requiring the consent of the girl's parents was very strict. For any young lover, who was so rash as to persuade his sweetheart to marry without the permission of her parents, was liable to be fined, imprisoned, or whipped, if he "inveigled the affections of any maid or maid servant." There is a record of a later date in the Court at New London, of one John Prentice against William Beebe, the latter being fined £5 for keeping company with Mercy Prentice and "endeavoring to gain her affections in order to a marriage without acquainting her parents, which is contrary to law." A breach of promise could be brought by either sex. An announcement of an intended marriage had to be publicly made three times within eight days before the ceremony could be legalized. A young woman not married before her twenty-fourth year was considered "ancient." It is not likely that there were many spinsters in any of the colonies, when we realize how soon widows remarried. There are records of some women having married many times, and one where the wedding took place twelve days after the death of her former husband.

Anne was the daughter of Rev. Robert and Anne Peck, and was born in Hingham, England, in 1619. She was baptized there in the Church of St. Andrews, and came to New England with her parents in 1638. The town clerk of Hingham of the Bay colony records their arrival as follows—"Mr. Robert Peck, preacher of the gospel in the town of Hingham, County Norfolk old England, with his wife and two children, and two servants, came over the sea and settled in this town of Hingham, and he was a teacher of the church." Robert Peck had fled from the persecutions of Bishop Laud, but at the beginning of the Long Parliament, his old parishioners in England persuaded him to return and once more become rector of St. Andrews. He with his wife and son Joseph sailed for their old home in October, 1641. He was of an old family dating back some twenty generations and his arms bore several quarterings. The Peck arms without quarterings, Anne Mason's seal, was often used by Major Mason in sealing his official papers. Two impressions of this seal are still extant in the files of the Connecticut state archives.

Robert Peck died in 1651, and in his will, which is dated July 23, of that year, he refers to his daughter Anne, as follows—"Item—I give to the children of Anne Mason, my daughter, wife of captain John Mason of Seabrook on the river Connecticut in New England, the sume of Forty pounds to be equally divided unto them and to be sent to my sonne John Mason to dispose of it for their use within two years after my death."

The marriage of John Mason and Anne Peck took place in Hingham in July, 1639. The ceremony was probably performed by one of the magistrates of the town, as ministers of the gospel were forbidden by law to act in that capacity. Anne Peck's family was of the gentry class, and her father the leading minister of Hingham, which created an unusual interest in her betrothal and marriage. That too, when the bridegroom was the victorious John Mason of Pequot war fame and the commander of the military forces of the colony. We have no account of the festivities that followed the ceremony, but we can imagine from what is known of the times that a gaiety rarely indulged in, must have been a break in the lives of the people of this settlement, as probably many who were present would never again see a wedding of such prominent people.

Many strange marriage customs were in order at that time in the colonies. For instance, the bride's garters were often scrambled for, presumably after they were removed in the bridal chamber, and the finder was assured of a good and happy future. "Sack posset" was often drunk in the bridal chamber, after which a psalm was read, and a prayer offered. It is said that in some cases, "the groom was led to the bride's bed, robed in a night gown of Broadcloth." Sometimes it was the custom for the brides-maids and groomsmen to put the wedding couple to bed. Also it was a common practice for the guests to enter the bridal chamber and all drink to their health.

In some communities the bride had the privilege of selecting the text for the Sunday sermon following her wedding, which was considered a great privilege. Another indulgence in some settlements that took place at the same service, was for the newly wedded couple to seat them-selves in a conspicuous place in the gallery when the meeting house could boast of one, and some time during the long sermon, rise, then turn slowly around so that every one present would be able to see all their new finery. This custom evidently came in vogue at a later date, and even in the cold meeting house in the dead of winter, the bride would throw off her coat to show her fine muslin gown to the congregation.

Within a few days after the wedding, the Major and his bride left for their home at Windsor. What a picture for an artist! All of the town folks, clad in their quaint finery, gathered at the Peck family home to wish the bridal couple God-speed. There were no doubt jokes and pleas-antries, perhaps a little broader than we would use to-day, which brought a smile and a blush to the face of the young bride. The leave-taking must have had its sad moments also, for Anne was leaving her family to go on what was then a long, hazardous journey, and a distance so great that only on rare occasions would there be opportunities to visit her old home. These thoughts must have crept into her mind as well as those of her parents, for she was the only daughter and one of the two children of the household. No doubt when the last good-byes were waved and the friends were lost to view, as the two passed into the cover of the forest, there was a feeling of relief. The strain was over, and as they rode along on their horses, close together, one can imagine the handsome young officer guiding his mount close to the one on which his wife was riding, placing his arm about her, drawing her close to him, and kissing away the tears.

On the 10th of October of that year, the Connecticut Court paid Major Mason, Deputy-Governor Ludlow, and four others, the honor of appointing them a committee to furnish the Court a record "of those passages of God's providence, which have been remarkable." This honor was renewed again in 1656, when Mason was appointed on another committee to serve in the same capacity, and it is probably due to this order that he wrote his history of the Pequot war.

The greatest advance the authorities made was in 1643, when they formed The United Colonies of New England, which included Massachusetts, Plymouth, Connecticut and New Haven. Each colony handled its own local affairs, but the Eight Commissioners of The United Colonies had entire charge of the dealings with the Indians and foreign powers. This confederation was no doubt the nucleus of the later union of the thirteen colonies in their struggle for freedom from England.

The first requirement to be a Commissioner was to be

a church member of good standing. If any question arose at their sessions wherein they could not agree, it was referred to the General Courts of the four colonies. All war expenses were to be paid by each colony regulated by the number of soldiers in each. This federation did not meet with approval in the mother-country, and when arguments arose there during Winslow's visit, he told them that "if we in America should forebear to unite for offense and defense against a common enemy till we have leave from England, our throats might be all cut before the messenger would be half seas through."

The colonies were growing in wealth and had better facilities for transportation. Two ships had been built in 1641 averaging 300 tons, one in Salem and the other in Boston. Spices, wines, ginger and other delicacies were brought to the settlements from Madeira and the West Indies. In spite of the growing prosperity, after the depression of the previous year there were many trying questions to be met, and the elders proclaimed a day of fasting, which was rigidly kept. Disturbing news regarding the trouble between the King and Parliament were continually reaching this side of the water, and with these troubles were added those with the Indians. The very trying weather conditions was affecting the crops, since it had rained for weeks so that the outlook for saving the corn seemed hopeless. But "it pleased God, that as soon as the fast was agreed upon, the weather changed, and proved fair after all."

There were other troubles besides the Indian outbreaks that disturbed the peace of the colonies in the early days of the settlements. Probably Anne Hutchinson's plain statements and actions regarding her views of religion caused more fear, at least among the church dignitaries, and certainly more anger, than any of those experienced with the Indians. Anne was looked upon in the same manner that the ancients did in the Old Testament, regarding the woman Jezebel, and this name, among others, they applied to her. The synod that had originally been planned to be held early in 1637, was postponed, owing to the Indian war, to the autumn, and was composed of twenty-five ministers, who gathered in Boston to bring action against this "woman of ready wit and bold spirit." The trial began November 7th, of that year. The judges were Governor Winthrop, John Endicott and Deputy-Governor Dudley, and the accusers were eight of the most prominent preachers, headed by John Wilson of Boston. Anne was forty-six, and though in poor health and about to become a mother, pleaded her own case, as she had no counsel. She had committed the unpardonable sin, at least in the eyes of the parsons of New England, of criticising the preachers and their sermons; of claiming "that the person of the Holy Ghost dwells in a justified person, and that no sanctification can help to evidence to us our justification"; of leaving the church before the sermons began, of holding and proclaiming interpretation of the Scriptures in a way much too liberal to be allowed to pass without condemnation, and her worst offense was her claim to have received divine revelations, a gift only to which the preachers had a right. She added that the ministers only taught forms, and not the spirit of religion.

Rev. John Cotton, probably the best educated and the most brilliant pastor of the New England colonies in his

day, with the possible exception of Rev. Hooker, and who
organized the Congregational Church, proved no longer
to be her friend.   His sermons in England had decided
Anne to come to the new country, and he, who at first
had been her spiritual guide and friend, turned against
her to save himself.   Captain Underhill, whose reputation
was not of the best, had spoken in her defense, and probably did much to prejudice the judges against her, and
for so doing, he lost his commission and citizenship.

After weeks of physical suffering due to the privations
she had to endure in her prison during the long, cold
winter months, and the mental tortures inflicted by her
accusers at the trial where she so capably defended herself,
she was condemned and banished from the colony, and
found a haven in Roger Williams' plantation in Rhode
Island.   She asked for no respite, though a few courageous
ones in the audience timidly suggested it.   Then the Rev.
Wilson arose and with great satisfaction pronounced the
sentence of excommunication.   "Therefore in the name
of the Lord Jesus Christ," he began, "and in the name
of the church, I do not only pronounce you worthy to be
cast out, but I do cast you out; and in the name of Christ
I do deliver you up to Satan, that you may have no more
blaspheme, to seduce and to lie; and I do account you
from this time forth to be a Heathen and a Publican, and
so to be held of all the Brethren and Sisters of this congregation and of others; therefore I command you in the
name of Christ Jesus and of this church as a Leper to
withdraw yourself out of this congregation."

When she passed down the aisle Mary Dyer, who was
said to have given birth to a monster owing to her affilia-

tion with Mistress Hutchinson, rose and walked out with the condemned woman. As Anne passed through the doorway of the church, some one standing by said, "The Lord sanctify this unto you." To whom she replied, "The Lord Judgeth not as man judgeth. Better to be cast out of the church than to deny Christ."

The Rev. Thomas Welde, who called her the "American Jezebel" in speaking of the manner in which she took her excommunication said, "she is not effected with any remorse, but glories in it, and fears not the vengeance of God, which she lies under." The strange irony of fate worked out in this case, when, three generations later, the grandchildren of the accused and accuser married. Nor did they have offspring with "horns, claws and scales," as was said to have been the case with poor Mary Dyer, the friend and follower of Anne Hutchinson, but left a progeny of worthwhile citizens, James Savage, the American historian being among them. Convincing proof to Anne Hutchinson and her followers that her religious interpretations were from the Lord, was when her house at Aquiday was shaken by an earthquake, proving that the Holy Ghost descended upon them as he did upon the apostles.

Today, after a lapse of three centuries, this courageous woman has been justified, and the statue of Anne Hutchinson stands in front of the Massachusetts State House and bears the inscription—"Courageous Exponent of Civil Liberty and Religious Toleration."

Among other statements Winthrop made at the trial was, "We see not that any should have authority to set up any other exercises besides what authority hath already set up," but in his statement of the proceedings at the trial of Coggshall, which he sent to England, he said that if Coggshall "had kept his judgement to himself, so as the public peace had not been troubled or endangered by it, we should have left him to himself, for we do not challenge power over men's consciences, but when seditious speeches and practices discovered such a corrupt conscience, it is our duty to use authority to reform both."

Winthrop's severity in these cases was the result of the pressure brought to bear on him by the clergy, Endicott, and Dudley, who claimed that he had been too lenient in former cases. It was due to such an interpretation of the law in previous cases that he was not reelected governor in May, 1635. Nevertheless in carrying out these intolerant decisions, directed by the clergy and magistrates, Winthrop's conscience troubled him. When he was dying some years later, and the never-compromising Dudley requested him to sign a document for the expulsion of some dissenters of the Puritan religion, he refused, making the pathetic statement "Of that work I have done too much already."

Young Governor Vane was of the same religious convictions as Mrs. Hutchinson, though owing to his official position, he was obliged to be more discreet than many of her professed followers. His disapproval and probable dislike for Winthrop was forcibly shown in the Lord Ley episode. When Vane was invited with others to attend a dinner to be given by the governor to Lord Ley, Vane sent his regrets, as his conscience forbade his acceptance. At the time of Winthrop's dinner, Vane, taking Lord Ley with him, dined with Mr. Maverick at Noddles Island. Winthrop was big enough to record the incident, regard-

less of the chagrin he must have felt. When Lord Ley
sailed for England many of the inhabitants of Boston
accompanied him to the ship, but Winthrop was not
among the number, though he had given orders that Ley
should be "honorably dismissed."

Another religious pestilence broke out and created more
hatred. It was owing to the arrival in the colonies in
July and August, 1656, of some Quakers. They were as
much hated by the Puritans as were the Catholics. Rev.
Wilson cried out from the pulpit—"I will carry fire in one
hand and fagots in the other, to burn all the Quakers in
the world!" The Quakers believed that God spoke
directly with men, and this, to the colonists, savored much
of the teachings of the Hutchinson woman, whom they had
banished. Rev. Higginson said that this "inner light
(was) as a a stinking vapour from hell."

Laws were passed forbidding any shipmaster to bring
Quakers to the colonies, under penalty of a heavy fine,
for the first offense, and whipping and imprisonment for
the second. When fines were imposed, it was a very bur-
densome verdict, as the difference in the value of the
pound made the average sentence of great importance.
The pound at that period would amount to twenty-five or
thirty times more than it was worth later. Fines were
paid mostly in wampum, beaver skins and other means of
barter. So it can be seen that when the law was enacted
in New England to fine all shipmasters who brought
Quakers to the colonies, it was one that most captains
of sea-going vessels respected. Nevertheless Quakers continued to arrive. If they returned after having been ban-

ished, they would be whipped, have their ears cut off, and for repeating this offense for the third time, have their tongues pierced by a hot iron. Later Endicott warned the Quakers to "take heed you break not our ecclesiastic laws for then you are sure to stretch." With such a sentiment, mercy was never shown members of this despised sect. When two of this faith, William Robinson and Marmaduke Stevenson, were hanged on Boston Common, Rev. Wilson cried out to them from the foot of the gallows, "The curse of God or Jesus go with thee!"

When a sentence was passed, it meant that before the execution the condemned was taken to the meeting house in chains to listen to a sermon on his life and crimes. Often, these sermons were printed and used as tracts, and met with as much popularity in the reading, as did the sermon when delivered. The public always turned out on these great days, as well as being present at the executions.

The Quakers in their turn did much to bring this curse upon themselves. They intruded themselves into the colony where they knew they were not wanted. They attended services in the meeting houses, and during the sermon would boo, ridicule and insult the minister and the congregation by calling out—"Thou firebrand! Thou mooncalf! Thou gormandizing priest! Thou bane of reason and beast of the earth!" Judge Sewall recorded in his diary under date of 1677—"A female Quaker, Margaret Brewster, in sermon time came in, in a canvas frock, her hair dishevelled loose like a Periwig, her face as black as ink, led by two other Quakers, and two other Quakers followed. It occasioned the greatest and most annoying uproar that I ever saw. They broke a glass bottle before the minister, shouting 'Thus will the Lord break thee in pieces. Parson, thou art an old fool!' "

Two Quaker women stripped themselves and went naked in the streets, but later, it was said that they were insane. An incident of the same nature occurred in England, where a Quakeress went into the church naked, being moved, she said, by the spirit, to appear as a sign to the people. Some of the followers of this sect seemed to fancy that clothes were a superfluity. Such incidents make it difficult for us to associate the kindly, peace-loving followers of this church in the present day with the founders. Yet with all of these exasperating annoyances, there was no justice shown by the Puritans in dealing with them in such a cruel manner. The preachers were up in arms, evidently fearing the usurping of their power and authority. Endicott was as callous and hard hearted as the ministers, and gave no mercy. Two women were imprisoned for causing disorder in the church, and kept three days without food, then whipped, and kept three more days with nothing to eat, though they offered to pay for food. Others were whipped then taken long distances into the wilderness and left to starve or make their way out the best that they could. Probably the most pathetic case of all was that of William Brend. He was arrested with several other Quakers, imprisoned, kept without food, and flogged. Then, as Brend refused to pay a fine that he considered unjust, he was put in irons, "neck and heel and lay for sixteen hours without food, on his miserable tortured back." Not content with this, the following day the jailer ordered Brend to do some

work, which he was much too weak to execute. Thereupon, he was taken out, flogged with a tar rope until it
broke, then dragged downstairs into the open where he
was given ninety-seven more lashes, then thrown back
into his cell more dead than alive. The citizens rose up
at this, and Endicott sent his physician, who told the governor that Brend would die, as his flesh would "rot from
his bones." The citizens demanded justice be done, and
the jailer punished. The Rev. Norton defended the governor and declared that Brend be whipped twice a week
if he refused to work, and at each whipping five more
lashes were to be added. This gives an opportunity to
compare the people with the governing preachers, and we
can be proud of our New England ancestors, and thankful
that they were not all like some of the divines. Otherwise
we might cover the past in darkness, instead of being glad
to have come from such sturdy, hardworking and cour
ageous people, who finally worked out their problems, and
freed themselves from the bondage of such insufferable
intolerance.

Cases of this kind were innumerable and the punishments appalling. After the death penalty was prohibited
in the colonies by England, for religious dissenters, the
tortures inflicted were increased which often caused death.
Rev. John Rayner was convulsed with joy when he saw
Mary Tompkins and Alice Ambrose cruelly whipped on
one of the coldest days of winter. Another cruel case of
the persecution of a Quaker family was that of Lawrence
Southwick and his wife Cassandra, who were imprisoned,
whipped, imprisoned again for weeks, all of their property
taken to cancel their fine for not attending meeting, when

it was impossible for them to do so when jailed. Finally they were banished, though they had nowhere to go. Their eldest son was tortured by being whipped through several towns at the cart's end, and died, while their two youngest children were sold into slavery by the authorities the day their parents were banished, in order to raise the money to pay the fine.

Some idea of the working of the clergy's minds can be gained when it is recalled that some years later, they were convinced that they had displeased the Lord by their leniency to the Quakers, and therefore the Lord had afflicted them by causing King Philip's War. Again when the United Colonies learned that Rhode Island had welcomed some Quaker missionaries, they rose in angry protest, and sent a warning to their Assembly to banish the followers of that sect for fear of the contagion spreading, and that if they didn't "wee apprehend that it will be our duty seriously to consider what further provision God may call us to make to prevent the aforesaid mischiefe." To which Rhode Island replied that they wished to be in loving relations with their neighbors, and added among other noble sentiments, that freedom of conscience "we still prize as the greatest happiness that men can possess in this world." And that Quakers were "Suffered to live in England: yea, even in the heart of the nation."

Maryland as well as Rhode Island had granted religious freedom previous to this period, while New Jersey and South Carolina followed by 1670, and Pennsylvania twelve years later, so that the "contagion" was happily spreading.

The Quakers were not the only religious sect that was persecuted. The same stringent laws were also enforced against the Antinomians, the Baptists and especially the followers of Gordon, and all other anti-Puritan societies. It was considered a religious duty, and a pleasure in the eyes of Christ, to punish all who differed from the Puritan doctrines. Rev. John Cotton, one of the most learned of the early preachers, looked upon such persecutions as carrying out the holy work of God. He stated that "The punishment executed upon all false prophets and seducing teachers doe bring down showers of God's blessings upon the civil state," and again, that, "it is an honor to God's Justice that such judgements are executed."

Another cruel case of religious persecution was that of Obadiah Holmes. A plea had been sent to the Baptist colony in Rhode Island by William Witter of Lynn, a member of the Baptist society, then old and blind, for some one to come and administer the communion. His call was answered by the Rev. John Clark, one of the prominent members of the Rhode Island colony, Rev. Obadiah Holmes, Gorton, and Crandall. They held a service in Witter's home on Sunday July 20, 1651, with closed doors, evidently hoping not to be seen or overheard by the citizens of the town who were antagonistic to any one who did not believe in infant baptism, the principal cause of the religious misunderstanding. Clark was said to be in the midst of his sermon, when two constables entered, serving warrants on the "erroneous persons being strangers." They were taken to the Puritan meeting house and forced to listen to the sermon, which, Gorton said, "was meat to be digested, but only by the heart or stomache of an ostrich." They wore their hats in church and caused other slight offenses, all of which they were accused of at the trial, which was only a farce as regards justice, as no evidence was heard. They were stigmatized as Anabaptists. Rev. Cotton, the most enlightened and polished of the preachers at that time, held forth that afternoon in a manner that is difficult to reconcile with the better part of his character. He claimed that if infant baptism was no longer a doctrine of the church that the church would be lost, that it was a capital crime, and the prisoners were "foul murtherers." This placed Endicott in a very embarrassing position, as he could not in justice condemn the men, and if he pardoned them, he, in turn would be condemned by the authorities. The latter fate had to be avoided, so the prisoners were sentenced to be fined, which they all refused to pay. Friends paid the fine for all except Holmes, who again refused all help. He said, "As I went from the bar, I exprest myself in these words—I bless God I am counted worthy to suffer for the name of Jesus; whereupon John Wilson strook me before the judgement seat, and cursed me, saying 'The curse of God . . . goe with thee,' so we were carried to the prison."

When he was taken to the place for punishment, he was stripped, and as the first blow of the three-thonged whip was given, he cried out, "Lord, lay not this sin unto their charge." He was given thirty lashes; his flesh was lacerated to such a degree that he could not bear to either sit or lie, and was obliged to prop himself on his hands and knees.

John Spur who shook Holmes's hand after the punishment, and for saying that he looked upon Holmes as a Godly man, was dealt the same punishment. In spite of these heathenish inflictions of the Baptists, Winslow when in London claimed that the Baptists who lived peaceably were not molested, while the preachers shouted that if the colonies were not rid of these "foul-murtherers" that the authority of the government would be ruined.

Within a year Rev. John Clark published his "Ill News from New England," giving "A Faithful and True Relation of the Persecution of Obadiah Holmes, John Crandall and John Clark mearly for Conscience towards God by the principal Members of the Church or Commonwealth," and to which is added, "Let him that readeth consider which church is most like the Church of Christ . . . The Persecuted or Persecuting." It explains clearly the cruel and unjust punishments inflicted on them in the name of religion. Some twenty-four years later, Samuel Gloom published his book, "A Glass for the People of New England," telling again of the cruelties practiced by The United Colonies against those of other religions.

The case of Mary Fisher and Anne Austin caused great excitement and dismay. They were imprisoned for weeks, half starved, and their literature burnt. They were returned to England. Later this same Mary Fisher went to Turkey to convert the Sultan who treated her with tolerance. Fiske says that "In Massachusetts the preaching of the Quaker doctrines might (and did) lead to a revolution; in Turkey it was harmless as the barking of dogs. Governor Endicott was afraid of Mary Fisher; Mahomet III was not."

In the time that has elapsed since the days of the Puritans, and we look back at their intolerance, we have still far to go before we can live up to and practice the rules given by the Emperor Akbar at the first Parliament of religion held in 1578, when he said—"If thou art a Mussulman, go stay with the Franks, if thou art a Shi'ite, go stay with the Schismatics; if a Jew, go fellowship with Christians. Whatever thy religion, associate with men who think differently from thee. If thou canst mix with them freely and art not angered at hearing their discourse, thou hast attained peace, and art a master of creation."

To quote also from a modern writer, the late Alfred Martin, who made the following remarks at the Religious meeting in Geneva in 1928: "Some one has said 'that Tolerance is the loveliest rose that blooms upon the bush of Liberalism.' We should, as a matter of fact, be ashamed to love but one flower and tolerate the rest without appreciating the subtle beauties of each and all. So, too, with the religions; of which each is the flowering of some aspect of the Truth."

One thing is forgotten in all of the criticism of the intolerance of the Puritans, and that is that they did not come to New England as a place for the free exercise of all religions. They came here for an asylum and haven for themselves, to practice and carry out their interpretation of divine laws. The followers of other beliefs were intruders, and our ancestors believed they had a right to banish and inflict punishment on those who were proselyting by teaching other religious beliefs. Winthrop held that the Puritans had come to America to carry out their own ideas, and those who did not agree with them should go elsewhere. He also said that it was right to persecute falsehood, and as he and the other settlers claimed they were right in their interpretation of the Scriptures, necessarily those not agreeing with them were wicked translators of the sacred word. Therefore they believed it was justifiable to shed the blood of the Quakers and other dissenters.

In September, 1661, Charles II commanded that these religious laws of New England be stopped, but this was revoked a year later. The letter that Sir Richard Saltonstall wrote from London to Rev. Cotton must have been humiliating. It ran—"It doth not a little grieve my spirit to heare what sadd things are reported dayly of your tyranny and persecution in New England; as that you fyne, whip, and imprison One for their consciences" and then added that their "rigid wayes have laid you very lowe in the hearts of the saynts." This letter was followed by many from the prominent members of the English clergy, who wrote to the governor and assembly to stop the persecutions.

It is strange that in all the bigotry and religious intolerance of the colonies, especially against the Catholics, they should have welcomed on different occasions representatives of that church. In 1642 a French shallop arrived in Boston with a crew of fourteen men, bringing letters from Governor La Tour. They remained a week, and were treated very kindly by the citizens, notwithstanding that they were Papists. Again in 1643, a Jesuit visited Massachusetts as an envoy from the French colony in Canada. He was well received, and even entertained in private homes. The same year two friars visited Boston. They, however, were more discreet and remained in the suburbs of the towns, for fear that their presence would give offense. However, they visited Rev. Cotton, who spoke of one of them as being a very learned man. On leaving, they made their adieus to the magistrates, and thanked them for the courtesies which had been extended. Still again three years later, a Monsieur D'Aubary, came to Boston with "two papists," and in 1650, Father Gabriel Druillet, a Catholic missionary, visited Maine and Massachusetts with Monsieur Godfay, a converted Indian. While in Charlestown they stopped with Edward Gibbons. What is most surprising of all, is that he was entertained by the magistrates at dinner, and made so favorable an impression that he was invited to supper as well. Endicott, who spoke French, acted as interpreter.

It seems they had been sent by the French governor of Canada, Monsieur D'Aillebout, who commissioned them to ask the authorities to join the French in warring on the Mohawks and Six Nations, as they had made war on the Christianized Arcadian Indians. That if the English would not take part in the war could the French have permission to pass through their territory to the Mohawk country. They were refused both requests as it was pointed out to the Frenchmen that they had no cause to antagonize the Mohawks with whom, at the time, they were on good terms. They also took advantage of this opportunity to tell the French representatives that they considered their bartering with the Indians with guns and ammunition was breaking the law of the country and would lead to disastrous results if continued.

From the very first settlement, the colonists were interested in having educational facilities for their children. The intense religious spirit may have been one of the causes of this early impulse, as one record seems to prove. It reads—"It being one chief project of that old deluded Sathan, to keepe men from knowledge of the Scriptures, as in former times keeping them in unknown tongue, so in these latter times by persuading them from the use of Tongues."

Many of the settlers were college graduates and men of learning. The writings of these men, the composition, and the penmanship all bear this out, together with the portraits, some of which have fortunately been preserved. It is not surprising therefore that Harvard was founded at such an early date as 1636, when the Massachusetts Court agreed to give £400 towards a school or college, which was to be erected at Newtowne. Shortly after this decision by the Court, Rev. John Harvard made a bequest to the colony of £779, 17s, 2d, and his library. He stated that his object was the "education of the English and Indian youth of this country in knowledge and goodness." It might be added, however, regardless of John Harvard's idea, that the principal thought of the authorities in establishing the college, was to insure "Pious ministers" to carry on the Puritan religion. Upon the receipt of this gift, it was decided to change the name of the college from Cambridge, the one borne by the university from which many of the colonists had been graduated in England, to Harvard. One Indian, Cheeshaheaumuch, is recorded as having taken advantage of John Harvard's interest in providing an opportunity for the education of his race. He graduated in 1665, taking the degree of Bachelor of Arts. This Indian was sufficiently conversant with the dead languages to write Latin, Greek, and to compose poetry, but unfortunately he did not live many years, and died of consumption. A brick dormitory was erected at Harvard at the time for the use of the Indians by the "Society for Propagating the Gospel." Only a few of the Indians took advantage of this opportunity. They wearied of a life so unnatural to them, while some, endeavoring to "stick it out," sickened and died.

This desire for the education of the children of the planters was general throughout New England. By 1647 a law was passed in all of the colonies in this group with the exception of Rhode Island, making it obligatory to erect schools in every settlement. This was the beginning of the wonderful and exceptional educational system of our country. No matter how small the community, a schoolhouse always testifies to the foresight and high aspirations of not only our ancestors, but of the present generation.

The lives of the Harvard students in the early days of the institution were far different from those living in the luxurious dormitories of the present period. The rooms were bare and cold in winter; the meals poor, and meager; the discipline strict, and the religious instructions were never neglected, nor any real or imaginary sacrilegious act went unpunished. A good illustration of this is the case of a student, Thomas Sargeant. Judge Sewall's diary gives an account of this incident as follows —"Thomas Sargeant was examined by the Corporation; finally the advice of Mr. Danforth, Mr. Stoughton, Mr. Thatcher, Mr. Mather was taken. This was his sentence. That being convicted of speaking blasphemous words concerning H. G. (The Holy Ghost), he should be therefore publicly whipped before all the Scholars. That he should be suspended as to taking his degree of Bachelor; Sit alone by himself in the Hall uncovered at meals during the pleasure of the President and the fellows, and be in all things obedient, doing what exercise was appointed him by the President, or else be finally expelled from the College. The first was presently put into execution in the Library . . . before the Scholars. He kneeled down and the instrument Good man Hely attended to the President's words as to the performance of his part of the work. Prayer was had before and after by the President."

It will be seen that the president of the college had not only in most cases to act as judge, but also as executioner. In 1644 when two students aged twenty, and sons of ministers, broke into two dwellings and stole fifteen pounds, the Court ordered them whipped, but since no law had been made for the punishment of robbery, they were simply whipped by the president, and then discharged, and supposedly expelled from the college.

Caste was recognized from the first in the college, the same as in the church, and the names of pupils were catalogued according to their social standing. The policy of cataloguing alphabetically was not inaugurated until 1773.

Nathaniel Eaton was in charge of the college when it was opened, and had the title of "professor." According to Neal's "History of New England," he was a man of high education, "but cruel in his nature, and lewed in his moral." He tells how one of the pupils was punished, but neglected to name the offense. He goes on to say that the youth was held down by two men, "till he had beat him almost to Death with a Cudjel," for which the

Court fined him, and expelled him from the college. Later, Eaton was accused of immoralities and banished.

After Eaton was expelled, Rev. Henry Dunston became the first president of Harvard, August 27, 1640, and at once established a high standard which it has always maintained. Fourteen years later his resignation was accepted with regret. The trouble was caused by Dunston's sympathy with the Anabaptist religious sect, and his objection to the baptism of children. This was sacrilegious to the Puritans and against the doctrines of their sect. The result was a trial in 1657, when he refused to have his child baptised.

Rev. Charles Chauncy became president of the college in 1654. He was a very conscientious and hard working man from his point of view. He rose every morning at four, both in summer and winter, and often worked far into the night. He was, however, quite as fanatical as the other preachers of the Puritan doctrines, and at the time that it appeared that six Quakers would be acquitted he said in his sermon at a Thursday lecture, "Suppose ye should catch six wolves in a trap, and ye cannot prove that they killed either sheep or lambs and now ye have them they will neither bark nor bite: yet they have the plain marks of the wolves. Now I leave it to your consideration whether ye will let them go alive, yea or nay."

Rev. Chauncy wrote many sermons and tracts, many of which had a sad and undignified fate. They were handed down to his grandson, whose widow married the second time, a man whose business was baking pies, and who found the pages of the manuscripts of President Chauncy's sermons fine for putting in the bottom of the pie pans.

How many students of today would be able to pass the rigid entrance examination that was required as early as 1645, as "When any scholar is able to understand Tully or such like classical Latin author extempore, and makes and speaks Latin in verse and prose . . . and decline perfectly the paradigms or nouns and verbs in the Greek tongue, let him then, and not before, be capable of admission into the college." The students upon entering Harvard were required to use Latin only, as English for the time was to be dropped. All of the ancient languages were included in the curriculum, as well as the higher branches of mathematics, physics, etc. In order to be considered fit to be dignified with his first degree, "the student had to be able to read the originals of the Old and New Testaments in the Latin tongue, and to resolve them logically." Every family in New England at this time was requested to give either a peck of corn or twelve pence toward the support of the college.

New England took the lead in establishing a high seat of learning in the community, and was followed fifty-seven years later by Virginia, when in 1693 the College of William and Mary was founded, and named in honor of the reigning monarchs of that time. Connecticut came next with the establishment of Yale in 1701, and before the Revolution four more of our now leading universities were founded. In spite of all the hardships with which the settlers had to contend, their desire to give posterity the best advantages of an education, and such as they had been able to acquire in the Old Country, seemed uppermost in their hearts. It was one of the first considerations and is illustrated by a New England mother who spoke to her boy thus—"Child, if God make thee a good Christian and a good scholar, thou hast all that thy mother ever asked for thee." We learn from Cotton Mather, grandson of John Cotton, in his noted work "Magnalia," that in describing the intellectual attainments of one man, he compared him to "a tree of knowledge, but so laden with fruit that he stooped for the very children to pick off the apples ready to drop into their mouths." While in Boston in 1649, a merchant gave his copy of Stephens' "Treasures" to Harvard College, but with the understanding that it should be returned to him, if ever he had a child "studious of Greek, and desirous of that book," which, it is related eventually occurred, and the book was returned.

The educational facilities were mostly for the male children, but the education of the girls was not entirely neglected. The teachers were women and taught the girls how to behave, how to learn all the complicated as well as easy stitches in sewing, how to make samplers, now so eagerly sought after by the antique collectors, and also their A. B. C.'s. The Psalm book and other religious works were the principal text books. They were taught to always be courteous to their elders, and to bow respectfully and stand aside when they passed.

The first printing press in New England was installed at Cambridge in 1639, and was under the control of the president of Harvard College. Rev. Glover who was bringing it to Massachusetts died on the passage and his assistant, Stephen Daye, set up the press. The first work from it was "The Psalms newly turned into metre," which was printed in 1640, and known as "the Bay Psalm Book." Previous to that time the "Psalm Book of Ainsworth,"

which the Pilgrims brought over with them from Holland,
had been used. "The Bay" book was very crude, both as
to spelling and punctuation, which made it grotesque, but
in spite of these defects it was in use for years, and in
1878 a copy sold for $1200. The first edition had printed
on the title page—"The Whole Book of Psalms, Faithfully
Translated into English Metre. Whereupon is prefixed a
discourse declaring not only the lawfulness, but also the
necessity of the Heavenly Ordinance of Singing Psalms in
the Churches of God." While the second edition added—
"For the Use, Edification and Comfort of the Saints, in
Public and Private, especially in New England."

One verse will give an idea of the conditions under
which the church members labored when using this now
famous book.

> *"And sat He would not then waste; had not*
> *Moses stood (whom He chose)*
> *'fore him i' th' breach; ye turn his wrath*
> *lest that he should waste those."*

The singing of these psalms without music and generally
lined by the preacher, must have been lengthy and tedious
affairs.

All was not harmony, however, in the established religion. There was dissension in the church at Hartford
at this time, and a general council was called in 1655-7
to adjust matters and reconcile the brethren who had
broken away from the church. Later, Mather wrote regarding these troubles—"From the fire of the altar, there
issued thunderings, and lightnings, and earthquakes,

through the colony." A reconciliation was reached and in November, 1660, a public thanksgiving was celebrated over the victory of the council which had succeeded in establishing peace.

CHAPTER X

CONNECTICUT was growing rapidly, new settlements were springing up on every side, and many of the original planters in that section were pushing north and west through the forests to establish new towns. With the increasing population, the duties of the officials became greater, and those of Mason's were no exception. His responsibilities, both public and private, became more strenuous as he approached middle life.

In 1641, his daughter Priscilla was born, and during the next five years his sons Samuel and John arrived, so that with the daughter Isabel by his first wife, the Masons had four children to add to their comforts and cares. Mason's military duties took much of his time, not only in training the militia, but in adjusting disputes that arose between the Indians, and occasionally between the Indians and the English. In 1645 the Court authorized him to assemble all of the trained bands of the colony once in every two years for a general review. In addition to this, he was a representative for his district from 1637 to 1641, when he was chosen Assistant or Magistrate, being reelected until 1659.

He was appointed with one other to investigate a rumor of the practice of witchcraft at Saybrook. No evidence was found to sustain these reports. There is, however, the record of a trial held in Lyme, when Balthaser De Wolf brought suit against Nichols and Margaret Jennings, who were accused of having bewitched his child to death. They were both acquitted.

The Indians, like their white brethren, believed in witches, and held "pow-wows" as they called them. The English openly accused them of being "partly wizards and witches, holding familiarity with Satan, that evil one." They were thought to be "partly physicians," as they practiced and performed cures with roots and herbs. These remedies were held "diabolical spells, mutterings, exorcism," and it was said that during these incantations, the Indians made "extraordinary strange motions with the bodies," which they sometimes kept up for hours, "foaming and swetting" in the meanwhile. The Indians were supposed to hold conferences with the Devil and were believed to be children of his satanic majesty. The English tried to prohibit the natives from continuing "such heathen practices," but it is doubtful whether much effect was made by this law.

While the colonists criticised the Indians' medical treatment, they had to admit that they were often successful, though they believed it was due to some mysterious evil power. There are records of the whites having sufficient faith in the herb remedies of the squaws to patronize them, and several women of the Indian tribes, at different times, attained a following, becoming well known among the settlements.

It is difficult to understand why the whites should have criticised the Indian doctors, when looking over the prescriptions then in vogue among the settlers. For example, toothache could be cured by hanging the teeth of a dead person about the neck, or, better still, to wear a necklace of fawn's teeth, or of a wolf's fangs.   A sure cure for the rickets was to mash some snails, and earthworms, mixed with many kinds of weeds, and this concoction was to be taken twice a day with four spoonfuls of beer.   Mashed snails should also be applied externally to hasten the recovery.   These prescriptions were not alone from the ignorant, as the following from Sir Kenelm Digby, said to have been a noted physician of London, proves.   He sent the following prescription to John Winthrop, Jr.   "For all sorts of agues, I have of late tried the following magnetical experiment with infallible success: Pare the patient's nails when the fit is coming on, and put the parings into a little bag of fine linen or sarsanet, and tie that about a live eel's neck in a tub of water.   The eel will die and the patient will recover, and if a dog or a pig eat that eel, they will die also."

If the patient survived some of these remedies, it must have been due to a wonderful constitution, plus great faith.   They believed that if the concoctions they made were applied to some article of clothing of a person wet with the patient's blood, though he lived in some remote place, that he would be benefited as much as though present.   Cotton Mather tells in his diary under date of April, 1699, of a cure by prayer.   Winthrop also records two incidents of this kind.

Many of the epidemics that have since cut down large numbers of the population in different parts of the world were prevalent at different periods during colonial times. Smallpox, as has been mentioned, diphtheria, typhoid, and various fevers, for which practically no efficient remedies were known, and on account of the extreme indulgence of drinking intoxicated liquors, bladder and kidney trouble claimed many victims. A gallon of rum was allowed a month to field hands, and both rum and whiskey were used in most of the households. The pathetic cases were those afflicted with mental diseases. There were no insane asylums nor almshouses until late in the eighteenth century, and the usual manner of treating the insane was to chain them in some out building. For instance, take the case recorded in Braintree in 1689, when the town board voted that the brother of the afflicted one should build "a little house, seven feet long and five wide, and set it by the house to secure his sister, good wife Witty, being distracted." The "Magnalia" gives an account of Elder Thomson, the man who killed the snake in the church during the synod at Cambridge, becoming "under the power of melancholy for the space of eight years" which was no doubt caused by the Devil. He became lucid during the last few hours of his life, which caused Mather to record in verse—

> "by his bed side an Hebrew sword there lay
> With which at last he drove the devil away.

If we criticise our ancestors for dealing with the insane in such a heartless manner, they at least did not look upon them as beings for the amusement of the crowds, as happened in other countries.

The physicians who were authors of medical books also wrote the cook books, anticipating the present-day dietary systems. One of the most noted of this kind, had the convincing title of "The Queen's Closet Opened, or The Pearl of Practice; Ancient, Physical, and Chirugical Receipts"; while another had an even more elaborate title, which read—"A Queen's Delight, or the Art of Preserving, Conserving and Candying, also the Right Knowledge of Making Perfumes, and Distilling the most Excellent Waters." These works were of course written for, and dedicated to the reigning queen, a courtesy that was hoped would be rewarded, for diplomacy and tact often brings the desired reward.

The Indians were not lacking in this respect, at least that gift belonged to Uncas. Although crafty, cunning and revengeful, he often used the silver tongue in his dealings with the English, as in July, 1638. He had shown unusual interest in some Pequots, whom he had entertained, and evidently fearing he might be criticised or suspected of having ulterior motives, he went to Boston with presents for the magistrates, which they first refused. Uncas appeared very much grieved, and pleaded his friendship with such sincerity that he convinced the authorities of his good faith, so that his gifts were finally accepted. Then the sachem of the Mohegans made a speech equal to a present-day politician. He promised to always obey the English in regard to the Pequots who had been adopted by his tribe, as well as with his dealings with the Narragansetts. Then laying his hand over his heart, he said, "This is not mine, but yours. Command me any difficult service, and I will do it. I have no men, but all are yours. I will never believe any Indian against the English any more. I would put him to death, were he never so dear to me." He only kept these promises so far as his dealings with the English were concerned. He was continually intriguing against the Narragansetts whom he hated.

Uncas left the court with a present of "a fine red coat" and a letter to protect him as he passed through the settlements on his return. The expenses of his men in Boston were paid, and they were given provisions for their tramp home.

Mason was in constant communication with the Indians, realizing the necessity of keeping watch over all of their movements to prevent any treacherous act. He had perfect faith in Uncas' loyalty, but not so with the Narragansetts. The latter had kept their treaty until after the Pequot war, when their powerful chief Miantonimo showed a spirit of unrest that was menacing. It was believed that in 1642 he had endeavored to warn all the Indian tribes, as Sassacus had done a few years previous, of the dangers of the encroaching English plantations, and to persuade them to form a union that would destroy the settlers. At first, the Bay colony would not give credence to this report, as the Indians were continually circulating wrong information in order to place their enemies in bad repute with the colonies. It was not until Plymouth warned them that the Bay authorities began to realize the seriousness of the situation. Then, every precaution was taken to prevent a surprise attack. The white inhabitants were thoroughly aroused throughout New England, and the fear became so acute that even a sudden cry or halloo at night would cause them to fear that some one had been captured and was being tortured by the Indians.

Miantonimo was described by the writers of his time as having a fine physique, tall, and well proportioned, and in temperament very subtle, and haughty in all of his dealing with the whites. He was sent for by the Boston authorities, when the rumors of his actions were learned, and he came at once. When questioned about the conspiracy, he demanded that his accusers be brought "face to face" with him. He argued, that if they could not prove their statements against him, that they should suffer the fate that would be dealt to him should he be proved guilty. He said that he could prove that the reports against him and his tribe were either started by Uncas, or one of his people. Miantonimo had a keen sense of justice, and demanded, that if they trusted the Mohegans, as they claimed, why had they taken their guns and ammunition from them. He would never speak or answer questions, unless in the presence of some of his own people, so that no false reports could be carried back to his tribe.

The hatred between the two sachems was very great, and each was looking for an opportunity to ruin the other. Matters came to a head when Uncas claimed that he had been assaulted by Sequesson, a sachem, and a friend of Miantonimo. He fought and killed him, as well as several of his band, wounded others, burnt their wigwams and took their belongings. Miantonimo at once sent a complaint to the Court at Hartford, in which he stated that Sequesson had not attempted to kill Uncas, but that the Mohegan chief had cut himself with a piece of flint in order to justify his dastardly accusation. The Court was cool to his appeal and only repeated what they had previously told both chiefs, that they would remain neutral in all quarrels between the two tribes. Undoubtedly, their sympathies were always with Uncas. Not wishing war, however, the Massachusetts colony had in the meantime raised an army. This convinced the Narragansett sachem of the hopelessness of his situation, and he signed a treaty of peace. The English soldiers were withdrawn, leaving only a few to protect Uncas.

Mason had no fear and went about among the Indians as freely as with the settlers. Often he was accompanied by either Thomas Stanton or Benedict Arnold who acted as his interpreters. During all this quarreling between Uncas and Miantonimo, the Major had used every effort to reconcile them, and establish a permanent peace between the two tribes, but unfortunately, without success.

The promise of the Narragansetts was not kept, and Miantonimo marched with several hundred of his warriors into the Mohegan country expecting to make a surprise attack on his old enemy. The wary Uncas always kept scouts in all directions, and was informed in advance of the approach of the Narragansetts as they forded the Yantic stream. Watch was kept as they pushed their way through the forest, and up the hill that overlooked the valley of the Yantic. In the meanwhile, Uncas had assembled his warriors, and instructed them in the course he intended to follow. When Miantonimo's army came in view, Uncas sent a messenger to him, asking for a talk, which the Narragansett sachem granted. The two men met in front of their respective armies, which seems more in keeping with the old-time battle lines of the whites, than between the aborigines of New England, who generally fought from ambush.

Uncas was the first to speak, and said to Miantonimo, "You have a number of men with you, and so have I with me. It is a great pity that such brave warriors should be

killed in a quarrel between us. Come like a man, as you
profess to be, and let us fight it out; if you kill me, my
men shall be yours, but if I kill you, your men shall be
mine."

Miantonimo replied, "My men came to fight, and they
shall fight!"

The Narragansetts stood waiting for the result of the
interview, but Uncas, acting upon his previously arranged
plan, fell flat on the ground which was the signal for his
men, who had their bows bent ready for action. They
shot over his body, and then made a mad rush on the
enemy before the Narragansetts had time to realize their
danger. There was only a short skirmish, before Miantonimo's men retreated in a panic, completely losing their
heads and forgetting that they far outnumbered the
Mohegans.

Tantaquieson, one of Uncas' chiefs, spied Miantonimo
in the confusion of the retreat, who was laboring under
heavy armor which he was wearing, and which had been
given to him by an Englishman, so that he was easily over-
taken by the swift runner of the Mohegans. However,
Tantaquieson only delayed the chief, waiting for Uncas
to come up to them, so that he could have the honor of
making him prisoner. During the rest of his life, Tantaquieson was a target for the Narragansetts, and several
attempts were made on his life. One time his enemies
nearly succeeded, when a Narragansett warrior crept into
his wigwam at night and seriously wounded him.

When Uncas reached Miantonimo, and touched him on
the shoulder, Miantonimo made no attempt to escape, but
submitted to his captor without a word. He did not even

speak when Uncas addressed him thus—"Had you taken me, I should have asked you for my life." But the great Narragansett sachem made no reply, as he evidently preferred death rather than to humble himself before his hated enemy.

The battle was short, but furious, and lasted only a few hours. There were a number of Narragansetts killed, and among them a brother of Miantonimo, and some others of his kin. Several were wounded in both tribes, including two sons of Cononicus.

In their frantic efforts to escape, the retreating band was pursued over several miles, and many are said to have leaped over the Yantic falls and were dashed to pieces on the rocks below, while others drowned in trying to swim the river. The retreat became a wild panic, and the Mohegans boasted that they found one of the Narragansett warriors in the reeds bordering the river, who believed himself in the water, and was trying to swim on land.

Uncas took his captive in triumph to his fort, midst great rejoicing of his people. He treated Miantonimo with every courtesy and kindness, which the prisoner acknowledged with gratitude.

It was a war strictly between the two tribes, in which the English took no part, but upon learning of the capture of Miantonimo, the authorities ordered Uncas to take the Narragansett chief to Hartford, where he was imprisoned, but a decision as to the verdict to be passed was left to the Commissioners of the United Colonies when they met in Boston in September. The Court claimed that Miantonimo had broken the treaty he had made with the authorities in 1638; that his attempt to unite all of the

Indian tribes in a conspiracy to annihilate the English was proven; that he had gotten a Pequot to shoot Uncas, which had only disabled the Mohegan's arm; and that he turned all the Indians, with whom he came in contact, against the English. After weighing all these facts, they were still undecided as to whether the crimes warranted his death. Finally they consulted with five of the principal ministers who were in favor of having the Narragansett executed. Their argument was to the effect that Uncas could not be safe while Miantonimo lived, that either by secret treachery or open warfare, his life would be constantly in danger, and "that he might justly put such a false and bloody enemy to death, but that it was to be done out of the jurisdiction of the English, and without cruelty or torture."

The prisoner was turned over to Uncas with a party of his warriors and two Englishmen, to see that the Court's instructions were carried out. The chief was taken just out of the jurisdiction of the English, when a Mohegan went up behind him and split his skull with a hatchet. Trumbull says, though other historians question his statement, that "Uncas cut out a large piece of his shoulder and ate it in savage triumph." He said, "It was the sweetest meat he ever ate; it made his heart strong." If this actually happened, as it was also said to have occurred when Kiswas was slain at Saybrook, it meant that Uncas, like many of the savages, believed that by so doing, he would be endowed with the strength of his slain enemy, as neither Uncas nor his people were cannibals.

Winthrop's account of the direction the Commissioners gave to Uncas was, that he was to take "Miantonimo along with him, in the way between Hartford and Windsor, (where Onkus hath some men dwell). Onkus brother following after Miantonimo, clave his head with an hatchet."

There have been many traditions as to the place where Miantonimo was executed, and a monument marks a spot known as Sachem's Point near Norwich, which, according to some authorities, is probably the spot where the battle began. It is well that later generations realized the great injustice that was done when this famous man of his tribe was slain. He had often performed friendly acts for the whites, and had assisted Mason during the Pequot war. The date on the monument records Miantonimo's death, September 28, 1643.

Savage's opinion of the murder of Miantonimo is that of most students of Indian history. He says, "Of several parts of this history (Winthrop's 'History of New England'), many readers will perhaps form an unfavorable judgment, but none has been so painful in the whole progress of my labours as this which relates to the treatment of Miantonimo by our fathers. Such a case of perfidy, cruelty, or both, it is impossible to pass without animadversion." Savage was also of the belief that the fact that the Narragansett chief had sold property to Gorton and his band had greatly to do with the decision of the court. Governor Stephen Hopkins wrote that "this was the end of Myantonomo, the most potent Indian prince the people of New England had ever any concern with; and this was the reward he received for assisting them seven years before, in their war with the Pequots."

Miantonimo's son Canonchet when captured during King Philip's War, and told that he was sentenced to death, showed the same spirit of courage with which his father was endowed, when he replied—"he liked it well that he should die before his heart was soft, or had spoken anything unworthy of himself."

The Narragansetts never forgave the authorities for this act, and their hatred for Uncas and his tribe was naturally increased, so that at the session of the General Court at Hartford in October of that year it commissioned eight soldiers to remain with Uncas, as they feared the vengeance of his enemies.   The New Haven colony sent six additional men.   At the time these resolutions were taking place at Hartford, Pessacus, Miantonimo's brother, was in Boston vowing his intention to take the life of Uncas—a vow he attempted to keep as long as he lived.   He claimed that Uncas had promised to free Miantonimo on the payment of a large amount of wampum, which he refused to do after receiving the specified sum, but instead, took him to the authorities at Hartford.   Uncas stated he had never made any such agreement, and that the only articles he had received were those Miantonimo had given him and his squaw for the kind treatment he had received while his prisoner.

In the spring of 1645, a large force of the Narragansetts led by Pessacus invaded the territory of the Mohegans, destroying crops, and, as their number was twice that of Uncas' force, the latter were obliged to flee to their fort for protection.   This fortress was so well situated on the banks of the river that Pessacus and his chiefs knew it would be difficult to take, and they also knew how poorly it was provisioned for a siege.   They stole the Mohegan canoes, so that, seemingly, there was no chance for those in the fort to escape, and they waited to starve them out.

It seemed impossible for Uncas to send any one for succor, but on a dark night, one of his braves succeeded in getting away unobserved, and sped across the country to the Saybrook fort where he made known the plight of his people, and Major Mason at once took means of sending provisions to the besieged. Trumbull states, "one, Thomas Leffingwell, an ensign at Saybrook, an enterprising, bold man, loaded a canoe with beef and corn and peas, and under cover of the night, paddled from Saybrook into the Thames; and had the address to get the whole into the fort."

A tradition states that the delay of Leffingwell, caused Uncas to go each night and watch the river from a rock which was a special vantage point, and since that time the place has been called "Uncas' Chair."

The advent of Leffingwell and the supplies he brought were received with shouts of joy, much to the astonishment of the Narragansetts, whose surprise was still greater when in the morning they saw a beef raised for their inspection across the water. The siege was abandoned, but their hatred for Uncas persisted. The Mohegan chief did not forget the good Samaritan act of Leffingwell, and he gave him quantities of skins and wampum. Many years later the Connecticut Court presented him with a farm of several acres to recompense him for his aid to the Mohegans.

Uncas had received so many favors from the English, that he became very arrogant in his dealings with the other tribes. He was unusually menacing toward the Nameaguges, a small band of Pequots that had resided for some time at the site that Winthrop and Peters had selected for the settlement which was later to be known as New London. These Indians had made their services of value to the new planters, and in return now felt secure from interference by Uncas. Their hopes in that direction were cruelly disappointed, as Uncas and his warriors continually annoyed and raided them, which caused much uneasiness among the English.

The following year the Narragansetts united with the Nunantics to war on Uncas. This combination became so threatening that in June, 1645, the Court found it necessary to raise an army of three hundred men, forty of whom were to be furnished by Connecticut. This decision of the English forced the chiefs Pessacus and Ninegret to sign a treaty August 27 of that year. Secret attempts were being continually made on Uncas' life. At one time a poison plot was discovered in time to save him from that fate.

These war scares took much of Mason's time. He was consulted on every occasion, and had to be continually on guard for the safety of the settlements. These duties together with those of his office of magistrate gave him little time to himself. He had to take every precaution against the Indians' getting possession of guns and ammunition, as they were secretly sold or bartered to the natives, though strictly forbidden by law. Yet, immediately following the first trial of Miantonimo, the Bay colony went contrary to its laws and the wishes of Mason, by returning the weapons to the Indians which had been taken from them. These arms had been purchased, for the most part, from the French and Dutch, "choosing," the magistrates said, "rather to trust God with their safety, than

secure themselves by an act of unrighteousness in with-
holding from the Indians that which was their own."
Mason's opinion of this unwise act can readily be guessed.
Affairs again came to a serious crisis in 1646, when Mr.
Peters had the friendly Nameaguges, led by their chief
they had nicknamed "Robin," to round up the deer so
that the planters would be able to obtain venison. Uncas
had been informed of the plan, and concealed a large
body of his men who attacked Robin's company. A quick
skirmish ensued, which resulted in wounding several of
Robin's tribe, and the burning and plundering of their
wigwams. When the matter was brought to the attention
of the Court of Commissioners, Uncas was let off with a
reprimand. Even the pleas of Winthrop the younger,
and sixty-two of the planters to allow Robin and his men
to be left under the jurisdiction of the English was refused.
Robin's tribe was placed under the control of Uncas—a
decision unjust and unnecessarily cruel.

This question was brought up again in 1651, but it
was not until sixteen years later that the matter was settled. The records state—"As for the Pequot Indians, they
are settled on a large tract of land for their planting and
subsistence, which we wish had been sooner attended,
but being now effected, we hope will satisfy our confed-
erates." They had a reservation of two thousand acres,
and Cassasinamon (Robin), was their ruler until his death
in 1692.

John Winthrop the younger with Thomas Peters laid
out the new plantation of New London. This settlement
was another bulwark of protection for the Mohegans, for
though the English were supposed to be neutral in all

Indian affairs, their partiality for the Mohegans could no longer be denied. The summer had not passed before Pessacus again attacked the Mohegans with an overpowering number, but Uncas with only forty men drove them off. A letter that Peters wrote at that time to Winthrop the elder, gives a good idea of the hazardous times through which the Indians as well as the whites were passing.

"I with your son were at Uncas fort where I dressed seventeen men and left plasters to dress seventeen more who were wounded in Uncas' brother's wigwam before we came. Two captains and one common soldier were buried, and since we came thence two captains and one common man more are dead, also most of which were wounded with bullets. Uncas and his brother told me, the Narragansetts had thirty guns which won them the day else they would not care a rush for them.

"They drove Uncas forces out by a wile, of forty appearing only, but one thousand in ambush, who pursued Uncas men into their own land where the battle was fought vario marte, till God put fresh spirit into the Mohegues, and so drove the Narragansetts back again."

Roger Williams was a strong ally of the Narragansetts. In all of the troubles between them and the Mohegans, he believed that the Narragansetts were in the right. Therefore, any one who championed Uncas and his tribe was under suspicion. This is very strongly brought out in a letter that he wrote to Winthrop in 1648-9, which is addressed to "His much honoured, kind friend, Mr. John Winthrop, at his howse at Nameug. These, Gawcawmsqussick Sir; Best salutations presented to you both with humble desires that since it pleaseth God to hinder your presence this way he may please for his infinite mercy sake in his sons blood to further our externall meeting in the presence of him that sits upon the Throne and the Lambe for ever, and that the hope thereof may be living and bring forth the fruits of love when it's possible and of lamenting for obstruction." Then goes on demonstrating the fruits of love by telling how he had sent a letter to Mason by a planter passing that way, in answer to some he had received from the Major, but not having heard from him, thought his missives must have gone astray, and continuing said, "and since I mention Capt. Mason (worthy Sir), I humbly beg of the Father of Lights to guide you in your converse and neighbourehood with him; In his letters to me he tells me some extraordinary lifts against Onkas that he will favoure him, but no more than religion and reason bids him. He promiseth to visit me in his passage this summer Eastward (I quere he meanes toward Plymmouth) I shall then argue (if God will) many things and how it stands with religion and reason that such monstrous hurrie and affrightment should be offered to an English town, either by Indians or English, unpunished. Sir, you have seen many parts of this Worlds snow ball, and never found ought but vanitie and vexation at Nameug you shall find no more except in the Fountaine of living waters: Sir heape coales of fire on Captain Masons head, conquer evil with good, but be not cowardly and overcome with any evil."

Williams wrote in another letter to Winthrop the same year in which he quotes from a letter he had received from Mason which refers to the menacing attitude of the Indians. "The Last night one Wequashcucks Pequts brought me very privately letters from Capt. Mason (and as he said from Onkas and Wequashcucks) the letters are very kind to myself acknowledging loving letters (and tokens which upon the burning of his howse) he had received from me etc. . . . he said the purport of his letter . . . seem to imply some present conclusions of hostilitie, the words of the letter are—'If nothing but blood will satisfie them I doubt not but they may have their fill:' and again— 'I perceeve such an obstinate willfullness joined with desperate malicious practices that I think and believe they are sealed to destruction'. "

In another letter that Williams wrote in defence of the Narragansetts he said—"I cannot yet learn that ever it pleased the Lord to permit the Narragansetts to stain their hands with any English blood, neither in open hostilities nor secret murders, as both Pequots and Long Island Indians did and Mohegans also in the Pequot war. It is true they are barbarians, but their greatest offences against the English have been matters of money, or petty revenging of themselves on some Indians, upon extreme provocations, but God kept them clean of our blood." It is evident that in the writer's love for this tribe, that he forgot when he made this statement, the Block Island murder of Captain Oldham, as well as the outrages they were committing in his own province; stealing, killing the planters' cattle, and harassing them in so many ways that the conditions became so severe in 1648, that the authorities of the colony applied to the Commissioners of the United Colonies, to be admitted into their federation. Only frightful, unbearable conditions could have driven the Rhode Island representatives to such extremes. How-

ever, they were saved this humiliation, and always remained an independent colony.

Williams' dislike for Uncas was no doubt well founded,
as the Mohegan chief was always in trouble or at war
with one or more of the numerous tribes. His treachery
and double-dealing often caused disputes, and perhaps at
times, a feeling between the different office holders, at least
they often disagreed when such occasions arose. A case in
point was when Uncas brought claim for twenty pounds
for rights of property that he claimed had been taken by
the English in the settlement of New London. At that
time Winthrop took the side of the planters, and Mason,
as usual, that of Uncas. The Indian eventually won out.
An agreement was made and the claim settled for fifteen
pounds. The occasion was a great event and celebrated
with much pomp and ceremony.

Numerous assaults and murders had been committed
by the savages from time to time, which kept the settlers
in a continual nervous state. Guards had to be kept on
watch day and night to prevent a surprise attack. One
of the conspicuous crimes was the attempt to slay an English woman in her home at Stamford a few years previous,
which resulted in the victim becoming insane. A threat
of a company of soldiers, and the holding of two sachems
of the tribe as hostages, resulted in the man being given
to the authorities. The gruesome description of his execution furnishes a good illustration of the Spartan-like
endurance of the natives. Trumbull's account which is
also given in the Connecticut records and Winthrop's
diary, states that "the executioner cut his head off with a
falchion: but it was cruelly done. He gave the Indian

eight blows, before he effected the execution. The Indian sat erect and motionless, until his head was severed from his body."

A murder that especially aroused the wrath of the English, was that of John Whitmore, also of Stamford, whose body was hidden for several weeks before it was discovered. These atrocities necessitated taking the stern measures advocated by Mason, and it was due to his precaution and foresight that the unfriendly Indians were kept in check.

Many changes were taking place in the plantations, and progress in most lines was being manifest, but not so with superstitions. This powerful ogre of the imagination held full sway. For example, 1645 was the coldest winter recorded since the founding of the northern colonies. It was said to be caused by "a strange sun phenomenon" that happened early in the year. In the town of Ipswich a calf was born with one head, three mouths, three nostrils, and six eyes. "What these prodiges portend," one preacher said, "the Lord only knows, which in his due time he will manifest."

A very religious woman of Boston was ungodly enough to take great pride in a parcel of fine linen that had been sent to her from London, which she had washed and pressed. Through the carelessness of a negro servant in snuffing a candle the linen was set on fire and consumed. The owner was consoled by being told that "it pleased God by the loss of this linen did her much good both in taking off her heart from worldly comforts, and in preparing her for a far greater affliction by the untimely death of her husband."

In a later generation, the great Cotton Mather knew that Satan visited his study and stole notes for his sermons. The judgment of God "appeared," when the ship *Mary Rose,* with her crew was blown up July 27, 1640. The captain and his men, the colonists claimed, "scoffered" at them, and refused to attend services on the Lord's day on land, stating they had as good service on board, and within two hours of this statement, the Lord avenged the insult by igniting twenty-one barrels of powder on the boat, which blew up the ship, and that was the end of the *Mary Rose* and all her people.

The tragedy of the *Mary Rose,* however, gave the inventive genius of a settler named Edward Bendall an inspiration to invent a diving bell. The owners of the ship had been notified, but made no attempt to salvage any part of the cargo that might have escaped destruction. Bendall took two large tubs, fastened them together, making them water tight, leaving an adjustable opening at one end. After weighting them heavily, he had the bell let down. The inventor sat inside and soon found himself in his water tight compartment at the bottom of the harbor. He was armed with two cords which he held. One was to notify the men above when to move the bell, and the other when to draw him up. More information as to the construction of the bell is not recorded, but that he obtained parts of the cargo proves that it was a success. The irony of the whole experience was that one of the guns brought to the surface seemed wedged, and in order to clear it, it was fired. To the dismay of the beholders gold coin dropped

into the water. Fortunately for Bendall some of it was
recovered from time to time at low tide, and the finders
were obliged to give the gold to him, by order of the
Court.

This marine tragedy was only one among several during
the first century of the settlement, though, perhaps, but
few were such proofs of the Lord's pleasure. Many of the
immigrants had not been able to survive the long, trying
voyages, and had died on their way to the promised land.
Storms had occurred, leaving in their wake wreckage and
death. There was another ship that arrived in 1636
crowded with men, women and children. After a voyage
of eighteen weeks on the water they found themselves
practically dying from thirst. Their beer had leaked out
a month before they landed. "So that they were forced
to stinking water (and that very little) mixt with sack or
vinegar." It is noted that a ship load of "scoffers" of
the settlers and their customs, suffered the judgment of
the Lord, as they fell into the hands of the Turks. Another ship load of the same caliber lost their all in a fire
set by their servants.

There was one rather humorous incident in all of these
troubles. That is, it is humorous after the passing of so
many years. The sinking of the *Angel Gabriel,* besides
its many fatalities, had a heart tragedy as well, and prevented a happy marriage of two young people. The suitor
had sailed to New England in the ill-fated vessel, and it
was planned that after he had built a home, his betrothed
would come to the New World and become his bride. But,
alas, when she learned of the tragedy that befell the *Angel
Gabriel,* she refused to run the risk of the voyage, and

remained in England. The would-be bridegroom also did not care to undertake the return voyage, after his unpleasant experience, and remained on this side, and thus the waters of the Atlantic ruined another romance.

The political changes in England affected her colonies. The emigration that had grown so large, suddenly ceased in 1640, and in the following few years, numbers of the planters returned to the mother-country to take part in the civil war.

In 1639 Archbishop Laud endeavored to establish the Church of England by law in Scotland. It was the final spark to fire the revolution in the north. Fortifications were reinforced, even women of high estate took part in the menial and difficult tasks. Charles sent two armies into Scotland, and two treaties were made, which only lasted a short time. The clergy and the prophetess Michelson, who was thought to talk direct to Christ, were urging military force. Arms were imported from foreign countries, while the homes of the nobility, or those who sided with the English, were raided and often destroyed. The treasury was empty. Laud was attacked in Lambeth Palace, which he had to fortify. Within a year he was impeached for high treason, and a few years later beheaded. Charles was taken prisoner, and sent to the Tower to follow Laud's fate, while the queen fled to Exeter in preparation to sail to France.

Cromwell was in power. Lord Fairfax headed the Parliamentary army, and was gaining victory after victory, defeating the King's troops at every encounter. Fairfax was a keen judge of men and their abilities, and in this war he needed men of the highest type to command his forces. It was then that he thought of his old war comrade of Belgium days, and sent for Major Mason to head one of his armies. It was a tempting offer, a compliment which probably no other of the military force in New England could boast, and yet, perhaps Mason had become so attached to his new home where he held such an honored place, that he could not bear to leave it. Or, perhaps, again, he preferred to be just plain Major-General John Mason of America, to any second place in England.

CHAPTER XI

THE military headquarters of Connecticut were located at Saybrook, which necessitated Major Mason's spending so much of his time in that vicinity, that in 1647, the Court requested that he would make Saybrook his permanent home. It was ordered that "captain Mason, should, for the peace, safety and good assurance of this commonwealth, have the command of all soldiers and inhabitants of Saybrook, and in case of alarm or danger by approach of our enemy, to draw forth a part of the said soldiers and inhabitants in such posture for the defence of the place as to him shall seem best." This order of the Court made Mason the actual dictator of the Saybrook settlement, a power he used to the betterment of the colonies, and which he never abused.

He moved with his family during the spring and they resided at Saybrook until 1659. Here his other three children, Rachel, Daniel and Elizabeth were born, and where also his eldest daughter, Isabelle, by his first wife, was married June 17, 1658, to John Bissell.

Saybrook, noted years later as the first seat of Yale University, was situated at the entrance to the Connecticut River, and commanded the northern part of that section of the colony. The first account recorded of it, is as early as 1614, when the place was visited by a Hollander named Adrien Bloch, and from that time the Dutch went there annually to trade with the Indians. Seeing the advantages

of the location, Governor Van Twiller of New Amsterdam
purchased the point of land for the West Indies Company,
and the name was changed from Pasbeshauke to Kieviet's
Hock, on account of the cry of the birds that gathered
there in large numbers, which the Dutch called, "kieviet."
For a few years the Dutch possessed the place without
protest, and it was not until the arrival of the representatives of the Earl of Warwick's patent that disputes arose.
This territory was included in Connecticut, and had been
granted in March, 1631, by the Earl, who was president
of the Plymouth Company, to Lord Say and Seal, Lord
Brook, and several others.

The patentees engaged Lyon Gardiner when in Rotter-
dam, as "Engineer and Master of works of Fortifications
in the legers of the Prince of Orange in the Low Countries," as he described himself, for four years at a salary
of £100 per annum.   He was to erect a fort and town at
the mouth of the Connecticut, which he named Saybrook
in honor of the two principal holders of the patent.   He
arrived in 1635, and was disappointed to find practically
no work done, and the three hundred men that had been
promised him, and who were to arrive the following year,
never materialized.   He said in his narrative that he found
only two men at the place, George Fenwick, one of the
proprietors, and another.   Disputes arose immediately as
to the rightful owners of the land, the result of which is
given in chapter two of this volume.   John Winthrop, the
younger, though only twenty-nine years of age, and who
had been appointed governor by the proprietors, before
he sailed, visited Saybrook for the first time the following
year.

The original plot on which the fort was located consisted of fifteen hundred acres, and stretching across the point of land which formed a peninsula was a palisade twelve feet high. George Fenwick had the use of the buildings, and was paid the duties on all exports for ten years. The ordinance requested that the masters of all vessels should stop at the fort and present Fenwick with a statement of the dutiable part of the cargo. At the end of the term specified, it was said that Fenwick had collected in this manner an amount of £1600. He was actually lord of the place, and acted as though he were the sole owner, so that the colony was glad to purchase his rights in 1644, and have the benefit of the customs.

Fenwick lost his wife during their residence at Saybrook, which was a loss to the colony, as well as to his family. Lady Fenwick was a woman of culture, and her presence in the settlement had a beneficial influence. She was buried in the fort inclosure, but in 1871 when the ruins of the fortifications were demolished, her bones were exhumed. They were wired by a physician, clothed in fine garments, her hair which was well preserved, was dressed, and she was then reinterred. The original monument is placed over the grave and can be seen from the Boston Post Road.

The church services were held in the great hall of the fort by the Rev. Hugh Peters. The second minister was James Fitch, who later became the son-in-law of Mason.

The first meeting house was erected in 1647, the year that the Masons moved there. All the men of the settlement always turned out in building the house of worship, as it was regarded as a great and patriotic event, and one in which they took great pride. They were plain and simple buildings at first. Never painted, and often built of logs, with chinks filled with clay, and the roofs were merely thatched, while the floors were often beaten clay. Later, when facilities and wealth permitted, wooden floors were installed, which were generally sanded. The meeting houses averaged about thirty feet in length with windows, at first filled with oil paper, but soon glass was imported. There were no shades, so that the glaring, hot rays of the summer's sun were often very trying. The seats were crude benches without backs, but as the congregation had to stand through the prayers, often an hour or two in length, their own backs may have welcomed the change.

Plenty of rum was always on tap at the raising of a new edifice, besides brown sugar and lemons, so, perhaps, our early ancestors brewed a concoction similar to our present-day cocktail. Sometimes the results of imbibing too much of the liquid refreshments ended disastrously to both the participants and the building, as there is more than one record which tells of the frame falling, and the men being injured. It is known that as many as several barrels of rum were consumed in the building of a meeting house. One of the most trying obstacles in erecting the first buildings in the colonies, was the scarcity of nails, and it is even said that buildings, temporarily vacant, were set on fire in the hopes of obtaining the necessary hardware.

When the meeting house of Saybrook was completed, it was voted that at the front door of the church should "be a guard of 8 men every Sabbath and Lecture day, complete in their arms." A sentinel was always on watch in the turret of the platform built on the roof. When there were rumors of Indian troubles, the guard would be doubled, and it was for this reason that men always sat at the door of the pew, when pews were introduced, to be instantly ready for defence, and to be able to make a quick exit. The sentinels were ordered to keep their matches always lighted, and to wear armor made of cotton wool, which was a protection against Indian arrows. It was also the law, though men went to services armed, they were never allowed to fire their guns except on wolves and Indians.

The experiences of the colonists who were occasionally imposed upon by impostors, claiming to be ministers of the gospel, and the possibility of a minister's becoming too liberal in his interpretation of the Scriptures, led to a law being enacted in 1658 by the General Court, preventing such possibilities. Later in 1679 a meeting house could not be erected without first obtaining permission from the freemen of the town or the General Court.

What the meeting houses and colonial churches have meant to posterity! These plain, white buildings, dominate the Green. The early ones with their box-like first attempts of a suggestion of a steeple, may have originated from the captain's lookout on the houses bordering the coast. Then the addition of the simple, narrow steeple, holding its own in among the green of the elms, was the beginning of the colonial architecture. Then came the ecclesiastical adaptation of the colonial preceding the Georgian period. These high, majestic, ornamental steeples that now grace so many of the New England towns, often viewed through the gothic arches of elms, are one of the greatest attractions of that delightful section of our country.

However merry the men were in erecting the houses of worship caused by the barrels of rum, they were obliged to suppress too much pleasantry, and in case of accident, not to let a slip of the tongue give forth a swear word, as it would have resulted in humiliating punishment. Swearing or using curse words were regarded as one of the greatest tricks in the devil's pack, and which was sure to lead to destruction. This could have been testified to, by two women. One for using profane language as "the Devil a bit," was severely punished; while another woman, named Goody Gregory of Springfield, became angry and said to her tormentor, "Before God, I could break thy head!" She was put in the stocks, and as one writer said, "suffered like a man."

The inhabitants of the settlements were called to meeting by the drum, and in some towns by the conch shell. Bells came later. The procession of the good folks going to church on Sunday must have been an interesting sight, and probably the artists who have painted such scenes have depicted them correctly. First came the father and mother, then the children, two by two, the eldest going first, and the line ended by the servants and negroes, as every soul in the community had to attend meeting. Church attendance in many cases must have been a great hardship. A long journey on horseback with generally two on the horse, so that progress was slow. On cold winter days it must have been painful. Then there was the "ride and tie" system, which meant a man and wife would ride a mile or two, then dismount, tie the horse to a tree, and go on foot, while another couple who had walked the first two miles, would mount the horse and go another two miles. So on until they had all ridden and walked, and finally reached the church. But what happened when the family was large, and horses scarce?

The Masons lived in a house adjoining the fort, and the first winter they were there, the house as well as the fort burnt. The family barely escaped with their lives. This necessitated building a new fortification which caused much dissatisfaction and disputes among the settlements. Hartford and especially Springfield were very much against the idea, as the Massachusetts Court wished those towns to be taxed for this purpose. Pynchon claimed that outsiders had no right to dictate to them, and that the fort at Saybrook gave them no protection. The matter was finally brought before a special session of the Commissioners of the United Colonies at Boston. Deputy-Governor Hopkins and Mason were the Commissioners from Connecticut. At the session Mason met his former antagonist Pynchon in debate, and again Mason won the victory. The new fort was built, and a dwelling house connected with it for the residence of Mason where he lived for the following ten years.

Mason and Winthrop the younger had exchanged many letters during the last several years relating principally to the Indian troubles. In 1643 the Major wrote—"I would not willingly neglect the service I owe, only in a word, there are strong plottings and endeavours, not only by Sowquesson and the Indians in our parts but allsoe, by the Nannogasetts, to procure the Mohawks to come against us, haueing sent them such quanities of wampom," and goes on to give the report of friendly Indians who had visited the plotters, and adds—"and is acknowledged by the Indians whoe are friends of them, their intendents and resolucons are as well against the English as the Monhege, only they are not yet resolved how to proceed, viz: whether to fall upon our plantacions where men are at work, or on the Lord's day, in time of meeting, or to come in a friendly way and ceese on our Sachems, as they term them: but for my part, I believe they will hardly dare to undertake such an enterprise, but I leave to God."

The Major wrote to Winthrop again in September of that year regarding the threatening trouble with the Indians, who, he said, had become "very insolent and heady. I belieue generally that the Mohawks will not meddle: and I verily belieue that they will not be so bold as to assault any English, well knowinge that they be open to apparent hazard as experience hauve somewhat taught: Yet I should encourage to the use of all meanes of defence, as if they weare in present view, but surely Sir, I am heartily sorry wee cannot afford you that supply that you desire. Truly wee are, for ought I know, not soe well furnished as I could wish, but doe intend to send up the Riuer; there is powder, I know, and match, I suppose. . . . You may command any thing wee canne possibly spare. . . . Sir, encourage your people, that they be not ouer much trobled; they scope at the monheags: they are lymited, and cannot goe beyond their tether.

"Sir be of good comfort. We hauc a Rock of Defence. If danger appeere, draw as neare together as you can; issue not out. Some are of a contrary mind, Viz: to sally out."

The threatening attitude of the Mohawks and Narragansetts was still a menace in 1648-9, and the correspondence of Mason and the governor was still filled with this subject. In a letter written in the year last mentioned, Mason assured Winthrop of the sincerity of an Indian named Wequashcucks who denied he had ever had "any hand with the Narragansetts in their plotting against Oncosor the English. I canne nothing but that he is reall. I have told Wequashcook, that if what he pretends prouve true, he need not feere any injury from the English, prouided hee keeps his couenant." He also stated that Thomas Stanton had met the Mohawks and that they had disbanded, "saying they never had any thing against us," and adds, "Sir, I will not yet conclude that the Mowhawks are gon, they are suttle."

In another letter he questions why Winthrop had imprisoned the sachem Weyquashcucks, and states that if the information he has received were correct that the chief had been bound by two "inferior men," that it was a matter of "great consequence." He had also been told that the Indian was imprisoned in Winthrop's house. "It is such a riddle that I doe not well understand, nor can I beleiue as yet. . . . I would wish he might be sett at liberty, if the case will beare it. If it be any thing that hath be (en) acted at Seebroke with mee, or in my presence, I shall be ready to answer, but if you apprehend the matter soe weighty that he cannot be sett free, then I shall desire hee may be carried to the common prison at Hartford. Sir, I would entreat this favor, that you would send me the true cause of Wequashcooks imprisonement by the bearer."

This interest in the behalf of a friendly Indian is only one of many kind acts that Mason did for the natives of New England.

The bitter feeling between the Mohegans and the Narragansetts never ceased. Both sides, and especially the leaders, were continually plotting and committing outrageous acts, even murder. On one occasion the boat of a Narragansett trader in the employ of an Englishman was driven by the wind into the Connecticut River for protection. "Onkas came aboard," writes Roger Williams to Winthrop, "and on a sudden groaned and cried out that the Narragansett had killed him! The Narragansett man denied it & Onkas showed a wound on his breast which bled fresh etc." Uncas bound the Narragansett and cut off two of his fingers which he sent to Mason. The Major came on board immediately, unbound the Indian and sent him to Hartford. Roger Williams gave what seemed proof in his letter, that the whole affair was faked by Uncas, who had wounded himself "and in a safe place" in order to get his enemies into trouble.

About the same time, Edward Hopkins wrote to Mason that the Commissioners at their last meeting at Plymouth resolved that the Pequots, who were then living at Naneag, must return to their reservation and "gave Uncas leave by violence and constraint to enforce them." Three or four men from Saybrook were to go with Uncas, and "that upon return to the Pequots to him, he due not over rule them with vigor or in a tiranicall manner, but so as they have no occasion to complaine."

These affairs were constantly happening, making continual trouble for Mason, who used every legitimate means to keep peace in the colony. The spring following his removal to Saybrook, he was ordered to go to Long Island to collect taxes from the Indians long over due. The

Island at that time was still a part, and under the jurisdiction of Connecticut.

Many of the Indians were loyal and faithful friends of
the English. The missionary work of Eliot and Stanton,
as well as others, in endeavoring to convert the Indians to
the Christian faith, met with some success, among the
poorer and scattered families, but the sachems were always
antagonistic to the missionaries. Many in later generations
embraced Christianity. The deluge that followed Fitch's
prayers for rain in 1676, made many converts. The converted natives soon became known to their fellow tribes-
men, and the whites, as the "praying Indians." One of
the most conspicuous of the converts was an Indian named
Wequashm who was so impressed by the victory of the
English in the Pequot war, that he at once embraced the
Christian religion. Later he became a preacher, and
taught his new religion among his people, only to be insulted by them, and at last poisoned. The Puritans
claimed in their hatred of the Quakers, that the "Friends"
tried to convert the Indians by giving them tracts, which
they said the Quakers claimed were better than the Bible.

The religion of the Indians consisted in worshipping
many gods, the sun, moon and planets, and some times
fire, but greater than these was one supreme spirit of all
goodness, named Mannitt. They also feared evil spirits,
especially one called Mattabo, and it seems, like their
white neighbors who came across the great waters, that
they feared Mattabo more than they loved Mannitt.
Thomas Mayhew who went as a missionary among the
Indians on Marthas Vineyard island in 1643, stated that
the natives did not believe in giving up their thirty-seven

gods for just one, though eventually he succeeded in making a few converts.

History was being made in other ways besides those of the disconcerting aborigines. At this time the preachers were having a synod in Cambridge to settle many important questions and in framing a code for church discipline, which resulted in the Westminster Confession being adopted as the doctrine of their faith. This gave the clergy complete power and control over the colony, as the inhabitants had to "obey their elders and submit themselves unto them in the Lord." The magistrates were directed to punish "idolatry, blasphemy, heresy," etc. Thus the Commonwealth of Massachusetts became a theocracy, and personal liberty was destroyed. And to quote from Brooks Adams—"the clergy held the state within their grasp, and shrank from no deed of blood to guard the interests of their order."

Connecticut and Rhode Island colonies both condemned these laws of the Bay colony, and it was owing to the stand they took against them, that the first rays of enlightenment began to spread over the New England settlements.

It was during this important convention of the clergy and in the midst of a sermon being delivered by the Rev. John Allen, that the famous serpent incident occurred, and which is best given in Winthrop's own words—

A serpent "came into the seat, where many of the elders sate behind the preacher. It came in at the door where people stood thick upon the stairs. Divers of the elders shifted from it, but Mr. Thomson, one of the elders of Brainstreet (a man of much faith), trod upon the head of it, and so held it with his foot and staff with a small pair of grains (a prong or fork, now obsolete) until it was killed. This being so remarkable, and nothing falling out but by divine providence, it is out of doubt the Lord discovered somewhat of his mind in it. The serpent is the devil: the synod, the representative of the churches of Christ in New England. The devil had formerly and lately attempted their disturbance and dissolution: but their faith in the seed of woman overcame his arm and crushed his head."

Another important happening in this year of 1648 was the first execution for witchcraft in the colonies which took place in June of that year. Margaret Jones of Charlestown was the victim. According to the records there were many proofs of her guilt. First of all she had a "malignant touch," and any man, woman or child who had the misfortune to be touched by her, whether with affection or displeasure, would become violently ill, vomit, and often be made deaf. Then she practiced medicine, and her simple remedies, which she herself claimed to be harmless, brought about such marvelous cures, that it was evident that she had diabolical powers derived from Satan, and it is said that she warned those who refused to take her concoctions, that otherwise they would never be healed. Even the best physicians or surgeons were therefore unable to break the spell or relieve the sufferer. These, with many other equally absurd statements resulted in the verdict of death, and Winthrop records in his diary, that "the same day and hour she was executed, there was a great tempest at Connexticut which blew down many trees." If the tempest was not sufficient proof of her guilt, the magistrates had further evidence, as following her execution a ship loaded with horses to be sent to the Barbados, and on which the husband of the "witch" had engaged passage, began rolling, and rolled for twelve hours.   There was much dismay at this, but the officer who had been sent to the ship to arrest Jones on account of his not having the money to pay for his passage, stated he had that which would stop the trouble and keep the ship quiet, and showed the warrant for Jones' arrest.   The result was magical, for no sooner was the poor widower put in prison than the rolling stopped.

The first record of a conviction for witchcraft in Connecticut was in 1651, "when Goodwife Basset" was convicted and hanged at Stratford, and Goodwife Knapp at Fairfield in 1653.   Winthrop records in his journal, of one that took place in Windsor in March, 1646-7, but there is no record to corroborate this statement.

The Salem witchcraft did not come until years later, when the terror had become so acute that no one felt safe from being accused of holding communion with the Devil, and having the evil eye to tempt, persecute and control others.   All the world was suffering from the same delusion at this period.   England could boast of having a "witchfinder," one Matthew Hopkins, who travelled about the country looking for the inhabitants who had sold their souls to the Devil.   For this work, he received good pay, which was doubled when he discovered a witch.   Such discoveries were very easy, as it was not difficult for him to find the riders by night on broomsticks.   All he had to do was to prick the body of the suspect with pins until he found a callous spot, which was the Devil's mark, and positive proof of the unfortunate's guilt. The more common practice was to bind the suspect, hand and foot, then throw her into a stream or pond. If she sank, she was innocent; if she floated, guilty, which meant death in either case. One of the last attempts to follow this procedure was in West Nyack, N. Y., early in the last century.

To permit a witch in a community was looked upon as dangerous as to allow a maniac or mad bull to be at large, and even worse, as the general belief was that such a criminal would win other souls to his satanic majesty. It seems almost unbelievable that such men as Luther, Kepler, Moore, Cranmer, Bacon and even Blackstone of law fame, believed in witches. The latter wrote in 1765, "To denye the possibility, nay, actual existence of witchcraft and sorcery, is at once flatly to contradict the revealed word of God in various passages both of the Old and New Testament; and the thing itself is a truth to which every nation in the world hath, in its time, borne testimony, either by example, seemingly well attested, or by prohibitory laws, which at least, suppose the possibility of commerce with evil spirits."

Not to believe in witches in Puritan days, was not to believe in God, and was the same as publicly declaring oneself an atheist, while the law read "if any man or woman be a witch, hath or consulted with a familiar spirit, shall be put to death." During this time John Eliot was attempting to convert the natives, and Anne Hutchinson was murdered in New Rochelle by the Indians.

Harvard College held its first commencement in 1642. Drunkenness in Maryland was fined by a payment of £100, while in Pennsylvania a law was passed abandoning prohibition. The Protestant Episcopal church was established at Marthas Vineyard, and Roger Williams' book, "The Bloody Tenet, a treaties against persecution," was printed. Roger Scott was tried "for common sleeping at the public services on the Lord's Day, and for striking him that waked him," and for which he was severely whipped. In New Hampshire a law was passed, that freemen and deputies were not obliged to be church members, and at the same time, Portsmouth of that colony, banished an Episcopalian minister. The New Amsterdam colony granted the "free exercise of religion to the Church of England," and in Virginia, the Episcopal church was established by law and dissenting was declared a crime. While in Maryland in 1648, Governor Thomas Greene, a Catholic, was removed and William Stone, a Protestant from Virginia was made governor. Fortunately he was very liberal in his views. During the same year, Mrs. Margaret Brent of Maryland went to the Assembly and "requested to have a vote in the house for herself and voice also."

Several attempts were made in the New England colonies to establish a more liberal government for equal rights and liberty of conscience. Among the first, William Vassal was the leader, and he endeavored to persuade the governor to put his proposition to a vote, but he was denied this privilege. Then several others joined in this petition, including Samuel Maverick, who entertained so freely and was so hospitable to all strangers. He called Winslow "a smooth tongued, cunning fellow who soon got himself into favor of those in supreme power, against whom it was in vain to strive." Winslow, however, was not as fortunate as Maverick made out, for when he went on a mission to

London he was imprisoned seventeen weeks in the Fleet for testifying against Morton. Then there were many others of note who joined this movement, as Doctor Chile, Thomas Burton and others almost as prominent, who signed the petition which asked "civil liberty and freedom be forthwith granted to all truly English . . . therefore humbly entreat you, in whose hands it is to help . . . for the glory of God . . . to give liberty to the members of the Church of England not scandalous." Then they went on to say that if their petition was not granted by the colonial government, they would petition Parliament. The result was that they were all heavily fined and either left of their own accord or were banished. Blackstone went into voluntary retirement.

Traveling became more general and taverns were more numerous, and were often kept by the best families. Boats along the shore were the most convenient manner of travel while in the interior the only means was by horseback, over narrow Indian paths. Women rode on pillions, which consisted of a cushion strapped on behind the man's saddle, and from which was suspended a platform or stirrup on which they could rest their feet. The "white hills" were first visited by an Irishman named Darby Field. His account of the sparkling white rocks, which was interpreted by his listeners as gold and diamonds, led to other adventurers to go to the White Mountains in search of the same. The Court appointed a special day for Thanksgiving. Endicott became governor of Massachusetts, and Connecticut's new code of laws was enacted.

The Dutch were having their troubles with the Indians,

which resulted in the massacre of both whites and red men. The trouble originated by an intoxicated Indian murdering a Dutchman. This enraged the Dutch settlers, but they were held in check by the governor, who was far-sighted enough to realize that the outlying settlements would suffer if war were declared. Since the citizens could not persuade the governor to act, they encouraged the Mohawks to make war on the offending tribe, killing large numbers of them. Then a Dutchman named Marine obtained permission from the governor to kill as many of the offending Indians as he could. Some historians say as many as eighty men, women and children were slain. This aroused, as Gardiner would have said, "the wasps" so that the whole of the Dutch colony was embroiled in a bloody Indian war; then, when it actually occurred, the inhabitants condemned the governor for causing it. His life for a time was in danger from the anger of his own people.

It seems that Marine's jealousy was aroused by the governor's calling in Captain Patrick, and he threatened the governor with his pistol, but was prevented firing, by another soldier. Then one of Marine's men fired at the governor, but missing, was caught, decapitated, and his head set on the gallows. Marine was sent a prisoner to Holland.

In an account given in a letter by Mason to Winthrop, dated Windsor, 1643, he tells how Captain Patrick, who took a prominent part in the Swamp Fight, had gotten himself in bad repute with the Dutch to whom he had fled after his trouble with the Massachusetts authorities. He had persuaded a large number of the Dutch colony to go against the Indians, with whom Patrick had had some misunderstanding. A quarrel resulted, and Patrick spoke roughly to the leader, spat in his face, and turned to leave. The Dutchman shot him in the head killing him instantly. This all took place in the house of Captain Underhill at Stanford on the Lord's Day, November 2, 1643. Winthrop records that Massachusetts had raised him to captain, admitted him to the church, made him a freeman, and paid him a salary, whereupon "he grew proud and vicious, for though he had a wife of his own, a good Dutch woman and comely, yet he despised her and followed after other women," which was the cause of his dismissal from that colony. This account tallies with the trouble Mason had with Patrick at the end of the Pequot War, when he endeavored to run matters to suit himself, and refused at first to allow the wounded to be taken on the shallop on which he and his men had sailed to Pequot harbor.

This same year the Puritans of Virginia asked for ministers of their faith to aid their cause, and the request was answered by four preachers sailing to that colony. They met with many hardships and were weeks en route, but had still greater trouble on their arrival, as the Church of England was established by the magistrates, and was the law of the land, so that it was not long before these "godly ministers" were driven from their new homes, and returned to New England. It was providential for them, as soon after the great Indian massacre occurred, April 18, 1644, when large numbers of the colonists were slain and their homes burned. It was following this trouble, that many migrated to the northern colonies.

During this period the French Captain La Tour made

several visits to the colonies, where he and his crew were treated with consideration, but criticism was aroused by the authorities permitting Papists such frequent inter-course with the planters, until finally the magistrates and deputies were called to discuss "whether it were lawful for christians to aid idolaters, and how far we may have com-munion with them?"   Also, there was a fear that by aiding La Tour they might offend France, with whom the captain was not on good terms, and the colonists could not afford to antagonize such a powerful nation, which might result in war.

In spite of the austerity of the times, where the Bible and book of Psalms were considered sufficient to supply the intellectual needs of the community, there were at-tempts at writing by some of the gifted, which was the beginning of literature in the northern English colonies. William Pynchon's book "the Meritorius price of our Re-demtion, Justification, Etc., clearing it from Common Error" was published at this time in London.   It shocked the magistrates and the public of the colonies because some of it was contrary to the doctrines of the church, and there-fore heretical.   It finally led to the author's returning to England where he remained the rest of his life.   Anne Bradstreet's poems appeared, and were relished by an in-tellectually starved people.   Knowing the prejudice against woman's attempts to aspire to any higher sphere than household duties, and to forestall such criticisms, she wrote in her prologue—

> "I am obnoxious to each carping tongue
> Who says my hand a needle better fits,
> A Poet's pen all scorn I thus should wrong.

For such despite they cast on Female wits;
If what I do prove well, it won't advance,
They'll say it's stoln, or else it was by
chance."

Even the preachers paid her compliments on her
achievement, and in the preface were several eulogies from
prominent ministers.   Rev. John Rogers wrote that he
had read the poems twice, "drank the nectar" of her verse,
and "weltered in delight."   Rev. Nathaniel Ward, who
believed in keeping woman in her place, wrote—

"It half revives my chil frost bitten blood,
To see a Woman once, do aught that's good;
And chode by Chaucers Boot, and Homer's furs
Let Men look to't, least Women wear the Spurs."

In her poem entitled "The Four Monarchies" which
gives Raleigh's "History of the World" in rhyme, she again
speaks in defence of her own sex when referring to Elizabeth, and which was very daring for her time.   It reads:

"She hath wiped off th' aspersions of her sex
That women wisdom lack to play the Rex.

.   .   .   .

"Now say, have women worth? or have they none?
Or had they some, but with our queen is't gone?
Nay, Masculine, you have thus taxed us long;
But she, though dead, will vindicate our wrong.
Let such as say our Sex is void of reason,
Know 'tis Slander now, but once was Treason."

Verse was used upon every occasion at this period. On elegies, epitaphs, acrostics and anagrams, and even puns about the dead were often passed about for the amusement of the survivors. Lady Mary Montagu said all England was a jingle, and that verse making was as common as taking snuff. While Tyler adds, that in "New England, it was much more common than taking snuff, since there were some who did not take snuff." The vogue had followed the settlers to the new country, and even Captain John Smith lapsed into verse in his histories of his voyages. Poems of length were only attempted by the few, but jingling rhymes seemed contagious and were used for births, marriages, deaths, or funerals, as the old tombstones of past years can testify. The preachers were no exception to this habit, and the Rev. John Wilson, who was so bitter against Anne Hutchinson and the Quakers, never allowed an opportunity to pass without commemorating the event by some verse, which is referred to on his epitaph, as follows—

"His care to guide his flock and feed his lambs,
  By words, works, prayers, psalms, alms and anagrams."

The first few lines of the epitaph of Jonathan Mitchell are—

  "Here lies the darling of his time
    Mitchell expired in his prime;
    Who four years short of fifty-seven,
    Was found full ripe and plucked for heaven."

In 1642, the first representative Assembly was held in the colonies, and in Rhode Island the first declaration of democracy was declared, when the citizens adopted a constitution giving "civil liberty, justice and equality to all." Some time before this, in 1641 to be exact, Roger Williams' colony had declared "that it is ordered that none shall be accounted a delinquent for doctrine." Even after the abuse the Boston authorities had heaped on the Rhode Island settlers, many of whom it had banished, they tried to persuade them to return to the Puritan fold, and when they refused, Boston tabulated them as "Heathens and Publicans." Most of the doctrines of tolerance originated with Roger Williams who carried on his work as peace-maker not only in New England, but also in the Dutch colony where he established peace between the Dutch and the Mohawks, and which was celebrated in New Amsterdam by a Thanksgiving day. The abuse and unfair treatment of the Indians in New Amsterdam was a repetition of what occurred in all of the other colonies, and which always led to bloodshed. The planters of Rhode Island, in spite of their friendliness towards the natives, had many occasions not only to complain, but were sufficiently outraged by them, to have gone to war. All of this trouble the planters of that settlement attributed to the indulgence the Puritans gave to the Mohegans, and a planter named Holly openly accused the New Englanders in his letter to Winthrop of encouraging "the outrageous Uncas," and his band of perpetrating crime in the Rhode Island territory.

In a letter that Williams wrote to Winthrop about this time, one detects a bit of sarcasm, as the Rhode Islander could never become reconciled to the Captain's friendship for Uncas. "Pardon," he wrote, "if I request you in my name to transfer the papers to Capt. Mason, who saith he loves me; God is love in him, only I desire to be yours forever."

The planters saw the need of encouraging manufacturing, and three hundred acres were offered to any one who would erect an iron factory in Massachusetts introducing the industrial age for which New England would be noted. Young Winthrop was one of the first to take an active part in this line of work.

What was happening in the rest of the world, then so far away from New England, the new country that now claimed twelve independent groups, and twenty-one thousand inhabitants. Coffee, that delicious stimulant, was first introduced in Europe by the Dutch. The Thirty Years War was still going on, though nearing its end, while the civil war in England was practically over with the execution of King Charles. Germany had invented the magic lantern, and had made the first map of the moon. The pendulum was made by Galileo. The Irish celebrated a St. Ignatius day, by killing thousands of Protestants. The London Gazette was published and John Evelyn was writing his diary. The famous painter Van Dyck died. In France Richelieu still ruled under Louis who was having his platonic affairs with mademoiselles Louise de la Fayette and Marie d'Hautefort, one of whom retired to a convent, and the other lived in exile. Then came Cinq-Mars, the handsome young man, who was first loaded with wealth and honors, but ended on the scaffold. When writing to his mother just previous to the fatal hour, he said, "Now that I make not a single step which does not lead me to death, I am more capable than anybody else, of estimating the value of the things of this world." Anne of Austria, Louis' queen, was intriguing against him with his enemy, Philip of Spain. Then came the infant Louis Fourteenth to the throne, and Cardinal Mazarin was in power.

Little New England so far away was growing, and was already recognized as a power in the commercial world with her exports of furs, horses, lumber, hemp and grain, prophesying the flourishing years to come.

The success and prosperity of the Connecticut colony once more aroused a feeling in Massachusetts of jealousy. They still claimed their rights to the Pequot territory, basing the same on the aid they claimed they had given during the Indian war. At the session of the Court in 1657, Major Mason, as the legal representative for Connecticut, stated the claims of his colony. He said the land was in the patent given by the original proprietors,— by the apparent consent to Connecticut's ownership for the last several years—by the right of conquest, as the men of his colony had won the Pequot war. The Massachusetts authorities were equally as positive in their claims of ownership, one of the proofs was to the effect that the country had been occupied first by one of their planters, who erected a house on the land, and that Winthrop who was of their colony and a magistrate of it at the time, had settled on the west side of the river. To which Mason replied—"You mention a possession house; which house was in the Pequot country, being on the west side of the river, and again deserted and most of it carried away by yourselves before any English again possessed it." He also argued that the Pequots had no right to the land west of the river, and as to the claim that Massachusetts had any rights from the result of the Pequot war, he added—"If the English should have beaten the Flemings out of Flanders and they fly into another domain;—if the French there meet the English and join with them to pursue the Flemings, would that give the French a right to Flanders?" The matter was not finally adjusted until 1665.

CHAPTER XII

JOHN WINTHROP, governor of Massachusetts, died March 26, 1649, and was one of the first of the original leaders of the Puritans to be taken by the Grim Reaper. The longevity of the early settlers is evidence of the sturdy constitutions which these people had, or they could not have survived so many years under the strains and hardships of the pioneer's life. Winthrop came from an old English family, and therefore had the intellectual advantages that affluence gives. Losing his position as a magistrate in 1629, owing to his Puritanical leanings, he became interested in the Massachusetts Company, and was one of several hundred passengers who sailed to New England in 1630. From the first he took a prominent part in the affairs of the settlement. He was elected governor twelve times, and history regards him as one of the most enlightened men of his time in the colony. Although of a kindly nature in private, in public office he was a dictator, and he encroached upon the power of the deputies, as he was convinced that his way was right. He felt the importance of his position, and regardless of his pronounced religious convictions, never appeared in public without wearing his ruff, and being attended by sergeants carrying halberds. At the session of the Court in March, 1635, it was ordered that at every General Court, six men chosen by the governor were to attend on him with halberds and swords. His portrait, ascribed to Van Dyck, hangs in the

Massachusetts senate room.   His diary, generally referred
to as "the Winthrop Papers," throws much light on the
customs and history of the early colony.   The decisions he
made against Anne Hutchinson, are, perhaps, the greatest
criticism that can be held against him.

It was appropriate that a man holding such a position
in the government and who was looked upon as the father
and chief founder of the colony, should be buried with
all the honors befitting a man of his standing.   Military
honors were given at the burial of prominent men.   The
militia with Major Mason as the leader of the Connecticut
forces, and a Commissioner as well, and all of the other
prominent people of the United Colonies were present at
Winthrop's burial.   A barrel of powder was used to do
honor to the great man's name.

It was the custom for the militia when present at burials
to fire a salute over the graves, and it is recorded that this
honor on special occasions had even been paid at the
graves of women.   Gloves were always given away at
funerals, and as early as 1635 it had become a habit to such
an extent that later it was known that as many as three
thousand pairs were given at one funeral.   Rev. Eliot of
the North Church of Boston had collected two thousand,
nine hundred and forty pairs of gloves in a period of
thirty-two years, and as he could not use them himself, and
having an eye to economy, sold the lot for an amount of
£140.   At the same time he was able to sell a quantity of
mourning rings that had also been given to him.   Rings
were another funeral custom of the day.   These mourning
rings were often quite elaborate, sometimes plain gold, but
often enameled in black and white with death's heads, a

coffin, or a skeleton engraved upon them. They also often had such cheerful mottoes as "prepare for death," and the like, while some rings bore the family coat-of-arms.

Meats and liquid refreshments were always plentiful at funerals, and sometimes to the detriment of the solemnity of the occasion. It is even suspected that this may have been the reason for the always large attendance. This was well illustrated when the custom slowly died out, as temperance came in, by an old gentleman's exclaiming— "Temperance has done for funerals!"

It is not possible to pass this subject without referring to Judge Sewall's diary, as he seemed fascinated with that morbid subject. It was customary for him to visit the family tomb and he states, when doing so, that he was "entertained" by the coffins of his "Father and Mother" and his six own children, and adds— " 'Twas an awful, yet pleasing treat."

The poorer people, however, could not indulge in all that went with the funerals of the rich, but the event was one of great reverence and much curiosity, as there was so little at the time to break the monotony. There was always the making of wills, if the patient was still able to make one, and in such cases, the first paragraph stated that the dying man gave his soul to God, etc., and then there would be a list of gifts, which today are the inventories of the households of the colonists. Such articles as a spoon to one heir, a gown to another, told of the meager furnishings and personal property of the planters. The dead were generally carried on biers to their last resting place on the shoulders of friends, and sometimes they were brought some distance from their homes in the country to the settlements, as private cemeteries or burying grounds were not common in the first days of the settlements, though later they were numerous.

If our worthy ancestors were tempted to attend funerals owing to the repasts offered, they can be pardoned, for New England soon gained renown for its hospitality and well-filled larders. Tables were said to groan with the good things to eat. Sewall records a dinner his wife gave to some professional nurses when the menu consisted of "boiled Pork, Beef, Fowls; a very good roast Beef, Turkey-Pye, Tarts." This repast seems equal to one described by Samuel Pepys as "being poor," as they only had "a couple of fowles, some venison pasty, a leg of lamb," etc. It must not be forgotten that our ancestors did not have many of the dainties of today. There was no tea, nor coffee at first, while sugar and molasses were only had in small quantities until the Barbados and West Indies trade was opened about 1660.

There were other distractions besides funerals to enliven the monotony of work and worship, and this too, even though a law was passed in 1656 which read "that any person or persons, of what rank or quality so ever, in the Jurisdiction shall, after publication of this order, play at Cards, Dice," or any other games would be subject to a heavy fine. Christmas and other holidays were also forbidden, as they were thought to savor too much of papacy. This prejudice against holy days became more pronounced in the passing of time until in 1659, when a law was passed that any one observing Christmas would be fined five shillings. In Narragansett, which was settled by members of the Church of England, two weeks were devoted to celebrating this festive occasion. April fool's day jokes were practiced, though condemned by the clergy, who never saw any good in pleasure, and only a few of them had any sense of humor. Thanksgiving days were proclaimed in the autumn, and then, like now, great feasts were held. Hunting and fishing were always encouraged, but they were looked upon as a necessity, and not regarded as sport.

Some of the so-called sports were brought over from England where they had been popular for years, so that wolf baiting was practiced in all of its cruelty. Josselyn gives the following account of such an event: "A great mastiff held the wolf. . . . Tying him to a stake, we bated him with small doggs, and had excellent sport, but his hind leggs being broken, we soon knocked his brains out." The carcases of dead animals often found in the woods showed that they had been trapped in a barbarous manner, such as mackerel hooks in a piece of meat.

Four greyhounds had been brought over from Ireland to help destroy wolves. Later other breeds from England were especially imported for this "sport," and they soon became so numerous that they were a pest. Trained to pursue Indians and wolves, they became vicious and killed cattle as well, so that laws were enacted to destroy many of them.

In spite of laws, youth could not be kept from the enjoyment of the dance which gradually came in. Those who first attempted anything so frivolous and unreligious, must have done so with fear, and possessed great courage and daring. Such gaieties did not continue long before a law was passed to make some discrimination, so that in

1651 all "mixt and unmixed" dancing at weddings given in taverns was forbidden.   One description of a dance is worth relating, which took place in New London in the latter part of the eighteenth century.   There were 92 jigs, 50 contra-dances, 43 minuets and 17 hornpipes, so that it is a fair question to ask when the dance began and ended. But gay affairs were often broken by a day or week of solemn prayer.   In 1655, a day of prayer and fasting was observed on account of reports in England that Quakers would destroy all the churches in the land.   Two weeks later two women missionaries of that sect arrived and received anything but a kindly welcome.   This resulted in a new law being put in force a few months later fining any town or person who entertained "Quakers, Ranters, Adamites, or such like notorious heritiques," if they permitted them to remain in the town over fourteen days.

Some years previous to this time, namely in 1652, a party of the citizens of New Haven decided after much argument and meditation, to move to Delaware, and desiring a competent leader, wished Major Mason to act in that capacity.   No sooner had the magistrates learned of this than they requested Mason to give up the idea and remain the head of the military staff.   A Court record dated October 9, 1651, mentioned receiving a letter from Mason regarding the proposed Delaware settlement.   The magistrates replied, stating that it was their desire of the "Whole court, that he would not entertain thoughts of removing his abode out of this colony, whereunto they can give the least allowance of approbation, yet if his own desire be for the present service of that place, and their importunities continue for his employment there, the court can not wholly deny him to them; the work being that which they are willing to promote; but are content he shall attend the service three months, provided he will engage himself to return within that time and continue his abode as formerly."

Messages had been sent to Governor Stuyvesant announcing the decision of the colonists to make a settlement at Delaware, which so enraged the Dutch governor that he arrested the messengers, and notified the New Haven authorities that if any of the English went to Delaware, he would not only seize their property, but arrest them and send them prisoners to Holland. The Connecticut authorities told the proposed emigrants that Connecticut could not spare any men who could bear arms. It was impossible to overcome all of these obstacles, and consequently the Delaware settlement never took place.

In 1653 and the year following there was much agitation in New England caused by the declaration of war between England and Holland. All of the colonies, save Massachusetts, realized that the war would be carried to this side of the water, and prepared at once to strengthen their defenses, but it took time which was usually the case, before the Bay state could be made to recognize the danger. Cromwell had anticipated this situation and had sent Major Sedgwick and Captain Leverett with a small fleet and land force to combat the Dutch. At the request of Sedgwick, the Court sent Mason and Mr. Cullick to plan the defense. They were also commissioned to go to Boston and endeavor to persuade Massachusetts to raise five hundred men to help meet the emergency. But as peace was declared after the Dutch fleet was defeated in the English channel, the commission was abandoned.

The Connecticut colony had had trouble from the first with the Dutch, and as time passed the situation became more acute. When Peter Stuyvesant arrived as governor of Manhattan in May, 1647, succeeding Governor Kieft, instead of the disputes being adjusted, they grew to such proportions that they became a menace to the peace of the two colonies. In 1648, Stuyvesant ordered the Dutch to seize an English boat owned by one Westhouse, and imprisoned the crew. Some murders were committed, and matters reached a crucial point. Finally, after several invitations, Governor Stuyvesant went to Hartford in September, 1650, to meet the Commissioners, when it was hoped that the difficulties could be adjusted satisfactorily to all concerned, and the meeting seemingly ended harmoniously. However, the same year a Dutchman named Augustus Harriman was arrested at Saybrook "for illicit trading with the Indians." He was fined £40. According to the English version, Stuyvesant was again aggressive in 1653 when it was claimed he made an agreement with the Indians to enlist their services in war on the English, with the hope of exterminating them, or at least conquering the country. That Ninigret the sachem of the Nihanticks, who had caused continual trouble between the different tribes, and who had become a pest to the planters, was said to be an ally of Stuyvesant's. That he had spent the previous winter with him in New Amsterdam. That he even visited the tribes west of the Hudson to enlist them in the anticipated war against the English colonies.

In the meanwhile the Dutch governor wrote letters of admiration to the Connecticut Court in which he expressed surprise that they would believe the statements of several Indians of different tribes. The English claimed they had investigated the report that had come to them regarding the plans of the Dutch, who, they believed, were waiting reinforcements from Holland before beginning actual warfare. Stuyvesant denied all of the accusations brought against him by the Connecticut Court. The fact that he had willingly gone to Hartford to meet the Commissioners, that he had appointed two Englishmen who resided in Dutch territory to represent him in negotiating a treaty of peace, and that he had offered to go to Boston at the request of the Commissioners, together with the conciliatory letters he wrote, indicates that there were two sides to the question.

The magistrates of Connecticut had realized the danger of this combination of the Dutch and Ninigret's Indians, and had used every argument to convince the Bay colony of the necessity of their aid, but they were deaf to all entreaties, and appeared not to care that the settlers of the Connecticut valley were worn out keeping watch day and night. In speaking of this criminal neglect by Massachusetts, Trumbull said—"Few instances occur in history, of so flagrant and obstinate a violation of a covenant, so solemnly made, as this of the general court of Massachusetts. . . . What interest Massachusetts made by thus favoring the Dutch, is not known." Fortunately the defeat of the Dutch fleet, and the death of Admiral Tromp, resulted in the Dutch suing for peace, which was concluded in April, 1654.

Many of the Connecticut settlers were still so incensed by the actions of their Dutch neighbors that they wished to go to war even though peace had been established between the two mother-countries. Roger Ludlow was the leading spirit among these dissenters and owing to the active part he had taken to attack the Dutch without authority resulted in his moving with his family to Virginia, and the historians state that he took the Fairfield town records with him. It was not until August, 1664, that the Dutch capitulated to the English and New Amsterdam became New York, named in honor of the Duke of York, brother of the king.

The troubles with the Dutch were not the only menace to the peace in the Connecticut valley, as the natives were always plotting against each other which generally resulted in murder or war between some of the tribes. Ninigret, a sachem of the Nihantics, who had married his daughter to the brother of Sassacus, to strengthen his influence over the intriguing Indians, was the cause of continual trouble for the whites. He united the Pocomtocks, and Mohawks, and other tribes to war on the English and to destroy the Mohegans. His machinations and secret warfare was the greatest Indian menace since the Pequot war. When the authorities learned of this federation and their plans, they sent Thomas Stanton, the well-known interpreter, to consult with Ninigret as they wished to prevent an Indian war. Stanton discovered that the Indians were actually prepared for war, having four hundred firearms and plenty of ammunition. The Mohawks did not keep their pledge, the Pocomtocks, though well armed, hesitated to go to war when they learned that the English were prepared to meet them, and the Narragansetts were obliged to abandon their purpose at that time, but never the idea. They were troubling the settlers of Rhode Island, in spite of the good services of Roger Williams, and had proven that they were not to be trusted. Ninigret had planned to reestablish the Pequot Indians on their old lands, and defy the English, but after some time the remaining members of the Pequots asked to be freed from the control of Uncas, to end their connections with Ninigret, and to be under the jurisdiction of the English. This arrangement was finally made, giving them a grant of land on the Mystic River. They made two settlements, each having its own Indian chief. The whites made special laws for them among which they were forbidden to practice witchcraft against the colonists.

Ninigret was committing outrages against the Indians on Long Island. When he was asked to give his oath against warring on them, he refused, saying that the Indians there had begun the trouble by killing his son and sixty of his men. Therefore, would the English governor ask a commission the privilege of avenging the murder of his son? He said he would not go to Hartford, nor would he stop attacking his enemies on the Island.

Massachusetts again hesitated to aid the other settlements against the rising danger of Ninigret's federation, leaving all the work to the other plantations. When they sent Major Willard to attack Ninigret's band, he simply returned upon learning that the Indians had hidden in the swamps, which gave greater confidence to the savages, as it proved to them the timidity of the whites, and resulted in greater trouble later. In all of the Indian conflicts in New England, it is known that had Massachusetts acted with more promptness and sincerity, and had joined the other colonies, much bloodshed and expense would have been prevented. The Massachusetts authorities vacillated, and left it to the other settlements to stand the brunt of the difficulties they were continually encountering.

When the Indian hostilities broke out anew on Long Island, Major Mason was ordered there once more to try and establish peace and break up the league, which he apparently did at the time. But again, three years later he was obliged to undertake the same task, and this time was more successful. The Court showed their appreciation of the services Mason rendered to the colony when they sent word to him that "We do not judge it convenient that you should in your own person make after any Indian in the woods." And again at the session of the Court at Hartford, May 16, 1650, which consisted of thirty-two members, a grant was made to Mason of a thousand acres of land for his valuable services in the Pequot war. Of this amount, five hundred were to be given to his officers and men, and five hundred for himself. The acreage given to Mason's soldiers was to be laid out in plots in the Pequot country. The following year the Court granted Mason in addition to what they had already given him, Chippahauge Island, since known as Mason Island, in Mystic bay, and a hundred and ten acres of land at Mystic.

A strange message was sent to the settlers from Oliver Cromwell by Goodkin in 1665. Which was, "that since the English had captured Jamaica, why would it not be a good idea for the people of New England, who were so harassed by the natives and weather conditions in the northern colonies, to remove and settle in this land of perpetual sunshine and summer," and added, that "it would have the tendency to the destruction of the man of sin." Governor Eaton on whom special persuasion had been brought to bear to carry out this idea, and who had consulted the other settlements, wrote at the order of the Court the following decision—"that, though they could not but acknowledge the love, care and tender respect of his highness the Lord Protector, to New England in general, and to this colony (New Haven), in particular, yet, for divers reasons they cannot conclude that God calls them to a present remove thither." It is evident that Cromwell had more political reasons for wishing this emigration than for propagating his religon. He had previously made a similar proposal after he had conquered Ireland, for them to move to that island.

Uncas at this time was causing trouble for the planters. He assaulted different Indians of other tribes, seeming to believe that he was a law unto himself, since he had the protection of the whites. He antagonized the Podunks, Norwootucks, and continually scoffed at the Narragansetts, ridiculing their dead sachem. He even leagued with the impossible Ninigret at times, in committing the same kind of outrages. The Court censured him severely, and threatened punishment unless he mended his conduct. Besides the troubles the planters were having with Ninigret, Uncas and the Narragansetts, members of other tribes were also committing murders of a most revolting kind. There was never any surety of unbroken peace. There was always the threat and fear of an Indian outbreak or massacre. We can scarcely imagine what indomitable courage our ancestors possessed to enable them to overcome constant danger, strife and almost insurmountable obstacles.

Letters were continually passing between Mason and Winthrop. Sometimes the Major addressed the governor as "The Right Worshipful, John Winthrop, Esq.," and some times "To the Worshipful, my much honored friend, Mr. Jno. Winthrop in Nameage these with trusts." Mason always used this formality when writing to any office holder, and invariably did so when addressing Winthrop, notwithstanding the warm friendship existing between them. He generally sent his regards to Mrs. Winthrop, and sometimes his love to all. It is evident that the two familes exchanged visits. In a letter Mason wrote to Mrs. Elizabeth Winthrop, he tells of sending her ten apple trees and thirty grafted ones. In 1648 he recounts the arrival of a ship from London after a six weeks' passage, which "brought many printed proclamations concerning the peace being concluded between the States of England and the Netherlands, with many letters tending to that purpose."

May 27, 1654, the Major wrote Winthrop—"We received your letter with the physick, which you are pleased to send to my wife, for which, as alsoe sundry other favours, we stand deeply engaged, but in any measure to requite, at present I see it not; yet we shall not remaine altogether foregetfull nor ungratefull. My wife as yet remaineth ill, yet some times a little re (u)ouein with the addition of somewhat more strength. Newes there is little." In several of his letters he refers to Winthrop's interest in his wife's health, and expresses his appreciation for the medicine he has sent her, as Winthrop had acquired a reputation as a physician in the colony and often treated the sick. In one missive, Mason wrote that his wife was no better since the Governor had last seen her, and he pathetically adds, "my wife is yet under the afflicting hand of God."

There were always troubles to be adjusted between individuals of both races, and Mason wrote the governor how his servant had unlawfully taken a canoe from the Indian Wequashcook. In another he told of an Indian woman being murdered by the "Nayantuck" tribe which occurred in 1657, and continuing said that she was killed by some of Ninigret's men, who "were always sculkinge near our townes; truly, Sir, I looke at it as a matter unreasonable, as alsoe very unsafe to suffer Indians to manage and maineteine a seat of warre at and in our very bowells; not making it appeer that they haue any ground to make warre at all; and if they should make cleere that they haue beene wronged, then I conceiue that those that live amongs us should eyther make the injured due satisfaction, or be enforced to depart from our borders. In my apprehension we act like men eyther a sleepe or affrayed. Certainly there is a great apathy and confusion amongs us, and if the Lord help not, we may soon feele the smart of it."

August 22, 1659, Mason wrote Winthrop that the sachem Namcet and fifty men went to the house of Benjamin Brewster, accused him of "entertaining Mohegans," ransacked the house, stole articles, etc., and added, "I shall say little, because I know it is to little purpose; yet am very apt to think if Annumpequum had beene thoroughly dealt with upon his shamefull intollerable abuse of our men at Pocomptuck, his barbarous plunderings at

Hockananco and his extreame pryde and insolency at Tunxis; but I hope those whoe are soe sollicitous to preuent a warre with theyre lenity and forbearance, will be as forward to proscecute.   You now understand what to expect from them, Viz—If they doe but pretend that theire enemies are in any Eng. howse they will forcibily make search, and allsoe plunder at pleasure, where they can preuayle.   Ouermuch lenity, as I haue often said, proues just security, etc but I ceese, fearing list I troble."   Then adds a postscript saying that no Indians were found in Mr. Brewster's house as "they made search."   It would seem by this letter that the country, even at that time, had its "sob sisters."

When Mason referred in his letter to Winthrop to his wife still being under the "afflicting hand of God," he reflected the belief of the people regarding chastisements, for according to the training of the Puritans, everything good or bad emanated from the desire of the Lord. If it was good, it was his blessing; if it was bad, it was proof that they needed chastisement, and when they were chastised, they should submit with grace to the affliction bestowed.   Such idolatry and fear is not to be wondered at when one realizes that from the child's earliest years, it was taught the terrors of death and the pitfalls that lead to eternal damnation.   Perhaps this idea of blessings and afflictions is well illustrated by the following incident recorded of our early ancestors.

In describing the attractions of New England, Josselyn said, that they had "heaps upon heaps of the Richests of Christ's tender compassionate mercies, being turned off from his dangling knees, began to read their approaching rod in the bend of his brows and frowns of his former favorable countenance toward them," and goes on to say "Also the Lord was pleased to awaken us with an army of catterpillars, that had he not suddenly rebuked them, they had surely destroyed the husbandman's hopes—When they fell upon trees, they left them winter wasting cold, here, and naked." Then later the Lord "cast them into the high ways, that the Cartwheels in their passing were painted green with running over the great swarms of them —in some fields they devoured the leaves of the peas." And again, "also the Lord was pleased to command the world and Seas to give us a jog on the elbow, by sinking the very chief of our shipping in the deep, and splitting them to slivers against the shores."

In the summer of 1648 there were unusual phenomena in the animal world, or such they appeared to the planters. One was evidently the seventeen-year locusts, judging from the description given by Winthrop, which hc said, "filled the woods from Connecticut to Sudbury with a great noise." The other was flocks of pigeons that came in such numbers that they obstructed the sunlight, and were so numerous that they were killed in enormous quantities, eight or ten dozen to the man, and one shot would kill several birds, which was an illustration "as how the Lord could make a blessing of that which formerly was a curse."

The disturbed political conditions in England were learned by the arrival of every ship, and the changes taking place had their effect on the colonies. It had already become known that Charles II had been invited to Scotland and had led an army into England only to be defeated, so that he was obliged to flee to Normandy. This showed the change that was coming over the people in the homeland, and as usual, the northern country was taking the lead.   Charles settled for a while in Paris where his mother lived.   Neither of them received much recognition from the French court, and they were so reduced financially, that often during the cold winter months the ex-queen of England, the daughter of Henry IV of France, was obliged to remain in bed in order to keep warm.   The English parliament which was so remiss in forwarding the queen her pension pretended to resent this treatment of their former ruler's consort, and they took the occasion to show their anger by seizing supplies being shipped to France.   The feeling became so strained against the exiles in France that Charles left the country of his own will, rather than be asked to go.

Winthrop and Mason were seriously watching the politics of England, realizing the effects they might have on New England.   Winthrop had been chosen governor of Connecticut in 1657.   Like his father, the late governor of Massachusetts, he was a man of culture.   When still a young man he had been admitted to the bar in England.   Tiring of that, he joined the navy, and served under the Duke of Buckingham in his attack on Rochelle.   He soon decided that being an officer in the British Admiralty was not to his liking, so that for the next fourteen months he traveled over Europe, even going to Turkey, and ended his trip at Boston, in 1631.   Three years later he returned to the mother-country, but in 1635 he was commissioned governor of the Warwick patent of Connecticut and set sail once more for the American colonies.   This time he remained until 1641 when he made a two years' visit to

London. While there he became one of the founders of
the Royal Society. Winthrop was a highly educated man
and had a library of over a thousand volumes. His tact,
and pleasing personality, together with his progressive
ideas and promotion of all public interest for the public
good, endeared him to the planters. He became their
choice for governor in 1657, filling that position, with the
exception of one term, for many years to come. He was
the founder of New London, later removed to New Haven,
but when he became governor of Connecticut, he was requested to settle at Hartford. Up to this time he had also
been a magistrate of Massachusetts, and following his one
year as governor he became deputy-governor. He was so
popular that the law was changed and public officers were
allowed to succeed themselves, which made it possible for
Winthrop to remain governor of Connecticut until his
death in 1676. Keeping up the position was as difficult,
apparently in the early colonial days as later, for in 1667
when Winthrop refused to again accept the nomination as
chief executive, he stated that he could not continue to
hold the office in justice to himself and family, as the finan-
cial tax was too great a drain on his resources. The assembly agreed to free him from all taxation, and in addition
to grant him one hundred and ten pounds out of the public treasury. He was finally prevailed to remain in office.

An interesting anecdote regarding Winthrop when he
resided in New London, gives another side of his character. It was forbidden for a couple to be married outside
of their parish, as well as requiring the ceremony to be
performed by a magistrate in the same precinct. Gen-

erally there were no occasions to dispute this ruling, but in March, 1672, when one Thomas Rudd and his sweetheart of Lyme wished to wed, they found that the magistrates were away. Winthrop was the nearest one holding an official position, but he resided in New London. It was then that Winthrop aided the lovers, by standing on one side of the stream that divided the two parishes, and the wedding couple on the other. In this way, he kept within the strict rules of the law, and performed the ceremony that united the happy couple.

At the election that made Winthrop Governor, May 17, 1660, Mason was elected Deputy-Governor, an office he held until his health gave out shortly before his death.

Cromwell's power in England was recognized throughout all Christendom, in which he made alliances or war. Even the haughty Cardinal Mazarin, who hated the Protector, appeared humble and paid court. Cromwell's stubbornness combined with his crudeness and lack of tact and his gross attempts at humor undermined him in the hearts of the people, causing many of his followers, and even those he raised to high positions, to drop away. The Protector's power lay with the soldiers, but when he lost their confidence the end of his dominion was near. Conditions became so intolerable that he no longer trusted his spies, and the fear of the assassin's knife haunted his imagination like a hideous nightmare, so that when death came in 1658 it proved a blessing.

All of these conditions seeped through many sources to the colonies, much exaggerated, but always containing grains of truth. The people in the plantations, like those in the mother-country, were speculating as to the changes that were about to take place, and as to how it would affect them.

The proclamation that raised Richard Cromwell, the eldest son of the late Protector as a successor to his father, was of small consolation. He was a man unknown to the world—one who had hitherto led a private life and was quite uninterested and uninformed regarding politics. The soldiers forsook his banner, many of them joining Fleetwood's forces, among them such supporters of the late Protector as Fitz, Mason, Moss and Farley. Richard was soon deposed. An incident happened soon after this event when Richard, traveling under an assumed name on the Continent, was introduced to the Prince of Conti. The Prince expressed great admiration of the late Protector when the conversation turned on England. He considered Cromwell a great man. "But," he added, "what has become of that poor, pitiful fellow Richard? How could he be such a blockhead as to reap no greater benefit from all of his father's crimes and success?"

The reports of the great changes that were occurring in England caused Winthrop and Mason to watch every move as best they could at that distance. They anticipated events with a foresight that was later crowned with success. With the advent of General Monk's invasion of England, his successful encounters against the Parliamentary forces, these two executives at the head of their colony realized that it meant the restoration of the Stuarts on the throne. What result that would have on New England, as Mason said, "was a riddle." It was decided by Winthrop and Mason, backed by the Connecticut authorities, for the Governor to go to England with a petition to the King, for a charter, forestalling their being deprived of their rights.   During Winthrop's absence, Mason filled the executive office.

CHAPTER XIII

SEVERAL of the planters of Saybrook, including Rev. James Fitch, had joined Major Mason in his project to form a settlement in the Yantic valley. The idea had originated with the Major, who, as one of the founders of Windsor, and whose presence had awakened interest in the settlement at Saybrook, combined with his authority as a leader, made him, as Miss Caulkins said, "the prime mover and ruling spirit of the undertaking." His dealings with the Indians had taken him several times to their country with which he had become well acquainted. This, together with his friendship with Uncas, assured safety for the establishment of a settlement in that outlying district. The idea had been considered for some time, but no definite steps were taken until the spring of 1659, when on May 20, the Court at Hartford considered the "petition presented by the inhabitants of Saybrook, doe declare yet they approve and consent to what is desired by ye petitioners, respecting Mohegan, provided yt within ye space of three years they doe effect a plantation in ye place propounded." There is no doubt but what the authorities were pleased to have a settlement established in the Indian country, as it would form another bulwark against invasions from the unfriendly tribes farther north. The petitioners did not wait the prescribed time, but on June 6 of that year, they purchased a plot of land nine miles square from Uncas and his sons, for seventy pounds. Mason acted as the Commissioner for the Court, and the deed was signed by Uncas and his brother Wawequam. The sachem's signature was a stags-skull. Sometime later one of Uncas' men when intoxicated burnt the Norwich jail, and the Indians were fined for the crime, which they canceled by deeding six hundred additional acres to the town.

Roger Wolcott records the account of the purchase of the land in the following verse—

"On just and equal terms the land was gained;
No force of arms hath any right obtained."

The town of Norwich was legalized by the Court May 16, 1662. In the early days the name was recorded as Norridge, Norwick and various spellings, according to the intelligence or education of the town clerk. The name Norwich is supposed to be of Saxon origin from Northwic, meaning North Castle.

It is not known why this exodus from Saybrook was made, nor why the Yantic valley was selected. It is thought that probably the fertile land, the plain for pasturage, and the advantages of being located on a river that flowed into the Sound within a few miles, may have been the determining factors. Whatever the reason, no more beautiful location could have been chosen, with its picturesque hills and valley, several streams winding through the land, and emptying over the falls into the Thames, then known as the "Great River." The land was unusually fertile and abounded in springs of pure water, while sections of the plot were clear of trees, which permitted early cultivation.

The forests furnished game and the river was of a depth to permit large boats of that period to navigate to the new town, as well as supplying the planters with many varieties of fish. Even sturgeon of a very large size were caught there during many years, as the taste for caviar was not known, and consequently the demand for the roe did not cause the destruction of the sturgeon as it is doing in our day.

Tradition gives another reason for the removal from Saybrook. It is stated that the inhabitants were practically driven from that territory by the blackbirds and crows which settled in large flocks on the newly planted fields. They destroyed the young corn, undoing all the hard work of the planters, and leaving ruin in their wake. Laws to destroy these pests were enacted in several settlements which required all males of sixteen years and over to kill at least a dozen grain-devouring birds a year, and the heads of which had to be delivered to the magistrates.

This was Norwich in the beginning, and the question arises again why it was so named? Mason was the prime mover in the project, and it is natural to suppose that the choice of naming the town was his. Again, was Norwich, the capital of Norfolk County, England, the city from which he came? Another coincidence is that Norwich in Connecticut, like the town of that name in England, is surrounded by a river, which may have been one of the reasons for selecting that site, and also suggested the name for the new plantation, to one who had formerly lived there.

The descendants of this interesting old town, rich in

traditions and history, can be proud that the land was not taken by force, but purchased in a legal manner. Not as much can be said of the Pequots to whom it had formerly belonged, for according to their traditions, they had gotten possession by conquest, and had forced the former owners from the land. In 1663 the Commissioners of the United Colonies appointed a committee to learn what claims Uncas had to the Pequot territory. They talked with several "old and creditable chiefs," from whom the above facts were learned.

The town was laid out in the one conventional New England, long street, but in this case, it was irregular, as it wound around the hills, following the course of the Yantic River, and in the center of the settlement was the village Green or Common, on which the train band drilled.

The only attempt at the settlement the first year, was a plan for the town, and a cabin in which the surveyors camped while at their work. It was there that the attempt was made on Mason's life, where the five Englishmen slept, as Mason was of the party to superintend the project. It was not until the following spring that the real settlement began. The first house to be erected was for the Major, while Rev. James Fitch's home was the next to be built, and was located on the opposite side of the roadway from the house of his future father-in-law. Both fronted the Green, and their land sloped to the river. They were the two most noted founders of the town, both remarkable men, says the historian of Norwich. Mason's home lot, which comprised eight acres, later became the site of the

Court house, and that in turn gave place to a school house.[1]   In addition to the home lot, every planter had a plot of land for pasturage.

The first meeting house was built on the rocks that overlooked the surrounding country, and therefore was a good vantage point in case of a surprise attack by Indians. The Congregational church held sway for years, as the first Episcopal church was not built until 1726.   A grist mill was soon in operation, a blacksmith was persuaded to join the colony, and the first thirty-five settlers began building the town, making one of which the citizens could be proud.

The military defense was one of the first considerations of the founders, and a lookout was erected on one of the highest hills, consisting of a house in which when there was fear of an uprising, several soldiers kept watch.   They were able to warn the planters of the approach of an enemy.   The train band of the town had the advantage of always being under the supervision of the Major, and no doubt profited by this privilege.   The law stated that a band of thirty-two soldiers were entitled to a lieutenant as its leader, and not until the company numbered sixty-four, could it have an officer who ranked as captain.

Yet even with all these precautions for their safety, it was most venturesome for these planters to move into the wilds, though the neighboring Indians were the friendly Mohegans.   It was due, no doubt, to the friendship of the whites that saved Uncas and his tribe from being annihi-

---

[1] Known as the "Town Street School," but at tht request of the Founder's Society of Norwich was changed in 1934 to the "John Mason School."   In former years the whipping post and pillory were near this school site.

lated, a fact which Uncas probably realized.   Mason's
judgment and understanding of the Indians, together with
his practical control of Uncas, assured comparative safety
for his followers.

The planters at Norwich, as well as in the other towns,
had much trouble for some time in keeping track of their
cattle, as the herds soon grew into large numbers.   Fences
were difficult to make and keep in repair, so that a law
was passed and enforced, obliging all owners to brand
their cattle on the ear, each with the owner's device, and
which was recorded in the Court.   Another menace were
the wolves that killed their cattle and threatened the lives
of the planters when out at night, so that wolf hunts were
organized to rid the plantations of these pests.   But the
worst of all in this new settlement were the rattlesnakes
that abounded in that section, sunning themselves on the
rocks during the summer season, and hiding in the long
meadow grass, so that precaution always had to be taken
in the fields and woods, especially at night.   They were
said to have been the cause of several deaths in that section.

Norwich soon became a popular town for visitors,
owing, perhaps, or at least in part, to Mason's holding
court in his home.   A tavern was opened to accommodate
transients who came in numbers at that time.   The
Tavernder, as the proprietor was called, had to be a man
of high standing and respectability.   There are no records
of his being unpopular, so that we can believe that the
board groaned with the good things that the river and
fields brought forth, and the lodging quarters were ac-
ceptable.   We have no account regarding the taverns in
New England of having been obliged to put up signs, as

was usual in some New York hostelries at that time, that "not more than five could sleep in a bed."

The quarrels and wars in which Mason had taken such a prominent part since the founding of the colonies, made it impossible for him to avoid having enemies, and the surprising part is, that there is but one record of an attempt on his life. The account of this is given in a letter dated June 9, 1660, sent to the Commissioners of The United Colonies and reads—"One night, at ye New Plantation at Munheage (Norwich), some Indians, (as it will appear), of the Narragansetts, shot 11 bullets into a house of your English there, in Hopes, as they boasted, to have slaine him whome we have cause to honor, whose safety we cannot but take ourselves bound to promote, our Deputy-Go'R Major Mason." The Records of the Commissioners in a complaint presented by the English living at the new plantation at Mohegan, states "that some Indians did in the dead time of night shoot eight bullets into an English house & fired the same, wherein five Englishmen were asleep."

Fortunately Mason was not injured. While this was the only known instance of an attempt on his life, he suffered, like other prominent men, from malicious gossip probably prompted by jealousy. What the insinuations were, is not known, but at the Court held in May, 1663, it declared that "not withstanding the uncomfortable debates that have been respecting the Major, that the Major stands clear and is in a fit posture to carry on the affairs of the Court, which the Court doth desire and rejust him forthwith to attend, according as place requires."

At the same session the Court granted Mason five hundred acres of land for a farm which he had the privilege of choosing. However, it was not to trespass on another's property, nor to have more than fifty acres of meadow land. He took possession of this property the following year. Three years previous, when he first moved to Norwich, he returned to the colony the land Uncas and another chief of his tribe had given him.

Land was so cheap in those days, and given away so generously, that one wonders how in succeeding generations it was possible to learn the correct boundaries. For example, land that was purchased or given away, was designated as "where he chooses"—"where he can find it"—"over the river"—"at any place free from engagement to another," until the surveyors in later times must have become lost in confusion endeavoring to discover the correct boundaries. To add to this mix-up, owing to the lack of foresight of the original settlers, no dates were recorded of the deeds, and the boundary lines were often a tree that had long since been cut down, or a stone that had been removed. For instance, "December 31, 1669 ordered by the town concerning the outlands that then shall be only one allotement for the said lands and every man shall take his allotement in the place where God for his Providence shall cast it, Mr. Fitch only excepted," which probably meant that Fitch had his choice, and the others took what the Lord gave. No property could be sold without the permission of the town, which kept out undesirables. There is a case where one of this class did buy land in Norwich, but he was later obliged to leave the community, as he did not live up to the standard required of the citizens.

Regardless of the careless manner in which the lots and farms were given to the original settlers, they immediately began erecting dwellings of a simple nature, though a far better type than those in other towns. These were gradually followed by the fine old ones which still stand around the Green, marked with the dates when they were built, which gives the dignified and delightful charm for which Norwich Town is noted.

The early houses had a small, square hall, with a staircase leading to the upper stories, which usually made several turns in order to be placed in that small, compact space. The large spacious halls that ran through the houses did not come until a later period of the early Georgian architecture. On both sides of the hall were the two principal rooms. One the parlor only to be used on Sundays and state occasions. The rest of the time it was kept dark and was almost hermetically sealed. On the opposite side was the living room, often serving as the dining room. The kitchen was in the rear, generally in a lean-to with a sloping roof that reached within eight or ten feet from the ground. The upper floors were used for the sleeping chambers.

One wonders how it was possible to erect the mansions at that time which still bear testimony to the fine taste of the owners. How were they able to bring the beautiful woodwork and mantels to the outlying districts with such limited means of transportation?—poor roads and worse wagons. The Sound and rivers gave the only practical means of shipment, and many of the settlements were too far inland to be easily reached in this way. Houses of the better class, that still rank as mansions, were erected in

some of the most distant plantations.   In Northampton
the home built in 1656 for Cornet Joseph Parsons and his
wife Mary Bliss, when the town occupied but a small plot
in a forest, inhabited by Indians, is still standing and apparently in as perfect condition as when it was first built.
This fine, old house is so well preserved that it is difficult
to realize that it is the oldest residence in the town.   Unfortunately, the original small window panes have been
removed, and replaced by modern ones.   This house, like
many others of that period, has its traditions and memories
of witchcraft days.   Cornet Parsons had made a fortune
with Pynchon in the fur trade, and he and his wife Mary,
a woman of superior attainments, aroused jealousy in
some of their less fortunate neighbors.   Finally, envious
criticism of her fine new clothes, furniture, etc., developed
into more serious gossip, until people began calling her
a witch.   A sick child in the vicinity said that Mrs. Parsons
sat on a shelf in his room and caused all his sufferings, and
when she went out, that a little, black mouse followed her.
Then some cattle belonging to a neighbor with whom she
had some altercations, suddenly died from a strange disease, and she was accused of having bewitched them.
Finally Mary Bliss Parsons was arrested, taken over the
rough forest paths to Boston, where she was imprisoned during three long months.   At her trial she made
her own defense, and so convincingly, that she was acquitted.

The mansions built in that day still standing are a
pleasure to see and study, built on lines of true architectural beauty.   It must not be forgotten that saw mills
were few in New England, and those few were very widely

scattered. The heavy, hand-hewed rafters and sills are still in perfect condition, which speaks well for the carpenters of that time. In spite of the beautiful architecture, there were few comforts, and no sanitary arrangements. A small ewer and bowl served for a bathroom. Not much more could be said of the sanitary conditions in England. In spite of the handsomely embroidered velvet and silk clothes of Samuel Pepys, he records in his diary that "My wife cleaned herself with warm water today and found it very pleasant."

The only heat was from the open fireplaces, so that in extremely cold weather they were roasted on one side and frozen on the other. Cotton Mather wrote in 1697 how he watched a great fire, the "juice forced out at the end of short billets of wood by the heat of flames on which they were laid, yet froze into ice on their coming out." While Judge Sewall noted in his diary twenty years later that it was so cold that "the bread froze on the Lord's Table," and yet a child was baptized, and that evening at six he said, "my ink freezes so that I can hardly write by a good fire."

Some idea of the hardships of travel in that day can be had from the account the Widow Margaret Bliss gave of her experience when she moved with her household goods and cattle from Hartford to Springfield in 1643, a distance of thirty miles, which took five days to make the journey. Also in 1659, the year that Norwich was purchased, Lieutenant William Clark moved with his family from Dorchester, Mass., to Northampton the same state. His wife rode on horseback with two baskets, called panniers, slung across the horse, carrying one child in each, and one in her lap, while her husband, a man fifty years old, preceded on foot. Then the famous diary of Madam Knight tells of her trip from Boston to New York in the first of the eighteenth century, which she made on horseback with a young man as a guide. Paths so narrow in places that the branches of the trees nearly brushed her off the horse; swamps and streams to cross, and altogether a most trying trip for a man, and much more so for a woman.

Horseback was the principal means of travel; wagons came later, as few roads would permit of teams before the first quarter of the eighteenth century. It was many years before the advent of the chaise and gigs. The first chaise in Norwich was probably owned by Col. Simon Lathrop, and this "effeminacy" was pardoned on account of his wife's ill health.

The first turnpike in the United States is said to be the one between New London and Norwich, and while the Boston Post Road between Boston and New York was laid out in the early part of the eighteenth century, it was not formally opened until 1792 by the order of Washington. The first postoffice was established in New England in December, 1657, and a monthly post in 1672. Parliament made New London the chief postoffice, and while it was 110 miles from Boston and 156 from New York, it was looked upon as the halfway place, and one of the principal towns in which to break the journey. Hartford took a practical way to raise money for building a turnpike, by having a lottery. The road was opened in the latter part of the eighteenth century and had a toll-gate.

The love of flowers was early in evidence in the colonies,

and especially so at Norwich known as the "Rose of New England." Seeds from the home lands were soon bringing forth of their kind in the house gardens of the new settlements. Box-bordered beds, as in old England, were filled with sweet william, fox-glove bells, johnny jump-ups, old man's love, bleeding hearts and bachelor buttons. Roses were probably not imported until a later date, but these blooms of delicious fragrance were soon sought for. Slips, likely descended from the roses cultivated by the Chinese and early Egyptians thousands of years before, were blooming in the home lots of our New England ancestors. It is curious to note, when speaking of this flower, cultivated and loved since the birth of civilization, that it was not until the first part of the nineteenth century that hand pollenization was practiced by Dupont in the employ of the Empress Josephine, and due to her interest, the first rose show was held at her home at Malmaison.

The servant question was a problem in the early days of Norwich, and slavery was introduced when the town was still in its infancy. Owing to the opulence of the inhabitants they were more numerous there than in many of the larger colonies. They brought high prices, some as much as two and three hundred pounds. The slaves were generally well treated, and many were given their liberty, as in the case of the Perkins family, which was probably the largest slaveholder in that vicinity. In two cases that are known, the Perkins family not only gave two of its slaves their liberty, but also small plots of ground with houses in which to live. Slavery was legally abolished there in 1784.

The fine houses were not the only evidence of the growing wealth of the colonists.   Such homes had to have fine furnishings, and then began the making of the chests, tables, and chairs that have ever since been cherished as prized heirlooms.   The fine houses also required fine clothes for the owners, and this manifestation of vanity aroused the ire of the clergymen, giving them another opportunity to express their wrath from the pulpits.   Not satisfied in condemning the wearers of rich apparel, they instigated laws that would punish any one so lacking in respect to the Lord, and who ignored the edicts of the Puritan doctrines.

One preacher said in his Sunday sermon—"The special sin of woman is pride and haughtiness, and that because they are generally more ignorant and worthless."   While another equally eloquent minister of the gospel cried out from the pulpit when referring to the finery of the fair sex, "Artificial deformed Marypowls, fit to furnish her (like) a Stage play should represent Some Hagge of Hell," and the Rev. Nathaniel Ward gave the following in his Sunday tirade, as well as in his published sermons, introducing the subject by saying that he would "borrow some of their loosed tongue liberty and misspend a word or two upon their long waisted, but short skirted patience . . . but for the women who live but to ape the newest court fashions, I look at her as the very gizzard of a trifle, the product of a quarter of a cipher, the epitome of nothing, fitted to be kicked if she were of a kickable substance than either honored or humored.   To speak moderately, I truly confess, it is beyond my understanding to conceive how these women should have any grace or valuable virtue, that have so little wit as to disfigure themselves with exotic garbes, as not only dismantles their native lovely lustre, but transclouts them into gaunt bar-gees ill shapen shotton shelfish, Egyptian hieroglyphics, or at best into French flirts of the pastry, which a proper English woman should scorn with her heels. It is no marvel they wear drails on their hinder part of their heads; having nothing, it seems, in the forepart, but a few squirrels' brains to help them frisk from one ill favored fashion to another."

The men did not escape the scathing from the divines in their crushing pronouncements against the new fashions. This was especially the case when wigs were imported and first began to be worn. It might seem strange that any one should have been bald in those days, any more than in our own, since they had just as wonderful panaceas for correcting that misfortune. One prescription that was infallible in making hair grow on a bald head was to "take sum fire flies, sum Red wormes & black snayles & sum hume bees and dri them and pound them & mixt them in milk or Water." This remedy it was claimed never failed in producing a fine growth of hair.

The clergy, with one or two pronounced exceptions, who were known to fall for this new mode, damned the artificial headdress. Wigs came in and became popular with men of means. The preachers could call the fashion the work of the devil, but heads covered with the growth of other heads, were more and more in evidence. When long hair was preached against, though "it was allowed to grow a little below the ear for warmth," what could be said for wigs?

In a later generation, Judge Sewall, the Pepys of the

colonies, and who hated wigs as the devil is said to hate holy water, expressed himself on the subject when a friend of his died. He wrote—"A Rare instance of Piety, Health, Strength, Serviceableness. The Welfare of the Providence was much upon his spirit. He abominated Perriwigs."

The Rev. Cotton Mather, also of Sewall's generation, and who was considered the handsomest man in New England, devoted a sermon in favor of wigs with which he adorned himself, and ended his sermon by saying, "one sign of a hypocrit was for a man to strain at a Gnat and swallow a Camel."

The curse of finery appeared as early as 1634, when a law was passed forbidding any man or woman "to buy any apparel . . . with any lace on it, silver or gold, or thread under the penalty of forfeiture of the said clothes." Nor were members of either sex allowed under the law to have clothes with more than "one slash each, and another in the back." Embroideries, needlework gold or silver girdles, hatbands, bath ruffs, beaver hats, "were forbidden to be bought and worn hereafter." They were allowed to wear out such as they then possessed. Probably this permission gave a loophole in the law that some of the bravest may have used to their advantage. Five years later the law against finery became even more stringent, when "immoderate great breeches, knots or ryban, broad shoulders bands and sayler, silk ruses, double ruffles and caps," came under the ban. Still there were citizens of the towns who dared appear in the new fashions of the day that were brought over in the ships from England. They did not seem to fear the warning of some of the preachers who predicted all manner of evil that would befall those who

gave up to such vanities, such as fire, war, baldness, cater-
pillars and all of the other afflictions in the catalogue of
horrors, as they "drew iniquity with a cord of vanity and
sin with a cart rope."

Finally in 1651 the Court denounced the new modes,
especially that men and women of "mean condition, education and callings should take upon themselves the garbe
of gentlemen by the wearinge of gold or silver lace or
buttons, or poynts at their knees, to walk in great boots,
or women of the same rank to wear silk or tiffany hoods
or scarfs."

The line of distinction in clothing according to the rank
or wealth of the individual was closely drawn. The Massachusetts law of 1651 forbade the use of silk to persons
whose estate was not valued at £200. Later six young
women were tried by the Court for this offense, and two
of them "for wearing it in a flounting manner and excess
of apparel, to the offense of sober people."   What an
opportunity for arousing jealousy!

These ideas of caste and forbidding rich wearing apparel
to the lower classes, was common in Europe.   In France
at this time, the Court forbade the bourgeoisie to wear
trimmings of gold and silver.   Madame de Maintenon in
writing to her brother, who was not born of the nobility,
when speaking of his wife, said—"When I spoke of a
simple dressing gown for summer, she answered, 'What?
Without any gold or silver?'   One would think she had
always been covered with it, and yet, it is only a week
since she has worn it."

One incident of the dress and habits of some of the
women in the colony was brought out in the trial of

Captain Underhill in defense of his affair with Mistress Wildboro. She was accused of going to meeting with "wanton open-work gloves slit at the thumbs and fingers for the purpose of taking snuff." The Captain claimed that this was a great injustice, saying that the practice of enjoying the "good creature called tobacco," could not harm any one.

From the very earliest times of the Puritan religion, they had to "contend" with woman's vanity and pride of dress. The good preacher Johnson, the leader of the flock in Holland, was unfortunate enough to have his own wife criticized in this respect. Her clothes were judged to be scarcely of the religious standard by the women of her husband's congregation. They said that "her bodies tied to the petticote with points as men do their doublets and hose; contrary to I Thess. v. 22, conferred with Deut. xx, II"; that she wore "lawn coives, busks, whalebones in the petticote bodies, a velvet hoode" and "a long white brest" and "a topish hat." That she "stood gazing, bracing and vaunting in the shop doors" and that "men called her a bouncing girl."

The topish hat which seemed most of all to enrage the enemies of the minister's wife, was described by Ainsworth of the Psalm book fame, "though velvet in its nature were not topish, yet, if common mariners should wear such, it would be a sign of pride and topishness in them. Also a gilded rapier and a feather are not topish, in their nature, neither in a captain to weare them, and yet if a minister should weare them they would be signs of great vanity, topishness and lightness." Talleyrand expressed the idea in a concise way, but which would have been too abbreviated to suit the early preachers, and would have spoiled many a long sermon, when he wrote, "C'est prodigieux, ce que la vanité devore d'esprit."

Our ancestors must have appeared very attractive in the costumes of that day, in spite of the laws. The men wore for every day, leather breeches of deer skin, and for best, short and loose ones tied just above the knees with ribbons, as silver buckles had not come into fashion in the colonies, and were probably prohibited. Long, straight coats reaching to the knee, cut loose at the neck to display the linen stock, which was fastened at the back. Green, and later, red waistcoats, red stockings and low shoes were worn by the gentry, topped off with wide-brimmed and steeple-crowned hats. The poorer classes wore woolen caps of buff or red. When in full dress, swords were always carried, as was the custom in England and on the Continent.

Perhaps the women did not appear quite so colorful in the plain gowns they wore at meeting, as the men, but even so, the plain full and quilted petticoats, linen aprons and collars were charming in their simplicity. However on great occasions the women could flaunt finery quite as gorgeous as the men. Their faces, partly hidden in huge bonnets, appeared very demure, and they looked as picturesque as one sometimes sees in Europe today.

Cosmetics were not used at first and could not be bought, at least, not openly, so that the good housewives of that time had to manufacture their own, as well as their perfumes. This new sign of the devil's work brought out more invectives from the pulpits, and the addicts to this evil habit were warned of the fate that befell those who used these beautifiers. One preacher said in denouncing this sin, that "at the resurrection of the Just there will be no such sight be met with as Angels carrying Painted Ladies in their arms." And Johnson of "Wonder Working Providence" fame was shocked when he found this sin was practiced by the Indian squaws, "For beauty," he said, "the Indians esteeme black beyond any color. Wherefore the Squaws use that sinful art of painting their Faces in the hollow of their Eyes and Nose, with shining black, out of which their tip of their Nose appears very deformed, and their cheek bone, being of a lighter swart black, on which they have a blew crosse dyed very deepe."

It was all work at first in the new plantations, the building of the homes, the clearing of the forests, and in the mcantime obtaining food from the streams and woods, as probably when they emigrated, they brought but few provisions, save corn and cattle.

Gaieties must have been very rare, so that when Priscilla Mason was married to the Rev. James Fitch in October, 1664, there was a pleasant break in the monotony for the people of Norwich. Probably the ceremony was performed by her father, as he was the chief magistrate in the town. It would be interesting to learn of the repast that followed. The settlers of Norwich never lacked for food, game and fish were plenty, and the fertile soil produced crops in abundance. There must have been plenty to tempt the palates at this feast. Perhaps among the tempting dishes were the corn cakes and succotash, learned from the Indians, and doubtless one of those famous puddings that was placed over the fire at night, and kept boiling until served the following noon. They were very large, conical shapes and were carved from the top. It was said that on one festive occasion, the pudding was so large and heavy, that it toppled over and knocked down some of the guests.

Priscilla Mason must have been deeply in love, as well as endowed with an abundance of courage to wed Fitch, as he was a widower with five children, the eldest being fifteen years of age. This was the first marriage to take place in Norwich, and as it united the two principal families, was an event of some importance, not only in that town, but in Connecticut. Rev. Fitch stood very high in the communities in which he lived, and he was much beloved by his congregations. This was proven by the following he had on moving to Norwich. He took great interest in the welfare of the Indians, and by hard study he learned their language, so that he could preach understandingly to them. His trust and confidence in the red men were often abused and shaken, and it is evident that he did not have the highest opinion of Uncas. Especially when he learned in 1674 that Uncas had sent a message to Eliot, stating that "Uncas is not well pleased that the English should pass over the Mohegan river, to call his Indians to pray to God."

After the prayer for rain, he referred to Uncas as "double dealing," and of breaking all his promises to the English; of being hostile to them in regard to all their laws and religion. He added, "The great opponent of soul's good and concernment to his people and abounding more and more in dancings and all manner of heathenish impieties since the wars, and vilifying what hath been done by the English, and attributing the victory to their Indian helpes." Goodkin was even more severe in pronouncing judgment on the Indian sachem, who, after all, had been of great help to the English. He writes in his history, when speaking of this chief—"Unkus, an old and wicked, wilful man, a drunkard and otherwise very vicious; who hath always been opposer and underminer of prayer to God."

No doubt many of these prejudices were derived from the missionaries, who were unable to have the chief accept their religious views, and also, it must not be forgotten to ask from whom Uncas obtained the intoxicating "fire water." A pleasanter picture to record is Miss Caulkin's opinion of the man, as she probably was better informed of the character of the Indian than most historians. She writes—"He manifested a certain degree of native talent, a more than common share of worldly wisdom, and a persevering activity in securing the independence of his tribe. Moreover, the generous and kindly treatment which the Narragansett prince received from him, while in his power as a captive, ought to be placed to the credit of the Mohegan chief. Miantonimo confessed that he had nothing to complain of in this respect, and that the courtesy he had experienced was beyond the common degree of consideration in such cases." It is fortunate that in the passing of time, the unpleasant characteristics of the great sachem are forgotten, and that a monument was raised over his grave in Norwich, the cornerstone of which was laid in position by a President of the United States in 1833, when Jackson visited the "Rose of New England."

Fitch wrote several religious books, one of which was

entitled "some Help for the Indians" and several sermons, also the new Covenant for the Norwich church which gives special reference to the religious training of children. His best known work today is the sermon he preached at the time of the death of his wife's mother. A copy of this work is now in the library of Harvard University.

Norwich, like all the towns in Connecticut, with the exception of New Haven, rejoiced at the news received from Governor Winthrop in London, telling of his success in obtaining a charter for their state. New Haven had up to that time been an independent colony and at first rebelled at the idea of becoming absorbed in the larger one.

The feeling ran high in the New Haven colony regarding this consolidation. Session after session was held by that assembly, and every argument and persuasion that could be brought to bear was employed. Many of the settlers resented the matter so keenly that they removed from New England. The most conspicuous migration of this kind was when the Rev. Mr. Pierson joined by practically all of his congregation, removed to Newark, New Jersey, taking with them the town and church records. Most of these people had lived in New Haven since it was founded twenty-five years previous, so that when they left, the settlement seemed depopulated. Eventually the consolidation of the two colonies was beneficial to both as time has proven.

During Winthrop's absence in England, Mason had the responsibilities of the chief executive added to his other duties, but they could not have been left in better hands. No doubt but what he was glad to receive the welcome news which told of Winthrop's return. The letter referred to was dated London, 1662, and gave details in regard to the charter he had been endeavoring to obtain from King Charles, and in which he states—"the charter for our colony of Connecticut which hath newly passed the great seal, and is as full and large for bonds and privileges as could be desired, so as I hope all will be well satisfied about the charge that has been necessary for the effecting and prosecuting a business of such consequences, which is to the full settlement of the colony for them and their prosperity." He took every precaution to see that the merchants who had furnished the loan to him in London should be promptly paid, as it must have been owing to Winthrop's personality that he was able to have the money advanced. Consequently he ordered that 2000 bushels of wheat and 1200 bushels of peas, dried and in good condition and ready for shipment be at the port of New London by the following November.

There are many traditions regarding the manner in which it is claimed that Winthrop obtained from King Charles such a favorable charter for Connecticut. One is to the effect that he succeeded in gaining to his cause the Duchess of Castlemain, one of Charles' mistresses, by giving her some quaint Indian deeds that she coveted. Another is that Winthrop showed the king a ring that had been given to him by his majesty's father, and proved his appreciation by granting to Connecticut, owing to the elder Winthrop's loyalty, many privileges not allowed to the other colonies. Perhaps, too, Winthrop may have discovered what Isaac Alliston found when he went to London to secure the Plymouth charter, and who wrote from there, that he had learned at the court of Charles, "that many lockes must be opened with a silver key, nay golden key."

The charter arrived in May, 1662, to the great joy of the people. Winthrop was appointed Governor and Mason Deputy-Governor by King Charles, and all promised well for the colony.

In the poem Roger Wolcott wrote giving "a brief account of the agency of the honorable John Winthrop, Esq., in the Court of King Charles the Second, in 1662," refers to Mason as follows—

> "The army now drew up. To be their head
> Our valiant Mason was commissioned;
> Whose name is never mentioned by me,
> Without a special note of dignity."

The poem ends with the king's reply to Winthrop's request—

> "Be it so then, and we ourselves decree
> Connecticut shall be a colony.
> Enfranchised with such ample liberties.
> As thou, Their friend, shall best for them devise;
> And further know our royal pleasure thus,
> And so it is determined by us.
> Chief in the patent, Winthrop, thou shalt stand,
> And valiant Mason place at thy next hand."

CHAPTER XIV

THE plantation at Norwich had grown to be a good-sized town with the arrival of new settlers, and improvements were keeping pace with the increase of the population. The planters had one great annoyance and that was with their friendly neighbors, the Mohegans. It was not a case of fearing Indian attacks or war, but of their continually loitering about. The men had never worked, save to fight and hunt, leaving all the menial and difficult tasks of drudgery to the squaws. This habitual idleness, with the slow extinction of game in the immediate neighborhood, often led to drunkenness, though it was strictly against the law to sell intoxicants to the natives. It was impossible for the Indians to adapt themselves to the civilization of the whites, for the two races were totally unlike in their ideas and customs. Having always shared their belongings, and where practically everything was held in common, they carried out these ideas when associating with the whites. The Indians would encamp on private property in Norwich and insist upon remaining, though ordered off. They helped themselves to the goods of the English, which the Court condemned as stealing, and with these thieveries they learned to "exaggerate the truth" to such an extent, that it was difficult to know when they were lying.

Uncas, who the Indians said "the English made him high," realized that it was the close proxmity of the whites

295

that protected him and his people.   Otherwise, with the powerful Narragansetts so near, the Mohegans would have been annihilated.   Even at this time, marauding bands would attack Uncas' tribe from the north, or when small bands of the Mohegans were away on a hunting expedition.

Some three years previous to the settlement of Norwich, Pessacus had again attempted to revenge the murder of his brother Miantonimo and attacked Uncas in his new quarters at Nayantick.   He was only saved by the appearance of an armed body of English led by Mr. Brewster and Lieutenant Avery.   This attack caused Mason to give an account of the skirmish at the next session of the General Court, and Mr. Brewster, who had come to the help of Uncas, was authorized to go to his assistance in case of need.   The Commissioners of The United Colonies, however, did not sanction Mason's idea, and ordered that no colony or individual should in any way mix in the quarrels of the Indians.

This decision of the Court must have been learned by the Narragansetts, as two years later they combined with the Pecomtucks, and pushed their way into Uncas' territory.   Most of the marauders plundered and burnt wigwams, while several pursued a Mohegan who had fired on them, into the Brewster home, where they slew him in the presence of its mistress.   Such scenes as these must have tried the nerves and courage of the bravest, and in this case, an account states that "Mistress Brewster" saw the slaying "with great affrightment."   For this offense the Narragansetts were fined eighty fathoms of wampum, and in return they came later in the summer and avenged themselves by robbing Brewster of household goods and corn.

There were many pathetic incidents due to the subjection of the Indians. The remnant of the Pequots rebelled against the tyranny of Uncas, claiming that he did "tricks" to get them into trouble with the whites. John Gallup testified before the authorities that the Pequots told him that "they would go to the Mohawk's country to live, that they had soe much trouble here that they wearied of it." These conditions and statements were confirmed by John Stanton who said that he had often heard the Pequots discuss this matter among themselves. Continuing, he added, "Nesomet some time last summer did say to mee, that they were now desperate. They did not now care where they now went to live or where they died."

In a letter that Captain George Denison wrote to Winthrop at Stonington, under date of October 27, 1666, in which he sought justice for the Indians, he says—"My faith to my trust, and the Honour of God and the Authority, I am under, (as I conceive) being Conserned; together the presing and opresing necessity of the poor Indians, who can find no resting place for the sole of their feet, not with standing the many ingruegements, orders and grants they have (by your help) obtained and have relied upon, yet it seems all in vaine."

The Court in Winthrop's absence voided all those orders and said that the Indians must be removed next April from Cowisattuck. He went on to state that the Indians had no liberty, and were not allowed to speak for themselves, and he prayed that they might have that privilege at the next Court in May. "And I wish they had not caus to reproach the English. . . . I pray Sir, doe some thing which may bee effectuall for there relefe, that there lives and comforts may not bee offered in sacrifise to the wills of men."

James Noyes also wrote to Winthrop in behalf of the Indians, saying, "The Indians are now breaking up more ground, otherwise they cannot live, for what is ten acres to live on 5 or 6 families which is about the quanitie that is now broken."

The fate of the Indian in the Americas since the advent of the whites, is one of the saddest in history. He was only a savage, and could not understand the whites nor their ways. Nor was he able to compete with them in the contest for their lands. In spite of being a barbarian, there were many noble men among them—men of fore-sight and with a sense of justice. The greed of the white man and the advantages he had in warfare, made the contest unequal from the first. "To say that his lands were bought," to quote from James Truslow Adams, "and therefore, he was justly treated, is a mockery. To have expected sympathy, understanding, and justice in the situation as it developed in the seventeenth century is asking too much, both of human nature and of the period."

Yet in 1640 the colonies of Connecticut, New Haven, and Rhode Island sent a letter to the General Court of Massachusetts in which "they declared their dislike of such as would have the Indians rooted out," and expressing their desire "to gain them by justice and kindness."

But the greed for land, as Roger Williams said, had become "one of the gods of New England." They began pushing the Indians from the land desired by the whites.

Often they were dispossessed of their land on a suspicion that they were attempting to war on the English. Then there were the many unjust laws that were created that hounded the natives. They were held responsible for the damage done by the horses and cattle of the English that ruined the gardens of the Indians. If a native was found intoxicated he was obliged to work for the accuser several days. It is even said that part of the works on the forts of the planters was accomplished in this way.

The authorities at times endeavored to relieve these trying conditions, as in November, 1666, "it was voted that the townsmen shall with all expedition send unto those men which are ordered by the Court, deputed to lay out the Indians' land which are now at Cowissatuck; and to provide for their comfort." It was also ordered that Garrett, known as Wequash, was to be the governor of the reservation.

The English were also sincere in their endeavors to Christianize the Indians, and while their efforts met with small appreciation by the natives it proved the good intentions of the whites. The planters began to realize that it was difficult to convey any knowledge to the aborigines without a good interpreter, and therefore the Court made provision to have John Mynor of Pequot, who had some knowledge of the Pequot language, sent to Hartford to complete his education, for which the "court will provide for his maintenance and schooling," so that "the glory of God and the everlasting welfare of those poor, lost, naked sonnes of Adam" might be taught the gospel.

Daniel Goodkin and John Eliot practically gave up the best years of their lives in attempting to educate and in-

struct the Indians in the Christian religion. They often
pleaded their cases before the authorities, and used all
their efforts trying to prevent King Philip's War. Goodkin
was so earnest in this cause, and so misunderstood, that
he aroused the hatred of the populace and was hooted at
in the street. After living with the Indians, he wrote two
books describing his relations with them, which threw
much light on the character of the natives. One is entitled a "Historical Collection of the Indians in New
England," and the other "An Historical Account of the
Doings and Sufferings of the Christian Indians in New
England." He also wrote another history on this subject,
which was never published, and was eventually destroyed
in a fire. Eliot's labor of many years, in studying the
Indian language, was rewarded in 1663, by having his
translation of the Bible printed in their language.

In spite of the erroneous ideas held by the uneducated
classes, and the injustice of the whites in so many cases,
claims made by the Indians for lands they believed
belonged to them by inheritance or otherwise, were
taken up and given proper consideration by the magistrates. In later generations there were several notable
examples of this kind in Connecticut.

The religion of the founders was still conducted in the
same fanatical manner, if not stricter than when they first
landed. In some ways it did not reach its apex of intolerance until the third generation in New England. But
even at this early time, occasional gleams of light filtered
through the darkness of the closed eyes of the bigots. A
new law was proposed in 1665 which would permit all
men of "competent estates and of civil conversation," to

be freemen, and could hold both civil and military offices. Also, "that all persons of civil lives may freely enjoy the liberty of their conscience and the worship of God in that way which they think best." Charles II also issued an order at this time giving freedom to religious services.

Regardless of these seeming liberties, most of the original early laws were enforced. The masters of families were obliged to catechize their children and servants in religion at least once each week. "The New England Primer," which contained the "Westminster Catechism," and which was published in 1660, was used in every school in the colony. This work with Rev. Cotton's "Spiritual Milk for American Babes," was handed down as a text book for several generations. The following verse, as one writer said, was what the babes "were cheered and inspired with."

> *"There is a dreadful, fiery hell,*
> *Where wicked ones must always dwell;*
> *There is a heaven full of joy,*
> *Where goodly ones must always stay;*
> *To one of those my soul must fly,*
> *As in a moment when I die."*

While here is another verse equally inspiring—

> *"In the burying place may see*
> *Graves shorter than I,*
> *From death's arrest no age is free,*
> *Young children too must die;*
> *My God, may such an awful sight*
> *Awakening be to me."*

The following law seems less "gentle," for it states that "any child above sixteen years old, and of sufficient understanding, who shall curse his natural father or mother" should be put to death, and parents who did not rear their offspring in the fear of God, were subject to the same law.

The old "blue laws" were very generous in sentencing people to the other world. To blaspheme or to worship any but the Lord God, meant a sentence of death. It is not astonishing therefore, that corporal punishment was in vogue in the schools, since it was so often applied by those in authority for so many petty crimes. Captain Daniel Mason, one of the Major's sons, was the first school master in Norwich, and from all accounts seemed to have been popular and served several years.

The services in the churches consisted, besides the sermon and prayers, of singing the psalms. One can get some idea of the effect of this music, by the criticism in England of the singing there. This critic said " 'tis sad to hear what whining, toling, yelling or shrieking there is on country congregations." One can well understand that if church music was bad in the mother-country, where they at least had some advantages, such attempts must have been worse in New England. The congregations were limited to only a few tunes and were often led by one with a poor, though loud voice, and who had no knowledge of the art of singing. He had to "set" the tune. The Psalms were so poorly translated and versed that it would have taken a genius to produce harmony. Many of the Psalms were over a hundred lines long, some as many as one hundred and thirty. They were "lined" most always

by the preacher, and this, with the singing, often took
the greater part of an hour, during which the congregation stood. A story is told of one minister who announced
to his flock that he had forgotten his sermon, and that
while he returned to his home to get it, they should sing
the Psalm. The preacher lived some distance from the
meeting house, but he was back in his pulpit several minutes before the Psalm was finished.

It was necessary to have the Psalms "lined" or "dea-
coned," as often there were not more than two or three
copies of the "Bay Psalm Book" in the congregation. The
leaders who "set the tunes" had their difficulties which we
learn from Judge Sewall's diary, where he states—"I set
the Yorke tune and the congregation went out of it into
St. Davis in the very 2d going over." There is also a
touch of pathos in some of his records. When told to set
the tune, he writes, "I intended Windsor and fell into
High Dutch, and then essaying to set another tune, went
into a Key much too high. So I pray'd to Mr. White
to set it which he did well, Litchfield Tune. The Lord
Humble me and Instruct me that I should be the occasion
of an interruption in the worship of God." And it is still
more touching when he realized his voice had gone. He
wrote—"It seems to me an intimation for me to resign the
Praecentor's Place to a better voice. I have thought the
Divine Long Suffering and Favour done it for twenty-four
years and now God in his Providence seems to call me
off, my voice being enfeebled." But Judge Sewall lived
three generations later than the time of our history. During Mason's life a question arose among the church members as to whether or not women should be allowed to sing

at meeting. Since women were not allowed to speak in church, how could they be permitted to sing, as singing, was in a way, speaking? According to the interpretation of some, the Scriptures strictly forbade women to prophesy, and singing the Psalms was construed as a form of prophesying. Rev. John Cotton was able to satisfy the conscience of the fearful relating to this question, and the women were given the right to add to the harmony or discord of the church music. Likely they used their influence behind the scenes to win this privilege.

Such an innovation as having choirs or musical instruments as part of the church services would have caused a revolution among the God-fearing population. It is interesting to note how another critic was impressed by the choir singing, when first introduced. This Puritan expressed himself thus—"Choiresters bellow the tenor as it were oxen; bark a counterpart as it were a kennel of dogs; roar out a treble, as it were a number of hogs."

The fanaticism against permitting musical instruments in the churches reached such a height in England that in 1664 an organization known as the "Round Heads" went through the towns of England destroying the organs in the churches. Not even Westminster Abbey's organ escaped. It was said when the barbarians destroyed that instrument they shouted "Hark! How the organs go!" and "Mark what musick that is, that is lawful for a Puritan to dance."

In the fanaticism of the Puritans they hated everything that could suggest a love of objects, as to them, it savored of papacy. Their hatred of pictures and statuary seen in the churches of the Catholics made them forbid all forms of art that might suggest idolatry, for "in his intense desire to escape those dangers," one writer states, "the Puritan had really come to believe that the Lord loved angles better than curves, and ugliness was more pleasing in his sight than beauty."

It is, however, a misstatement that our ancestors had no eye for beauty or perfection, otherwise we would not have the fine, old mansions that they built on perfect lines of true architecture. Nor would we enjoy the pieces of furniture they designed and made, that are rated so high today by our connoisseurs. To be sure, dramatic art was looked upon as the Devil's work, so that the plays of the great authors, Shakespeare, Beaumont and Fletcher, and other noted writers, were not permitted in the colonies, though some could be found in a few private libraries, but were probably hidden from view. Poetry, as we have already seen, even from the beginning of the settlements, was greatly appreciated and used as a mode of expression.

With all of this church going, strictly enforced religious law, it was customary to not only furnish rum freely at the building of a meeting house, but to have portable bars at the church doors on festive occasions. At the ordination of ministers in later days, great feasts were held with bumpers of cider, beer, punch and grog, and the mixed drinks were often prepared on the doorsteps of the churches. Several preachers added to their mere pittance of a salary by having a still that manufactured the strongest kind of intoxicants. Very likely these concoctions gave some relaxation to the over-worked people.

In all of the religious controversies that were continually taking place, there is no instance of Mason's taking part.

His life was filled with the serious duties to which he was appointed, a Commissioner, a Judge, a Member of the Assembly, Deputy-Governor, and Commander of the Military forces. All of these duties gave him no time to enter into the disputes that lay outside his work. Yet with all of the trying problems that he had continually to solve, we find no occasion of his losing his poise. He was much admired and loved by the people, and in proof of their devotion they presented him with a sword marked with the inscription, "Vene, Vidi, Vici," which is now almost illegible. This sword was evidently given to the Major in honor of his victories over the Indians. It is a straight, two-edged blade, thirty-three inches long, and is still in a comparatively good condition. On the blade, close to the hilt, is a scroll work with the above inscription, and over the joining of the hilt and blade, is a silver filigree network. The guards have been broken off and it has no scabbard.

The sword has passed through many dangers during its long career, not the least of which was when it was loaned to the Centennial Celebration in Philadelphia in 1876. It was misdirected on being returned, and was lost for over a year. December 22, 1894, it was presented by its last owner, Asa Lyman Gallup, to the New London Historical Society.

According to family tradition there was another sword that also belonged to Major Mason. Both weapons were inherited by Captain Daniel Mason, the Major's youngest son, and were carried down in the male line for three generations. The one which is now in the possession of the Historical Society passed to the Gallup family, and the other came down through the male line to John Mason of Mason Island, part of the original grant to his ancestor.

During his latter years at Norwich, Mason, following the wishes of the Court, wrote his history of the Pequot war. He followed Caesar's example in his story of the conquest of Gaul, and wrote in the third person. In his modest preface addressed "To The Honorable The General Court of Connecticut" he states that though he was one of the chief actors, he wishes some one "better qualified might have undertaken the Task, for I am not unacquainted with my own Weakness; yet I shall endeavor in plainess and faithfulness impartially to declare the Matter, not taking the Crown from the Head of one and putting it upon another. There are several who have Wrote and also Printed at random on this Subject, greatly missing the Mark in many Things as I conceive."

In the introduction to the "Judicious Reader," he states —"I shall therefore, God helping, endeavor not so much to stir up the Affections of Men, as to declare in Truth and Plainess the Actions and Doings of Men; I shall therefore set down Matter in order as they Began and were carried on and Issued; that so I may not deceive the Reader in confounding the Things, but the Discourse may be both Plain and Easy."

This history was first published in 1677 by Increase Mather, in his "Relation of the Troubles" with the Indians, without the preface. The manuscript had been given to Mather by John Allyn who was the secretary of the colony. Mather supposed the history was the work of Mr. Allyn, and erroneously attributed it to him. It was not until 1736 that a second edition, edited by the Rev.

Thomas Prince, was printed with the prefaces.   Prince had obtained the manuscript from Captain John Mason of New London, a grandson of the Major.   A few copies of this edition are still extant.

Tyler in his "History of American Literature," in speaking of Mason's history states—"It is fortunate that he dashed off his little book without the expectation of printing it. . . . His style is that of a fighter rather than of a writer; there is an honest bluntness about it, an unaffected rough simplicity, a manly forth-rightness of diction, all the charm of authenticity and strength."

CHAPTER XV

NOTHING had disturbed the colonists so much, since the threat of war with the Dutch some time previous, as the information that reached them of the declaration of war between England and France. A letter received by the colonies, dated the 18th year of the reign of King Charles II, 1665-6, "desires the colony to apply themselves with all their force and skill, to the reduction of the French and Dutch possessions in America, to obedience to England."

The planters of New England realized that in their close proximity to the French colony in Canada, they would bear the brunt of the war, and be the first to suffer. They feared the marauding Indians of the North in the pay of the French. There was also fear of their own Indians taking advantage of this opportunity to massacre the whites. The Mohawks had attacked the settlement at Esopus in New York and were not defeated until sixty-five of the settlers had been killed. These fears were only too well realized when Indian warriors descended on Northampton. The same year, 1665, the French sent an army against the Mohawks, and a year later signed a treaty with the Five Nations. Another event of much consequence that occurred three years later, was the treaty at Aix-la-Chapelle, which ended the war between England and Spain. Unfortunately this did not occur until after St.

Augustine had been captured and plundered by the English.

The greatest question in all of these worries was the one of the protection of the inhabitants, and the need of an ample military force. All of these questions were brought to Major Mason to solve or pass on. One of many was whether or not it was better to reduce the "troops of Dagooniers" for the defence of the Colony to Foot companies, though a cavalry troop headed by Richard Lord as captain had had an important place up to that time. The first organized company of Horsemen was not founded until 1672.

The war between England and France, which had been such a strain on the colonies, was no sooner over than there were rumors of trouble with the Narragansetts. This meant extra duties for the militia and its commander. The responsibilities and cares were telling on the Major, as his birthdays multiplied. Information was continually coming to Mason of the menacing attitude of the Indians, and in a letter he wrote to Winthrop in 1668, he said when speaking of this subject—"I hear some of the Indians are going to Nannogansett with your passe. Good sir;— consider what you grant them on that account, ffor it is vehemently suspected, not upon slander grounds, that it hath beene and still there is a designe in all their acting." And continues to say that the Indians had had presents from the French and French Indians.

A letter dated June 29, the following year, from prominent citizens of Long Island to Major Mason tells of some important information that had been received from friendly Indians regarding a conspiracy that again consisted of a federation of all the tribes to destroy the English. Mason at once forwarded the letter to the governor and magistrates at Hartford with one of his own, in which he stated that he believed the assertions were given from an authentic source, and wrote—"Consider; it is high time to lay to heart what we should be and doe in such a season. T'is too apparent that there is a plot on foote between the French and almost all the Indians in the country." He refers to the well-known fact that the Northern and French Indians had been in the vicinity of the English colonies several times, and that "incredible sums of wampum have been given to Ninigret and other Indians." Mason suggested notifying Massachusetts and Plymouth to acquaint them of the danger—"without minceing; they are matters not to be dallyed with," and "whether it be not our best, to begin first with them." He thought that they should be "strictly examined, and if found guilty suitably dealt with, not as if we were afraid of them or the French. T'is good to kill such birds in the egg." Ninigret, he thought, "should be speedily apprehended and examined. The friendly Indians ought to be sent to the Mohawks to forbear any hostile attempt against the other Indians for the present." In a postscript he adds— "I had news from the Mohawks last night, who are very sorry that I came not to Albany." Mason was convinced that the Mohawks, with the exception of the Mohegans, were the best Indian friends the English had, and continuing said—"I question as matters now stand, whether you had not better deferre your speaking to either of them about this war at present. I wish we might some way signify favorable respect towards them. I verily believe the plott is deferred only till they have overtopt the Mohawks."

Mason suggested at another time that Ninigret be held for examination, and all arms belonging to the Indians be taken, though he still had faith in the Mohawks and Mohegans, but warned the authorities that a watch should be kept on those tribes as well as on all of the other Indians.

In July of that year (1669), Mason wrote to Winthrop that he had received a letter from England, "dated Mch. the third, from a man of knowne trust, whoe doth informe thus, that their liberties are great respecting Religion, and great expectations of more. The Parliament are to meet on the 4th of this instant, being tomorrow. Its thought they wilbee prorogued, if not disoliued, and writts for choyce of a new. The French hath great preparations at land and sea, but whether intended is rather uncertainely suspected then knowne. Its certain he hath an evill ey against the Dutch, and many suspect for England. His Embassadour hath been lately whipt and impris (oned) by the Turkish Emperour, some say slayne."

A little later, Mason forwarded to the authorities at Hartford a letter he had received from Thomas Stanton which confirmed the previous reports of the Indian uprising, and gave "divers and strange information concerning the Indians in these parts." He went on to state that Ninigret had sent messengers to all the leading sachems of the different tribes, inviting them to a great dance at Newport. "The truth is," the interpreter said, "thye ar verie hie of late and slite all athorietie of the English, but such as sutes with their own 'umores.'" It happened

Please cut pages !

that a youth named Osborne who lived at Cowsattack and was familiar with the Indian tongue, had been told by a squaw to warn his mother "in pity of her" the intention of the Indians to annihilate the English, and that the dance was only a blind to have all of the natives meet at a great concourse to plan the attack. Goodwife Osborne had been persuaded by her husband from communicating this information to the authorities for fear, he said, that "she should be counted a Twattler." The same statement came from a Pequot named Mosomp, who stood high with his people. He told young Osborne that Ninigret told him, that the Indians would have Cowsattack again, or it should cost the English their blood. Stanton said he "wondered" to see Uncas and Ninigret together at Robin's dance, "they who durst not looke each upon the other this twenty years, but at the nossell of a gun or at the head of an arrow or spear." Stanton also noted the discrimination Ninigret made in only entertaining men who were possible warriors, the others were sent back to their homes. Also that the Narragansetts were well furnished with ammunition.

Mason sent this letter, also, to Hartford with one of his own, in which he wrote, "Its not a time to be secure; if I am not stark blind in Indian matters, its not farre from as great a hazard as ever New England yet saw, whatever some of you may think and let us tell (you) though you send never soe many messengers, not one in twenty that be soe persuaded."

All of the resentment of the Narragansetts for the treatment they had received from the settlers, and which was now reaching a boiling point, was later to break out into the conflict between the two races and be known in history as King Philip's War. A war that occurred after Major Mason had gone to his last sleep, and one in which his young, gallant son and namesake, Captain John Mason, was to receive a mortal wound.

Besides all of these rumors of war, the colonists were suffering from fear of the Lord's anger. The bearded comet that appeared in 1664, and the severe earthquake the following year, were thought to be demonstrations of His displeasure. Another matter that concerned many of them at this time was the attempt of the English government to arrest Whalley and Goffe, two of the judges who had voted for the death of Charles I. They had escaped the net in England and had succeeded in reaching the colonies where they found refuge with the sympathizing Puritans, and although the search went on for years, they were never captured.

New laws against indulging immoderately in strong drink were more rigidly enforced. No one was permitted to remain more than half an hour in a house or tavern where liquor was sold, nor were the tavern keepers allowed to sell more than half a pint of wine at a time. Any one intoxicated was liable to a fine, imprisonment or to be confined in the stocks, though time for this punishment was not to exceed three hours. These laws much disturbed Josselyn and is commented on in his book. Any one found drinking in New Jersey after nine in the evening was fined. The strangest part of all was the one regarding ministers, which forbade the clergy to carouse and drink intoxicants, when it was known that several of them were brewing liquor in their stills. The keepers of the "Ordinaries" were obliged to keep their beverages up to the full strength according to law. There was the case of Nathaniel Ely of Springfield. He was a constable and swore when taking his officer's oath "by the great and dreadful name of the everlasting God" to faithfully perform his duties, but a little later he changed his occupation and kept an "Ordinary," thereby no longer being obliged to serve in the militia. He was called to account by the Court for not keeping beer constantly in his house, and for having "beere farr below" the strength, "that rule ye law."

Among other fears that were creeping in, was the power of the printing press, and a law was passed forbidding any press to be used in any place except in Cambridge. Another act was that all inhabitants should keep fire ladders ready for instant use. Owing to the houses being heated by open fire places, conflagrations were common and occurred more frequently on Sunday when all the inhabitants were at meeting. The authorities became so dictatorial that they even prescribed the number of servants one could keep in each household. Another rule was, that every town should be provided with a House of Correction, which proved that as the populations increased, so did the breaking of the laws. In Virginia negro slavery was growing as the planters could use slaves to greater advantage than in the north. They created an act that "the death of a slave from extremity of corrections was not accounted a felony," while in New England a man was severely whipped and fined for "immoderately correcting and cruel treatment of a negro so as to cause his death."

A law was passed in England at this time that affected the colonists, as it required all exports from Europe to pass through the British ports.

One of the trades that brought great profits to the settlers at an early date, was raising horses, which were shipped to Barbados and the West Indies. The result was that horses became so numerous, that in 1660 a law was passed that every horse had to be registered, giving the name of the owner and the age and mark of brand that the animal carried. Fences were few, in spite of the law to the contrary, and troops of horses roamed through the woods, often ruining the fields of the neighboring planters, causing friction and often lawsuits. This also gave ample opportunity to those of little conscience to trap horses during the night, remove the marks, and sell them for export at some distant port. If the thieves were caught they were fined and even whipped.

The great whale industry did not play an important part in the business world of Connecticut until many years later, though it formed a certain amount of profit in the early days. The first mention of whale fishing is recorded in the Hartford archives under date of 1647, when the privilege was given to a Mr. Whiting, who had the monopoly for the next seven years.

Changes were also taking place in the Old World. Europe had had its usual number of wars. England had fought the Dutch and won, so that New Netherlands had become New York in 1664, which established amicable relations between the colonies. France was being ruled by Louis XIV as an absolute monarchy, and Cardinal

Mazarin had fled to Italy long ago. The English government had treacherously made a secret treaty with the
King of Denmark, who invited the Dutch fleet to find a
haven in one of his harbors, so that it could be seized by the
English. It failed of its purpose, and the Danish monarch
turned tables and made an offensive alliance against the
English. Charles of England with Louis of France, after
many negotiations, some of them not of a high standard,
finally came to a break in 1665, which resulted in the war
to which we have already referred. Louis brought his
queen to Flanders at this time in all the glory of mediaeval
pageantry. It is thus described by one of the courtiers who
was present. "All that you have read about the mag-
nificence of Solomon, and the grandeur of the king of
Persia, is not to be compared with the pomp that attended
the king in his expedition. You see passing along the
streets nothing but plumes, gold laced uniforms, the chari-
ots, mules superbly harnessed, parade, horses, housings with
embroidery of gold," which bespoke the extravagances of
Louis' reign.

Although war was continued in one country or another,
and which almost seemed a case of normal conditions in
Europe, innovations and changes for betterment in the
social life were gradually taking place. In 1662 a great
event occurred when the omnibus appeared for the first
time. Coffee and chocolate were introduced and at once
became popular. A Jew named Jacobs in opening the
first coffee house in Oxford, little dreamed that he was
establishing a very important custom in the nation. Coffee
houses caught the fancy of the people and became the
literary clubs of the cities. At the same time vegetables

little known in England before, were introduced, such as asparagus, artichokes, cauliflower and other varieties. Pleasures of the table were not the only ones now handed out to the public. Izaak Walton had published "The Compleat Angler," and Richard Marvell had written his garden poems. John Dryden was later to be created laureate, as the king had evidently forgotten or forgiven the poet's eulogy on the death of Cromwell whose body was to be dragged from the tomb, hung on the gallows, and his head to be set on a spike at Westminster. At that time gibbets and gallows were often signs to mark the roads, and toll-gates and turnpikes were in use as early as 1660.

John Newton was making his discoveries of Differential Calculus. Bunyan was serving his twelve-year term in prison and writing the greatest allegory in the English language. Pepys had started his famous diary and recounts how in 1661, he saw a woman in a comedy, the first time he ever saw a woman on the stage. Soon, however, with the aid of Charles II, women made their triumphant way in the dramatic art. They always had the king's patronage, whose admiration often went beyond the applause in the playhouse. He had already introduced his mistress, Lady Castlemaine, to the Queen in the presence of the Court, and handsome Nell Gwynn, the former orange girl, held her sway over the monarch for a time. The king had re-opened the theatres in 1660, which the Puritans had closed when they came into power, as actors, according to their religious code, were rogues, though they had allowed an opera to be published in London during their time. So with the king's aid, Drury Lane was rebuilt from plans by Sir Christopher Wren in 1670 where play bills had been used in the theatre during the last seven years. While Sir Christopher Wren was making fame as well as fortune with his churches, Inigo Jones was having his trouble with Parliament, on account of having torn down buildings to make way for rebuilding St. Paul's Cathedral.

The restoration of the Stuarts meant the encouragement of all the arts, most of which had lain dormant for the last decade. Charles took great interest in patronizing the drama, literature, painting and music. The world once more became "merry England" under his reign. Quite a contrast to life under the Protector, as some one wrote—"gaiety and wit were proscribed; human learning despised; freedom of inquiry detested; cant and hypocrisy alone encouraged." This all reads well, but even Charles' proclamation giving freedom of conscience did not hold. George Fox, as an illustration of the freedom, was arrested simply for preaching against the "crime" of erecting steeples on meeting houses. In 1664 several witches were burned in England, and William Penn was arrested for proclaiming the doctrine of the Quakers.

Science was advancing amidst all of these prejudices. The Marquis of Worcester's "Century of Invention" prophesied the telegraph and steam as a motive power for propelling engines. The quest for gold was also an incentive for inventions to salvage the coins in boats long lost in Davy Jones' locker. In 1669 a diving bell was made in an effort to recover the gold of the Spanish Armada. Plate glass was manufactured for mirrors and coaches. The Royal Exchange was founded. Lighting the city of London by a lantern hung before every tenth door made the city quite luminous on dark nights between the hours of six and midnight. All of these improvements had to be paid for, and taxes were increased. A toll tax that was put in effect in 1667 taxed the lowly one shilling, and a duke one hundred pounds, the amount depending on the rank of the individual.

Students of history for the last two centuries, at least, must wonder if Portugal has not often regretted the part of the dowry that Catharine of Braganza took with her when she became the bride of Charles II, which gave Bombay to England. Another geographical change was made when England sold Dunkirk to France for four hundred thousand pounds in 1662.

The return of the Stuarts caused the downfall of many of the leaders under Cromwell. The last to suffer the death penalty was Sir Harry Vane, the timid youth who was once governor of the Massachusetts colony. He was much loved by the people of New England whose affections he held even after the stand he took in behalf of Anne Hutchinson in her trouble, which, though not openly proclaimed, was known. On the scaffold he showed no fear, for his faith in the promises of the New Testament consoled and strengthened him. His last words were lost, drowned by the drums, as the government did not wish his defense to be heard.

The medical profession had made but little progress at this time. Physicians did not believe in Harvey's great discovery of the circulation of the blood, and used every means to belittle him in the profession, as well as in the minds of the people. His practice suffered accordingly,

and his discovery was not recognized when he died, aged
79, in 1657.   But the world still believed in the healing
power of the king's touch for the cure of scrofula.

England was afflicted by the terrible plague that broke
out in London in 1665, and within a year over ninety
thousand died.   The king summoned parliament which
was held in Oxford, and which voted a large sum to alleviate the suffering.   The following year, London suffered
another misfortune in the great fire which destroyed over
thirteen thousand houses.   They were all built of wood,
all dry on account of the drought, and with a violent east
wind, once started, it was almost impossible to stop.   The
flames lapped up the homes of the inhabitants during
three days.   Often a great calamity of this kind unites the
people by closer ties, but sometimes it has the opposite
effect.   Such was the case after the great fire.   The conflagration was attributed to the hated Catholics, and even
a monument was erected with a tablet on which was engraved that statement; a proof of the intolerance which
wiped out reason and allowed emotions to hold sway.
They had not learned the principle so well expressed by
their great English novelist, George Eliot, some centuries
later, that "To be truly liberal one must learn to tolerate
intolerance."

In January, 1668, the Triple Alliance was signed at The
Hague, and demands were made at once of King Louis
of France.   But the King of France knew the weak nature
of the English monarch, and acted accordingly.   He sent
the Dutchess of Orleans, Charles' sister to visit him, and
with her she brought the charming, young woman named
Querouaille, a gift as a mistress from Louis.   Charles took

her to London and later made her Duchess of Portsmouth. These women won Charles over to Louis, and a secret treaty was made by them to conquer Holland. All of which promised anything but harmony for the immediate future.

CHAPTER XVI

TO ADD to the unrest that seemed to be contagious at this time, the Rhode Island planters were disturbed at the possibility that their colony might be absorbed by Connecticut or Massachusetts. Their fear was not only in losing their identity as an independent state, but also of their spiritual liberty. With this thought, Roger Williams wrote Mason, then Deputy-Governor, dated at Providence, June 22, 1670, a strong and sincere letter appealing for justice for Rhode Island, and stated that all they asked, was to be left as they were. It is evident that the misunderstanding Rogers once entertained for Mason in years past owing to their different points of view on the Indian question was fortunately fading out in the passing of time. The letter is nearly seven pages long. It reads in part as follows, and begins, "My honoured and deare and ancient friend my due respects and earnest desires to God for your eternall peace, etc.

"I crave your leave and patience to present you with some few considerations, occasioned by the late transactions between your colony and ours. The last year you were pleased, in one of your lines to me, to tell me that you longed to see my face once more, before you died. I embrace your love, though I feared my old lame bones and yours, had arrested travelling in this world, and therefore I was and am ready to lay hold on all occasions of writing, as I do at present.

"The occasion I confess is sorrowful, because I see your-selves with others embarqued in a resolution to invade and despoil your countriemen, in a wilderness, and your ancient friends of our temporal and soul liberties." Then he goes on to recount the effort he made to prevent the league of Indian tribes at the beginning of the Pequot war, which has been given in a previous chapter, and then con-tinues—"Alas, Sir, in calm midnight thoughts, what are these leaves and flowers, and smoke and shadows, and dreams of earthly nothings, about which we poore fools and children, as David saith, disquiet ourselves in Vain? Alas, what is all the scuffling of this world for but, come will you smoke it? What are all the contentions of wars of this world about, generally but for greater dishes and bowls of porridge, of which if we believe God's spirit in Scripture, Esau and Jacob were types. . . . If both desire, in a loving and calm spirit, to enjoy your rights. I promise you, with God's help, to help you to them in a fair and sweet and easy way; My receipt will not please you all. If it should so please God to frowne upon us that you should not like it, I can but humbly mourne, and say with the Prophet, that which must perish, must perish. And as to myself, in endeavouring after your temporall and spirituall place, I humbly desire to say, if I perish, I perish. It is but a shadow vanished, a bubble broke, a dream finish'd. To eternity will pay all.

"Sir, I am your old and true friend and servant, Roger Williams."

Williams explained that he had returned to England some years before and had obtained from Parliament a "charter for Rhode Island," but that the Massachusetts authorities were endeavoring to prove that they had one preceding Williams.' Fortunately, Rhode Island, which always had the courage in all emergencies to stand its grounds regardless of the other states, won out. It retained its liberty as an independent colony.

Mason sent the letter to John Allyn, then secretary to the colony, enclosing several others he had received from Williams, and in addition, gave his own ideas and suggestions regarding the controversy as had been requested. He advised, as usual, moderation, and his letter reads in part— "For my owne I am not very well acquainted with the matters in question respecting the rights of our Charters. Yet something I haue vnderstood; and more, I haue accidently mett with of late. I am apt to think the proper right of Narragansett country belongs to Connecticut. But there seems, notwithstanding to be soe many twistings in the matter: and how they may be interpreted, is doubtfulle and uncertaine; besides the many hazards that may attend the management of this affayre to a full issue, possibly to the effusion of blood, it is not soe already. Besides many other disasters which are not yet discerned. Tis alsoe possible the toll may proue to be more than the grist. A wise man reckons the cost before hee builds his house. Truly I am of that mind that the charge recouering what is aymed at, if should be gayned, will amount in reason to more than the whole country, as it now stands will be worth. ffor it is barrane in the general." He said that all the desirable land had been taken for large farms, some times "five, six, and ten miles square," and that all that remained "were rocks, swamps and sand heaps; facts," he stated he knew to be true, and added that if the matter was referred to England for a trial, that the cost would be excessive. "And in leive of this, we must erect a gouerment over a people that will come vnder no gouernment, neyther ciull or eclesiatic, they beinge already in dispersed corners like the Sweedes, soe that there is noe likelyhood of any Tollrable Christianlike society to be settled amongst them (and truely if it were otherwise), how incapable they are to attend, it is too well knowne to all men." He pointed out the high tax that would be placed which would be a hardship on all the inhabitants of the colony. Mason also told of two lawsuits being tried in England before he left, endeavoring to settle a dispute of a similar nature. "And therefore for us to take soe much troble and charges vpon soe great uncertaintyes to procure a nothinge, nay, truly, that which is worse than nothinge in my conception. . . . I speak not this that we may be dastardly cheated and befooled out of our rights, but that there may be a due and provident care so to demean ourselves that we may prevent after inconveniences. . . . I shall only commend this as at present to your serious consideration, for matters of moment, you know, should be handled with ripe advise, poysed consultation and solid conclusions."

Mason, while Deputy-Governor, was appointed chairman of a committee to try and settle amicably the joining of the Connecticut and New Haven colonies, and "to go down to New Haven to treat with our honored and loving friends about settling their union and incorporation with this colony of Connecticut." In 1663, a year later, he was again appointed chairman of another committee for the same purpose.

The Major was also one of a committee to settle the boundary between Connecticut and Massachusetts, and also the line between his colony and Rhode Island, and which led to the controversy with Roger Williams. The inhabitants of Mystic and Psukatuck were ordered in October, 1662, not to obey any instructions from any other colony, and in case of difficulties occurring, "to repair to our worshipful deputy-governor for help, and that they choose a constable for the year ensuing; and the constable to repair to our worshipful deputy-governor for his oath."

In the latter years of his life, Major Mason held court at his home in Norwich, and as he was the only magistrate in that section, it necessitated arguing most of the law-suits there. This caused some complaints of the hardships, for many had to travel long distances from their homes. He held the office until his death, and no appointment was made until two years after his decease.

Mason had his enemies, like all forceful characters, and at a setting of the Court in New London, June 6, 1671, he brought suit for one thousand pounds against one Amos Richardson, for slander and defamation for calling him "a traytor, and damning the colonies." A verdict of five hundred pounds was given. Richardson asked for a review of the case which was not granted until June the following year, some months after the death of the Major. When Richardson was summoned by the Court to either withdraw his suit or go on with the review, he replied that since Mason was dead, that the action died with him. Samuel and John Mason, sons of the Major, defended the action, and as Richardson made no defense, the original verdict remained in force. The Mason heirs subsequently levied an execution on the Richardson estate to satisfy the original judgment. Twelve mares were taken for which an allowance of £71 was allowed, although the plaintiff claimed they were worth much more. The matter was not settled until further litigations finally closed the case. It is interesting to note an incident that occurred at the court proceedings following Mason's death and which seems to index the character of Richardson, and the opinion in which he was held. He disputed the records of the Court, which resulted in his being arraigned for defaming the Court, by saying that a part of the record was not true, and he was fined eight pounds.

Mason's health had been failing the last few years, and he was a great sufferer from an incurable disease. At times he was in such pain that he was unable to hold court. However, he showed the same fortitude in combating his painful malady, as he did during the Indian wars. He presided at the sessions of the Court until September, 1670, which was his last appearance on the bench. A petition had been made to the Court in the previous autumn as follows—"that the county had been empowered to hold court yearly, in June and September, to consist of the Magistrates and the Commissioners; that it having pleased God so by his Providence to bless us with the enjoyment of only one Mason with our country, namely our honored Major Mason, who by God's visiting hand upon him in respect of weakness and sickness of body, hath not at all times been in a capacity to undergo the great trouble that attends our Courts, without assistance, whereby our Courts have been formerly much weakened, and prays the Court to point some one to his service."

The following paragraph is recorded under date of May 9, 1672, "Major Mason, who for many years, had been deputy-governor and rendered important service to the court, being far advanced in years and visited with many infirmities, about this time, excused himself from the services of the Commonwealth." This date is evidently an error, as Mason died in January of the preceding year.

A greater trial than had yet befallen Mason came when his wife passed away, but fortunately, the separation was not for long. Mrs. Mason's memorial service was preached by her son-in-law, Rev. James Fitch, and it was considered of such a high literary standard that it was published. In his eulogy of his mother-in-law, he said, "I need not tell you what a Dorcas you have lost; men, women and children are ready with weeping to acknowledge what works of mercy she hath done for them. . . . She was gifted with a measure of knowledge above what is usual in her sex." This was printed in 1672 and on the title pages states, "A Sermon preached upon the occasion of the Death and Decease of that piously affected and truely religious Matron, Mrs. Anne Mason, sometime wife of Major Mason, who not long after finished his course and is now at rest. By James Fitch, Pastor of the Church at Norwich."

This sermon is all that is known of the life of the Major's wife, but such a testimonial from her son-in-law conveys the idea of a gentle, loving nature. Also that her children were such fine characters testifies to the harmony of the home environment, and what a helpmate she was to her husband.

One wonders what Miss Caulkins' reaction would be could she see the burying ground today with its encroaching buildings.

The neglect of the hallowed place where the founders of their city sleep is in pitiful and humiliating contrast to the well-kept grave and monument of Mason's Indian friend Uncas.

A fitting marking for the monument that stands in the old burying ground would be a part of the introduction "to The Judicious Reader" in his History of the Pequot War, which is given in the first chapter of this volume, where it referred to "Drawing the Curtain" from the Casement so that Posterity might learn of the "Difficulties and Obstructions their Forefathers met with in their first settling these desert Parts of America."

1651

Jn o: Mason

The only record that refers to Major Mason's will is given in the book of County Court Trials, New London County Court, Vol. 3. (1670-1681), page 47, under date of June 4, 1672—"the Will and inventorie of Maj'r John Mason, Deseased exhibited for Court & ordered to be Recorded." Both the will and inventory are missing which is most regrettable.

In September, 1859, Norwich celebrated its two hundredth anniversary of the settlement of the town. Great enthusiasm for the patriotism of the founders was expressed on every side. A historical discourse was given by Daniel Coit Gilman, and the address on the "Life and Times of Major John Mason" was made by Rev. John A. Rockwell, in which he said, when paying tribute to the memory of Mason that "The war with the Pequots constitutes one of the most important events in the early history of the colonies, and while all participated in the beneficial results, the success of the undertaking is to be ascribed to the contributions and sacrifices of Connecticut alone, and most of all to the prudence, energy and indomitable valor of John Mason and the troops under his command. . . . I have described a hero and a statesman; a great man and a fit founder of a great nation; a leader in that class of men who impress their characters on future generations. He possessed all the elements of greatness. His purposes were high and noble; his will was strong and determined. He was possessed of remarkable firmness and promptitude, a courage which was absolutely fearless, united with prudence and moderation the most considerate and reflecting. There was a sternness and almost terrible rigor in his character, and yet he was as modest as a child. Never do you hear from him one word of boastfulness or vanity.

"Fierce and unrelenting as he showed himself in the bloody battle with the Pequots, he was yet a man of moderation and a friend of peace; and by his firm, cautious and resolute, and yet pacific course, he prevented, or checked in the outset, every tendency to disorder or violence.

"These high qualities made him not only a great soldier, but an admirable legislator and magistrate; and later periods furnished such shining examples in Washington and Grant.

"There is no manlier or more heroic figure than this in all our Colonial history."

BIBLIOGRAPHY

"History of the Pequot War," by Major John Mason.

"News from America," by Captain John Underhill.

"Leift Lion Gardener his relation of the Pequot Warres." Address by John A. Rockwell delivered at the Two Hundredth Anniversary of Norwich, Conn.

"Life of Major John Mason of Connecticut," by George E. Ellis.

"History of Norwich, Conn.," by Frances Manwaring Caulkins.

"History of The Major John Mason Statue."

"History of New England," by Thomas Prince.

"The Massachusetts Historical Society Collection."

"The History of the Indian Wars in New England," by Rev. William Hubbard.

"Antiquarian Researches Comprising a History of the Indian Wars," by E. Hoyt.

"The History of New England," by Daniel Neal.

Records of the Plymouth Colony.

"History of Connecticut," by Benjamin Trumbull.

"History of American Literature," by Moses Coit Tyler.

"Old Colonial Days," by Mary Alden Ward.

"History of the Plymouth Plantation," by William Bradford.

"Travels and Works" of Capt. John Smith.

"Three Episodes of Massachusetts History," by Charles Francis Adams.

"The Emancipation of New England," by Brooks Adams.

"The Founding of New England," by James Truslow Adams.

"History of the Great Indian Wars, 1675 and 1676," by Thomas Church.

Judge Sewall's Diary.

"History of New England," by Winthrop, edited by James Savage.

"History of New England," by J. G. Palfrey.

"Accounts of Two Voyages to New England," by John Josselyn.
"Customs and Fashions of New England," by Alice Earle.
"The Beginning of New England," by John Fiske.
Connecticut Records.
"A Connecticut Trilogy," by Margurite Arliss.
"Poetical Meditation, Being the Improvement of Some Vacant Hours," by Roger Wolcott.

INDEX

Adams, Brooks, quoted, 233
Adams, James Truslow, quoted, 298
Adams, Mrs. John, 148
Ainsworth, of Psalm book fame, 287
Aix-la-Chapelle, treaty of, 309
Akbar, Emperor, 186
Albany, N. Y., settled by the Dutch as Orange, 34
Allen, Rev. John, 233
Alliston, Isaac, of Plymouth colony, 293
Allyn, John, secretary of the Connecticut colony, 307, 325
America, earliest settlements made and attempted in, 18-19; voyages of discovery and settlements made after the beginning of the seventeenth century and various accounts of them, 26 ff.
Amusements and sports in the colonies, 251-253
Angel Gabriel, sinking of, in 1635, 44-46, 219
Anne of Austria, 87, 246
Antinomians, persecution of, in New England, 183
Avery, Parson, lost in wreck of the *Angel Gabriel*, 45-46

Bachelors, attitude toward, in the colonies, 48-49
Bacon, Lord, 236
Ballot, first use of, in America, 50
Baltimore, Lord, founding of Maryland by, 83
Bancroft, George, quoted, 166
Baptists, persecution of, in New England, 183-185
Bay Psalm Book, the, 194-195
Beaumont, Francis, 22, 305
Berghe, Count Henry de, 25-26
Bible, King James' version of, 22
Bissell, John, married to Mason's daughter Isabelle, 222
Black Hawk, 93
Blackman, Rev. Adam, 83
Blackstone, Lord, quoted, 236
Block Island, 99, 100, 101, 102
Bohemia, 20

Bois-le-Duc, Brabant, fall of, in 1630, 25-26
Bombay, acquirement of, by England, 320
Boston, Mass., founding of, 46; reconstruction of fortifications of, in 1634-1635, 67-68
Boston Post Road, laying out of, 281
Botanical Gardens, London, 22
Bradford, Governor William, 35, 39, 40, 42, 70, 71, 79; "History of Plymouth" by, 46, 66
Bradstreet, Anne, poems of, 241-242
Bradstreet, Rev. Simon, account of Mason's death, 330
Brass cannon, casting of the first, 82
Brent, Mrs. Margaret, requests a vote in the Maryland Assembly in 1648, 237
Brewster, Benjamin, 262, 263, 296-297
Brewster, William, of Plymouth colony, 46
Bromley, Hon. Isaac H., 136; tribute to Major Mason, 335
Brook, Lord, 71, 223
Brown, John, "The Pilgrim Fathers of New England and their Successors," vii n.
Buckingham, Duke of, favorite of Charles I, 24-25
Bull, Dixy, pirate, 53-54, 100
Bunyan, 318
Burton, Thomas, 238
Bushnell, David, his submarine, 22
Butler, Samuel, "Hudibras," 87

Canada, colonizing in, 31-32
Canonicus, chief of the Narragansett Indians, 92, 99, 101, 105, 106, 124, 125, 126
Cape Cod, discovery of, 33
Carver, John, of Plymouth colony, 46
Casanova, 117
Caste, recognition of, in the colonies, 56
Castlemaine, Lady, 318

339